GAIETY TRANSFIGURED

GAIETY TRANSFIGURED

Gay Self-Representation in American Literature

David Bergman

The University of Wisconsin Press

The University of Wisconsin Press
114 North Murray Street
Madison, Wisconsin 53715

3 Henrietta Street
London WC2E 8LU, England

5   4   3   2   1

Printed in the United States of America

Library of Congress Cataloging-in-Publication Data
Bergman, David, 1950–
    Gaiety transfigured: gay self-representation in American
literature / David Bergman.
    250 pp.   cm. — (The Wisconsin project on American writers)
    Includes bibliographical references and index.
    ISBN 0-299-13050-9
    1. Gays' writings, American—History and criticism. 2. American
literature—Men authors—History and criticism. 3. Homosexuality
and literature—United States. 4. Gay men in literature.
I. Title. II. Series.
PS153.G38B4   1991
810.9'9206642—dc20   91-50321
                                                    CIP

For Donald Craver
teacher, colleague, friend

They know that Hamlet and Lear are gay;
Gaiety transfiguring all that dread.
All men have aimed at, found and lost;
Black out; heaven blazing into the head:
Tragedy wrought to its uttermost.

W. B. Yeats, "Lapis Lazuli"

CONTENTS

GAIETY TRANSFIGURED

1

An Introduction by Way of Acknowledgments

E VEN in the stodgiest of academic books, the acknowledgments
offer an occasion for autobiography—the grateful bow to a
secretary of more than usual helpfulness, the obligatory salute to wife
and children for their saintly forbearance with the author's distrac-
tions and frustrations. Since I have neither wife nor children nor permanent secretary, I would like to take this opportunity to narrate the
genesis of this book as a way not only of expressing my gratitude to
the many people who have helped me, but also of explaining why the
book has taken its very queer shape.

Gaiety Transfigured has its origins in another decade. Shortly after
I had finished graduate studies, Karl Keller approached me with a
proposition to edit a collection of essays on camp. I was, he said, the
campiest person he knew. "Camp," which had seemed to be a term of
pregnant possibilities when Susan Sontag launched it into critical discourse in the late sixties, had by the late seventies fallen into such dis-
repute that it had become a term not to be spoken among academics.
Karl and I believed it still could be helpful in opening up a wide array
of critical strategies. We approached several scholars, some of whom
agreed to write essays for the book, and several publishers, all of
whom refused to publish it. The only products of this misadventure
were a short paper Karl published on "Walt Whitman Camping" and
the first draft of "Strategic Camp," not a word of which remains in the

3

current version. Karl, who succumbed to the effects of AIDS several years ago, is the person who planted the seeds of the present work and who encouraged me at a time when I needed all the encouragement I could get.

I should mention that in 1978 or 1979, when Karl and I conceived of a book on camp, books on homosexuality and the arts were rare. The gay studies movement had barely taken shape. Our topic was, as a campy friend once put it, "very *très*."

Several years later at the end of the first Reagan administration, when Anita Bryant had campaigned against the Miami fair housing and employment bill on the basis that gays were antifamily, Philip Church, an editor then of *The Kenyon Review,* asked me to write an essay about gay literature and the family. I wanted to write the essay because what little discussion existed about homosexual men and their families always emphasized the son's relationship to the mother, and I was particularly interested in the father-son relationship. I also felt that AIDS had begun to dominate the social, sexual, and artistic life of gay men, and that it was necessary to remind myself and the hetero-sexual community around me that being gay was more than being sick. I felt very strongly what W. H. Auden argued in "Musée des Beaux Arts," that as an artist and critic I needed to put suffering in its "human position," not to deny it, but to suggest that gay communities had more to share than the disease decimating them. "Alternative Ser-vice: Families in Recent American Gay Novels" was the first of the chapters I wrote, and I want to thank Phil Church and Galbraith Crump, two of the more extraordinary teachers I had at Kenyon Col-lege, for opening the pages of the *Review* for my study.

I had a third reason for writing "Alternative Service": to try to un-derstand what was happening to me as both a gay writer and a gay man. I was then engaged in a series of poems about the first homosex-uals I knew. Of the half dozen poems I projected for the series, I had completed only one. I was completely blocked on the second.

I now can see that I was caught in, what Diana Fuss calls "the ten-sion between the notions of 'developing' an identity and 'finding' an identity" (100). The tension derives from two stages of coming out, the process in which individuals come to accept themselves as homo-sexual and learn to integrate their sexuality into their lives. I knew per-sonally the vicissitudes of coming out and had watched a number of young men "find" their identities as homosexual. For a year or so, we were gay with a vengeance, associating exclusively with other homosexuals, adopting the most stereotypical attitudes and fashions. Having located a label for our feelings, we set ourselves to live, as Mary McIntosh has argued in her now classic essay, the homosexual role with all the theatrical flair and commitment of the young, since it "removes the element of anxious choice" (32). The phase passes usually when the young man has internalized being homosexual or has learned the difference between gay stereotypes and himself. The poems I was writing were about this process.

But then I was faced with the far more difficult task of "developing" my own sense of gayness, of finding out how my sexuality could play its part in my life, of going beyond my first envisioning of what it means to be gay. The reason that a gay man must go beyond this initial construction of his sexuality—must if he hopes to enjoy any share of the well-being that is the birthright of the individual—is that his initial construction is far too often built upon homophobic foundations, the conception of homosexuality fostered by "compulsory heterosexuality," as Adrienne Rich has termed it. The child who will become gay conceives his sexual self in isolation. I cannot think of another minority that is without cultural support in childhood. Jewish children, for example, from infancy are brought up with a looming sense of their religious identity just as black children from birth develop a sense of racial identity, or baby girls soon find what it means to be female. But gay children—who have a keen sense of being different— often have nothing and no one to show them what that difference consists of, or how one might integrate that difference into a way of life. When I came to write on gay lyric poetry and on the discourse of otherness, I came to understand how the absence of such a cultural heritage in childhood had affected me and my work.

Indeed, I came to understand how I was not unlike the vast majority of gay people; I grew up ignorant of any depictions of single-sexed domestic arrangements in literature, painting, or history. I first came to know about homosexuality from the yellowed pages of a copy of Krafft-Ebing that my parents kept in their bookcase. And since in those far-off days, the more graphic details remained in Latin, Latin became for me a language of forbidden erotic possibilities. I remember in my teens, a David Susskind program in which members of the Mattachine Society, shown in silhouette, discussed the need to lift the stigma of sexual difference, and the host's urgent plea to his viewers for compassion and understanding. Thus for me, as for most children of my generation, homosexuality was written in a foreign language or depicted in outline alone, its voice incomprehensible and its face shrouded in a darkness no one was brave enough to expose. It is important to remember that homophobic attitudes were perhaps stronger in the fifties than they had been in the twenties and early thirties. Evert Van der Veen has described the years from 1933 to 1967 as the "Hiding" period of gay publishing (15–21). Explicitly homosexual work was published quite freely in the early thirties—Forman Brown had no trouble with his editors when he published *Better Angel* in 1933, but Alfred Knopf refused to publish James Baldwin's *Giovanni's Room* in 1955 because, according to William Cole, "It was judged not the time for an out-an-out homosexual novel" (Weatherby, 135). When I grew up, I had little to choose from except pornography and silence.

I was not alone in coming to understand that I was gay by reading about homosexuality in Krafft-Ebing. Homosexuality, it is almost true to say, is a literary construct for many gay people. In his book on *Decadence,* Richard Gilman observes that it "like so many other categories of the 'abnormal' . . . makes itself known to us, at least in the beginning, in the form of a legend" (13). I learned to be queer through the legendary work of Krafft-Ebing. Others were affected by the legend of Oscar Wilde, whose martyrology has a secure place in the myths of modernity. Charles Henri Ford, who with Parker Tyler published in 1933 the groundbreaking novel of the New York homosexual underworld *The Young and the Evil,* recalls the impact of the Wilde myth: "I was seduced," he tells Ira Cohen, "when I was ten years old by an older man. But I did not take it as my sexual definition because I was still excited by little girls. So it was not until I reached adolescence and I read Oscar Wilde and I knew there was a whole other sexual side" (Ford and Cohen, 55). For Ford, the legendary has more impact on his development than does physical contact. The seductions of older men and little girls pale beside the vividness of the literary.

In a study published nearly twenty years ago, Barry M. Dank asked gay men in his survey group how they first came to recognize themselves as gay. While over 50 percent said that they made this realization after socializing with other gay men, 15 percent said that this understanding came from their reading (109). If one considers how little Americans read, the figure is quite astounding, showing both the importance of literature for developing gay identity, and how rare such discussions have been. It is significant that Dank, writing in 1971, does not ask his research population about film or television. Clearly, he assumes—and rightly—that one could learn nothing about homosexuality from mass media.

Gay men's reliance on literature has not, however, always been helpful. Even literature written by homosexuals has often presented gay life as a depressing, marginal, and unfulfilling experience dominated by violence, drugs, alcoholism, poverty, and prostitution. As Samuel R. Delany, the black science fiction writer, points out in an interview, gay men learned to speak about their sexuality in a rhetoric of despair and degradation. Confined to a mental hospital after a nervous breakdown, the twenty-two-year-old Delany found himself after much indecision confessing his homosexuality one day to his therapy group in terms far removed from his true experience:

> I'd talked like someone miserable, troubled, and sick over being gay; and that wasn't who I was. On the contrary . . . the gay aspects of my life, from the social to the sexual, were the most educational, the most supportive, the most creative, and the most opening parts of my life. . . . Where had all the things I'd said that morning come from?
>
> I began to understand where they'd come from that night. They'd come from a book by the infamous Dr. Burgler I had read as a teenager that had explained how homosexuals were psychically retarded. They came from an appendix to a book by Erich Fromme that told how homosexuals were all alcoholics who committed suicide. They had come from the section on "Inversion" by Havelock Ellis in *Psychopathia Sexualis* that I'd read;[1] some of it came from Vidal's *The City and the Pillar* and some from Andre Tellier's *The Twilight Men*. Some of it had come from the pathos of Theodore Sturgeon's science fiction story, "The World Well Lost," and his Western story, "Scars." And some had come from Cocteau's *The White Paper* and some came from Gide's *Corydon*. Some, even, had come from Baldwin's *Giovanni's Room*.
>
> When you talk about something openly for the first time—and that, certainly, was the first time I'd talked to a public *group* about being gay —for better or worse you use the public language you've been given. It's only later, alone in the night, that maybe, if you're a writer, you ask yourself, how closely that language reflects your experience. And that night I realized my experience had been betrayed. (196–97)

1. Delany has confused *Psychopathia Sexualis* by Krafft-Ebing with Havelock Ellis's *Studies in the Psychology of Sex.*

Delany's remarks reveal simply and dramatically the varied role literature about homosexuality and books by homosexuals played in the construction of gay selfhood. On the one hand, such literature was a principal way gay men came to understand themselves. On the other hand, gay authors' public statements were written in a language at once guarded and false, screening out what was particularly good about gay life even as it tried to make that life comprehensible and acceptable to a heterosexual readership. In a conversation with Edward Field, he discussed with me strategies that gay writers used in the late fifties and early sixties to break the barrier of silence that still surrounded homosexuality. In his first book, *Stand Up, Friend, With Me,* Field's only overt reference to homosexuality is a derogative one about "a faggot actor" his sister is dating. "Even if gays were dismissed," Field told me, "the fact that they could be talked about at all was thrilling. . . . A lot of authors wrote about [homosexuality] condemning it, but it was the only way they could get away with mentioning it." Furthermore, gay literature, by providing terms gay men could use to speak to the public, highlighted the discrepancies between public and private language about homosexuality. Finally, gay literature and the literature about homosexuality placed on the gay author a double burden: first, the responsibility to become aware of the gap between public and private discourse about being gay, and second, the responsibility to alter the public discourse so that it might better reflect the reality of the gay experience.

I must admit that my experience of reading *Psychopathia Sexualis* was very different than Delany's, although the difference might have been that Delany was a better and more systematic reader of Krafft-Ebing than I was. As I now recall it—and I have not gone back to those dim pages to verify—he is in the main utterly neutral in his presentation of the case histories, and I read only the case histories. He writes of the oddest people with a breathtaking clinical detachment. I did not notice at the time whether he provided any logical links between the cases, and in any event, my furtive reading habits led me to open the volume at random. As a result, a servant's fetish for lace underwear follows in my memory an account of Indian self-mutilation by simultaneously riding bareback and masturbating. The case of a general excited by men in parade comes after the story of a bookkeeper who frequented houses of prostitution. A person sexually aroused by the slaughter of chickens is jumbled in my mind with a farmer in love with the local priest. In short, Krafft-Ebing provided my adolescent mind with a lively panorama of sexual abandon, an X-rated picture out of Brueghel. Whatever I desired hardly compared to the florid elaboration of his case studies. Moreover, Krafft-Ebing gave equal measure in his case studies to biological and psychological causes. Whenever possible he would link his patients' psychological conditions to a physiological anomaly, but most often, as I recall, his examination showed his subjects to be physically normal. In my Krafft-Ebing, sex was a mystery whose forms resisted all attempts at classification or explanation, and though I now have a more detailed knowledge of various psychoanalytic, historical, anthropological, and physiological explanations of the phenomenon, I cling to the wonder and mystery of sexuality.

At issue is not that different gay youths read Krafft-Ebing differently, but rather that their sense of being gay relied so intensely on literary representations. Gay men's reliance on printed materials is reflected in the enormous volume and sophistication of the literature already published about AIDS. The medical profession has never before encountered a patient population so well informed about such esoteric matters as immunology, pharmacology, epidemiology, and drug testing. Local gay papers publish articles that regularly employ technical language found nowhere else but in scientific journals. In Van der Veen's 1986 survey of three hundred gay and lesbian periodicals around the world, 58 percent reported regularly on AIDS and 26 percent on moral general questions of science, while only 22 percent regularly reported on violence and hate crimes (28). Such technical information—written in the alphabet soup of medical acronyms—testifies to the gay community's reliance on literature for its information, despite the notorious gay grapevine whose speed (if not accuracy) remains a monument to oral folklore.

If I had to justify the value of studying gay literary representation, I could point to no better evidence for its significance than the disproportionate importance given to writing in gay communities. I don't mean that gay bars were, or have become, literary salons or lending libraries. But literary representation (and I use literary in its broadest sense) has been of greater importance for gay communities than for any other ethnic, national, or religious group. In the United States, there are more than one hundred gay and lesbian periodicals; worldwide, nearly two thousand (Van der Veen, 25). Hardly a major city on the East coast is without at least one gay bookstore, and since 1978— when Edmund White's *Nocturnes for the King of Naples,* Larry

Kramer's *Faggots,* and Andrew Holleran's *Dancer from the Dance* gained critical and commercial success—gay books have become a regular and increasingly large portion of trade publishers' lists.

Like Delany, I feel that developing a sense of what it is to be gay is of particular importance to me as a writer of both poetry and prose. I had stopped writing poetry altogether in my last years of college and my first years of graduate school. I was unable to write anything because I felt I could not write about being gay, the subject that most absorbed me at the time. Nor was I satisfied with the public language about homosexuality that was then available to me as a poet. Not until my lover at the time and I took a day trip to Harper's Ferry—that scene of another attempt at liberation—did language and emotion open, and out of the glove compartment of his rusted Beetle I took a piece of paper and wrote the beginning of a series of poems addressed to Walt Whitman. On a scrap of paper, I jotted "To be American is to be queer," and in so doing united the currents of the national spirit with my literary ancestry and my erotic desires.

Suddenly I felt that my sexuality, rather than marginalizing me in the traditions of American literature, actually placed me within its central channels. Being gay was empowering. Ten years later in studying F. O. Matthiessen, I came to see that I was not the first writer to find that to be American is to be queer. Indeed I had profited by the work of gay men before me, who had constructed the framework in which I could weave my own cultural productions.

The composition of "Alternative Service" was an attempt to write through the poetic blockages I was then experiencing, to retrace the labyrinth of "finding" my sexual identity in order to "develop" a sense of what I could do as a gay man at the end of the twentieth century.

I had no plans when I began writing "Alternative Service" of writing any more about gay literature. I did not intend to write a book. My experience of editing a collection of essays on camp had shown me the improbability of publishing book-length studies on gay literary subjects, and the mood of the country had taken an even more conservative turn since Karl Keller and I had tried to interest publishers in that project. The difficulty of publishing gay literary studies influenced the way *Gaiety Transfigured* evolved. At first one essay generated another to fill in or develop concepts left unelaborated, until the sheer number of essays began to form a mass large enough to suggest a book. I have tried to retain traces of the way this book developed for they testify to the uncertainty of gay literary studies, the political historical context in which it began, my own pressures of composition, and the far-from-settled concerns over gay literary methodology and canon. So spotty is the critical work even today, so incomplete the published record, so unexplored are the archives, that we are very far from ready to write a history of gay American literature; at least I am far from presuming so magisterial a position. I have not directly addressed the issue of homosexuality and the canon in this book.

A literature which gives Whitman, Melville, Thoreau, and Henry James significant places cannot be said to underrepresent homosexual writers. As I argue in the F. O. Matthiessen chapter, the canon of American literature has been fashioned in such a way as to give homosexual writers a privileged place. Yet it is also abundantly clear that those who have been elevated to canonical status have risen because they have been circumspect about their homosexuality and its depiction. In his old age, Whitman, the most explicit among them, went very far to cover up his sexual orientation. Thomas E. Yingling is, I think, correct when he says that gay writers have had to work through the basic "contradiction of being empowered to speak but unable to say" (26) and that for Crane, as well as other gay writers, "homosexuality needed to remain obscure—a 'private,' 'personal,' issue of no relevance to art" (109). Those who did make a public issue out of their sexuality—like Crane, Wilde, or Tennessee Williams— were harmed by such exposure. Williams seems to me the most glaring instance of a gay writer—arguably the greatest playwright this country has produced—unable to secure an unquestioned place in the canon because of the "scandal"of his sexuality, whose mark is unmistakable in his finest works.

The method I follow both implicitly acknowledges the canon and ignores it. Each essay places the text or texts it examines within a historical context and whenever possible with a gay genealogy of representation. I have paid little attention to genre since gay texts— even premodern ones—have played fast and loose with genre. One may argue that the very intermediateness of so many gay texts reflects the "intermediate sex" of their authors, but I have neither developed such an argument here with any consistency nor can espouse one without strain. More important for me is the introduction of authors who have been overlooked or not read in a gay light. I have devoted considerable space to such writers as Frances Grierson, Alain Locke, and Tobias Schneebaum, whose work deserves much greater attention than I think it has been given. But I have not tried to be encyclopedic. I have omitted many gay writers of genuine importance, such as Paul Bowles, Hart Crane, Allen Ginsberg, James Merrill, George Santayana, and Henry David Thoreau. These are omissions that come from lack of space and opportunity. My plan has never been to exhaust a subject, but to follow as best as I could certain currents within gay American literature. Consequently, after writing "Alternative Service" I realized that I needed to explore how homosexuality was related to death and to selfhood, but more urgently, I needed a working definition of homosexuality.

My attempt to define what was meant by the homosexual was aided by sustained study of feminist thought and critical practice. I would have begun such a study on my own had I not received a serendipitous invitation to join a Towson State University workshop whose aim was to integrate feminist scholarship into the sophomore level courses of the university, specifically, in my case, the Survey of British Literature. In its two years, the workshop I attended examined theoretical works on canon formation, language formation, ethical differences, male and female representation of gender. The program, funded by Fund for the Improvement of Postsecondary Education (FIPSE), and directed by Elaine Hedges and Sara Coulter, was instrumental in assisting me to work out many of the personal, theoretical, and practical problems of studying the representation of gender, and I want to thank both Professors Coulter (who directed the workshop in which I participated) and Hedges for their interest, support, and encouragement in this process and in my own reexamination of how, as a critic, teacher, and individual, I came to view gender differences and distinctions.

But although this study relies on feminist theory, methodology, and practice, I must admit that I speak of lesbian authors and material only briefly in this book. The reasons for this omission are varied. Psychoanalysis has given lesbianism a different—if related—etiology from male homosexuality. Insofar as this book rests on psychoanalytic understanding of gay male literature, those theories do not easily accommodate lesbian literature. Similarly, the history of lesbianism appears separately from the history of gay males. Although sodomy was regularly criminalized and punished, lesbianism does not have the same legislative history. To be sure, lesbians were punished as heretics and witches and, as such, suffered as long a history of oppression as homosexual men. But because they were punished as heretics and witches—

not as sodomites—their history and their literary representation followed a different path from homosexual men. As Monique Wittig has written in *The Lesbian Body:* "Lesbianism . . . is a theme which cannot even be described as a taboo, for it has no real existence in the history of literature. Male homosexual literature has a past, it has a present. The lesbians, for their part, are silent—just as all women are as women at all levels" (ix). Diana Collecott insists in her essay "What Is Not Said" on "the differences between homotextualities" (237), and Catharine R. Stimpson has pointedly argued, "If female and male gay writing have their differences, it is not only because one takes Sappho and the other Walt Whitman as its great precursor. They simply do not spring from the same physical presence in the world" (97). I agree. Only a few generalizations about gay men's writing can comfortably extend to lesbian literature. Moreover, a study of the interaction between gay male literary circles and lesbian literary circles deserves a book in itself and a very long book it will be. I do not pretend to be writing that book here. If what I say sheds light on lesbian literature, I am pleased, but I am not in a position now to assert such connections, though no doubt such connections can be made.

I have another reason for the omission. Simply put, I don't think I have the insight into lesbian literature that I have into gay men's literature. I don't have the same nuanced response. I feel that I lack this sensitivity at least in part because I am a man and, as such, have been acculturated outside of the codes women use to communicate their experience. I may be more conscious of my defects as a reader of lesbian literature because as a gay man I often am astonished by how insensitive ostensible heterosexual male critics are to the texture of gay literature. I may be missing less than I imagine, but I can't assess what I don't see. I felt some of the same reluctance when I began to explore black gay literature, namely, that as a white man I would fail to grasp the subtle—and not so subtle—differences between the black and gay experiences. I can't say now whether I have negotiated successfully across those barriers, but I feel a greater sympathy with the gayness of black men than many heterosexual blacks have expressed.

The omission of lesbian writers is just one of the lacunae in this study. Under the weight of my academic training—and as a graduate student at Johns Hopkins, the training was ponderous indeed—I used to feel somewhat guilty about my inability to take sides in the historicist/essentialist debate. Readers of these essays will find arguments that seem to be drawn from both sides of the debate. But we are learning that the split between nurture and nature, historicism and constructionism is not as irrevocable as it may seem. One may not need to choose between them; at least I have not chosen between them.

We might not need to choose because homosexual behavior is so widely distributed that it may derive from a variety of different origins. There is reason to think that some types of homosexual behavior may be genetic—or at least hormonal—while others are learned. Second, homosexuality may be a condition to which some are biologically predisposed but which manifests itself only under certain environmental conditions. Third, homosexual desire may be like certain linguistic abilities—such as making guttural sounds—a capacity which, if not exercised before the age of five, is lost entirely forever. Finally, and most important, whether the desire to have sexual relations with a person of one's sex is innate or learned, the manner of its expression is clearly historical.

David M. Halperin has argued that categorizing people on the basis of the sex of their sexual partners is as arbitrary as categorizing people by what they eat.

> Just as we tend to assume that human beings are not individuated at the level of dietary preference and that we all, despite many pronounced and frankly acknowledged differences from one another in dietary habits, share the same fundamental set of alimentary appetites, so most premodern and non-Western cultures . . . refuse to individuate human beings at the level of sexual preference and assume . . . that we all share the same fundamental set of sexual appetites. (27)

Halperin's analogy between sexual classifications and dietary classifications makes clear what part of any behavior might be biological and what learned, and as a child reared in a strictly kosher home, I find this analogy speaking rather forcefully to me. Certainly, we all get hungry; we have a drive to satisfy that hunger, but in some cultures strict rules govern what one may eat. The idea of eating a dog, for example, is repugnant to most Americans—we cannot think of dogs as food. We think of those people who eat dogs as unnatural or bestial, or despite the contradiction, as both. Similarly, in a chapter of his *Summa Theologica* on the unnaturalness of sodomy, Aquinas also refers to the eating of raw foods. For Aquinas, consuming any uncooked food other than milk was an unnatural use of a natural object.

What we think of as food and as appropriate ways of preparing it are learned, cultural categories even though hunger itself is biological.

Feminist theorists have taught us even more subtle ways that culture affects our sexual preferences even within the category of heterosexuality. Those who have studied male representations of the female body have noted that since the mid-nineteenth century pictures of the most sexually desirable women have shown progressively thinner torsos. Elizabethan men found a high forehead an almost irresistible part of a woman's anatomy. Chinese men seem to have taken a particular fancy to women with small, lotus-shaped feet. American heterosexual males don't seem to share their sexual interest in foreheads and feet. Are they, then, unnatural for failing to respond to such anatomical details? Of course not.

The truth is that virtually all theorists will claim that some aspects of sexual response are individual (for example, a preference for gap-toothed women), others are culturally instituted (a preference for thin blonds, for instance), and still others are innate and biological (the need for sexual release). Where one draws these lines differs, and the debate between constructionists and essentialists is fundamentally a debate on where those lines ought to be drawn. If I find myself siding at one point with constructionists and at other points with essentialists, it is because I am most concerned with the political leverage that one or the other argument gives me.

Even Halperin, who is closely associated with the constructionist school, admits that "constructionism may not turn out to be right in all its preliminary claims"; nevertheless, for Halperin, "by bracketing in effect our 'instinctive' and 'natural' assumptions, it makes it easier for us to highlight different historical configurations of desire and to distinguish various means . . . of institutionalizing them" (42). In short, the constructionist position is useful in placing into question the institutions—legal, religious, and ethical—that justify the oppression of homosexuals because they are, in the institutions' view, "unnatural."

However, when the religious Right takes the constructionist position to argue that homosexuality ought to be suppressed because (1) it can be taught to children (the recruiting theory of homosexuality), and (2) because homosexuals can change if given enough reason to change (the rehabilitation theory), then progay theorists find it easier to argue for the biological, instinctual, essentialist position of homosexuality.

I admit to equivocating as much as the next fellow. Nowhere is this equivocation more obvious than in my handling of the political potential of homosexuality. A friend wrote me that he finds it "curious . . . how sympathetic [I am] to the Carpenter/Whitman/Matthiessen dream of brotherhood/democracy/egalitarianism through homosexuality." And another questioned my "overly sanguine" attitude to the differences between the patriarchy and homosexual males. In both cases, they have read me as an essentialist, that merely being a homosexual privileges one to a particular political position. Of course, this is not the case. I am all too aware that homosexuality as a category cannot exist without the category of heterosexuality, that the two cannot be separated. But I am equally aware that because one is set up in opposition to the other, they cannot be so easily absorbed either by a general theory of bisexuality or by the intestinal fortitude of late capitalism. What I believe is that at best the feeling of "otherness" that patriarchy imposes on the homosexual can be a means by which gay people might, or could, and should understand themselves in relation to the institutions of power. In writing about Walt Whitman, Frances Grierson, Edward Carpenter, and F. O. Matthiessen, I was attempting to support a line of cultural work that may be of use to other gay people looking for a way positively to position their estrangement. But I have heard enough gay people utter misogynist, racist, anti-Semitic, and homophobic remarks to erase all hope that a homosexual orientation in itself can be the source of a higher, deeper, or more enlightened consciousness. I cannot escape the conclusion others have reached, that despite challenges from within the gay world remains firmly tied to the dominant order.

The nurture/nature controversy in gay studies is a reflection of the larger controversy about gender and gender identity, specifically in the issue of whether the "feminine" is a biological or a social construct, or whether some modes of masculine and feminine thought and behavior are innate and others cultural. Feminist theory and criticism are riddled with such contradictions—particularly the tension between post-structuralist or French feminism and pragmatic feminism of the Anglo-American variety. These tensions and conflicts in feminist theory are particularly important to the areas that intersect gay representation.

I have in mind the tension between Nancy Chodorow's psychoanalytic study of object formation as a sociological phenomenon and Julia Kristeva's psychoanalytic study of epistemology and language.

On the one hand, they both could be considered as constructionists since they claim that gender identity is developed after birth. Yet they differ markedly in two areas: what sorts of things are affected and effected in the first eighteen months of life, and how changes in child-rearing practices might alter the psychic structure of the child. Kristeva's position is more fatalistic: no matter how a child is reared the subject will, if it is to retain its sanity, develop the psychic distortions and confusions of language initiated in the mirror stage. She argues that "The symbolic destiny of the speaking animal . . . *seals off* . . . that archaic basis and the special jouissance it procures in being transferred to the symbolic. Privileged 'psychotic' moments . . . thus become necessary" (241, Kristeva's italics). Chodorow is less fatalistic. She contends that the distortion may be ameliorated by altering how children are reared. For Chodorow, insofar as society can change, the psychic landscape of the child can do so too. Kristeva's belief in the patriarchal nature of symbolic language always puts the feminine at a disadvantage in the manipulation of the sign, a disadvantage never compensated for by her closeness to the semiotic. "If it is true," Kristeva writes in "Motherhood According to Bellini," the penultimate essay in *Desire in Language,* "that every national language has its own dream language and unconscious, then each of the sexes—a division so much more archaic and fundamental than the one into languages—would have its own unconscious wherein the biological and social program of the species would be ciphered in confrontation with language" (241). Chodorow, though she contends that the female child in the patriarchal family is less capable at separating herself from those around her, believes that the female child is not necessarily a less efficient manipulator of signs. Those theorists who follow Kristeva tend to fall into essentialist arguments; those who follow Chodorow, into constructionism.

But rather than harming feminism, these seemingly opposed positions have benefited it, by placing at feminism's disposal essentialist and constructionist arguments and rhetoric for different, if overlapping, political needs. Both positions argue for change, but for different kinds of change. Constructionist rhetoric is aimed at the oppressor; it is the victim's argument for change in the victimizer. But if feminism had *only* constructionist arguments, it could represent women only as victims of institutional oppression, and although constructionists can wave the banner of egalitarianism and deploy its stirring rhetoric—thus tapping into the most firmly held of American ideals—it nevertheless can hardly celebrate womanhood in itself. That's where essentialist arguments become valuable and useful. They celebrate the unique virtues of women or, for that matter, any unfairly oppressed social segment. But although they tend to be celebratory, they are by no means pacifying. Essentialism argues for change within the oppressed group. It argues that the group must not only accept and celebrate its difference, but take those steps which strengthen these differences. Thus constructionist and essentialist arguments are complementary rather than oppositional. Indeed, as Diana Fuss has persuasively shown, essentialism rests on a constructionist position that these essential virtues have not been more fully developed because of social oppression; and constructionism rests on an essentialist position that all people are the same. These arguments are employed at different times to speak to different audiences and for different purposes.

As I look back on this book, I see how I have shifted strategically from one line of argument to another, and I have shown how gay writers take both sides on a single issue. This oscillation can be viewed as part of the general doubleness that is present in gay writing. In the chapter on camp, I argue that camp is a style that developed out of the doubleness of the gay writers' audience, that it provided a way to talk to heterosexual and homosexual readers simultaneously. Camp developed out of the need to hide homosexual implications from hostile heterosexual readers while entertaining one's fellow homosexuals. In its doubleness, camp is similar to the Signifyin(g) that Henry Louis Gates, Jr., finds in African-American literature as a way for black writers to communicate across and through vernacular and formal domains of language (44–51). Examining lesbian black writers such as Audre Lorde, Diana Collecott has noted, "Slaves, women, homosexuals, oppressed ethnic and religious groups, have always used forms of doubletalk to elude punishment, censorship, or mere ridicule" (242). Gay activists who wish to be free of any signs of accommodation have condemned camp as the terrible language of a people coping with oppression. Yet for others camp is the brilliant adaptation gay people have developed to deal with the hostile straight world, the protective and beautifully elaborated coloring that has helped gay people survive. If I favor the latter of these approaches, it is because it provides me more room in which to operate as both a gay man and a writer.

Since the eighteenth century, various forms of constructionist and essentialist arguments have competed for the support of gay people.

Homosexuals were involved in creating the biological model—an essentialist model—to counteract the oppression of the religious model that considered sodomy an acquired sin. Uranianism, the theory formulated by Karl Heinrich Ulrichs, a German lawyer, and embraced by John Addington Symonds and Edward Carpenter, was a useful concept because it might keep homosexuals out of jail. If, as Uranians argued, homosexuals were feminine souls trapped in male bodies, no amount of prison could alter their constitution. Uranians might be freaks of nature, but not criminals. But very soon, courts and the families of gay men began to use this biological model to force "treatment" for the "disease" of homosexuality. Gay men and women were subjected to a whole array of procedures, including electro- and insulin shock, hormone and aversion therapies. Against such a background, sociological theory became popular as a way out of mental hospitals. Homosexuality, such theories argued, was a label imposed, a self-fulfilling prophecy at once learned and intractable to correction. Theories about the origins of homosexuality have arisen dialectically in response to changes in legislation, medicine, and ethics.

As I worked through the materials that have become this book, I realized that I was interested less in their truth and aesthetic values, than I was in their effectiveness as cultural production; that is, I was most interested in viewing these works, in Alan Sinfield's words, "as contests between the stories that we tell ourselves about ourselves and the world" (153). I am particularly interested in the cultural productions of oppressed subcultures, and Sinfield's position is similar to my own:

> A subculture is a group collaboration to build a common story and establish it against rivals. . . . Subcultures are not founded always, or even particularly, in opposition and resistance; more mundanely, they are *ways of coping*. They afford to those who live them stories of their own identities and significance. They help groups who are ill at ease in the dominant culture to manage the diverse, often contradictory, histories and demands that they have experienced. (153, Sinfield's italics)

The four terms I develop as part of the structure of how gay people speak about themselves—otherness, genuineness, permanence, and equality—are not always the terms that gay people would have chosen had they been free to choose. For example, gay men often live a lifelong struggle against the feeling of otherness that they feel has been imposed upon them. Yet in building up cultural products that reinforce such terms either implicitly or explicitly, gay writers have developed a tradition, a mythology, and a common language that help gay men live out their lives with some shared sense of community, dignity, and continuity.

I received in the mail today *The Healing Notebooks* sent by its author Kenny Fries, whose work up to now I did not know. *The Healing Notebooks* is a lyric sequence written while Fries's lover struggled with the consequences of HIV infection:

> Begin with scraps of paper, odd
> sentences, someone else's phrases—
>
> *There is always something to be made*
> *of pain.* But art is once removed,
>
> The widow knitting scarves
> The lover quilting names,
>
> where was I in 1981? '82? '83? *Ask*
> *whose signature is stamped on the orders?*
>
> Sarah says, *People with AIDS need drugs*
> *not fiction about AIDS.* There I use
>
> the name in someone else's name.
> *Not one of my poems ever saved*
>
> *one Jew.* And still I sit all day as if
> choosing the right word could save your life.
>
> (section 12)

The Healing Notebooks is an exemplary cultural product not only because it provides a way of coping with the disease, but also because it interweaves its voice with other gay voices, locating itself by triangulation in the linguistic geography of inversion. Only in "someone else's name" can Fries find the licence to speak the word AIDS. Like the quilt the lover sews, the poem is a series of quotations stitched together, quotations taken mostly from other gay authors, such as Adrienne Rich, Sarah Schulman, and W. H. Auden. Fries finds, not a consistent position in these voices, but a way to connect himself to the gay community at a time when his grief threatens to separate him from it.

Similarly *Gaiety Transfigured* is itself a cultural production, situating my voice within the chorus of other gay voices, establishing an artistic and critical tradition which would give it both resonance and a means to cope with and negotiate through the thinly disguised homophobia within the critical and academic community.

The first two chapters which follow this introduction were written and rewritten several times, at intervals of months or even years. But by the time I had finished the chapter on the structure of homosexual discourse, I saw that I had developed enough material for several related chapters, and I began to work on them in a more systematic manner.

I began to explore the political position which early gay activists had tried to chart. I was interested in looking at Whitman and several of his English disciples, Edward Carpenter, Goldsworthy Lowes Dickinson, and C. R. Ashbee. Accident led me to Frances Grierson's all but forgotten work; a friend stumbled upon him in the course of reading about Abraham Lincoln in Edmund Wilson's *Patriotic Gore*. I want to thank Daniel Mark Epstein, my friend and colleague, for setting me on Grierson's trail, and for his enormous personal and intellectual support throughout the years.

Yet another friend who made an enormous contribution to the book is Dr. Louis A. Ross. During the period in which I was working on the chapter on ego structure and the lyric voice ("Choosing Our Fathers"), Louis Ross, a psychiatrist, was a frequent visitor to my home as he commuted between Washington where he lived and Baltimore, where he continued seeing patients and completed research of his own. He lent me several books and, though often bone tired, listened attentively to my developing ideas, gently steering me away from the more obvious pitfalls in the psychoanalytic material. His friendship and encouragement helped me bridge the wide gap between the object-relations theory I wished to develop and the literary criticism with which I was familiar. I also need to thank Alma Nugent, Claude Summers, and Gordon Hutner for reading the manuscript of this chapter and making valuable suggestions.

As teachers, we like to say that we learn from our classes, but often it is hard to say exactly what we have learned from them. The chapter on cannibalism and homosexuality is an example of a subject that directly evolved from a student's question. I once taught a course called Images of Masculinity, whose focus was men's autobiographies and autobiographical novels, and during a discussion of the cannibal-istic fantasy in Mishima's *Confessions of a Mask,* a student asked whether such fantasies were common in gay literature. Although my initial reaction was no, I realized that I could cite a half-dozen exam-ples off the top of my head. And although the students quickly moved to another topic—they were as disturbed by the idea as I was—I could not forget this puzzling conjunction of concepts. Only several years later, in the spring of 1989, when Towson State University granted me a sabbatical to complete this book had I the time to explore the rela-tionship between homosexuality and cannibalism. Several people were particularly helpful. I want to thank Professor Barbara Leons at Towson State, an anthropologist, whose interest in Latin American political organization did not keep her from spending many hours ex-plaining to me the anthropological problems of my materials and my analysis. She taught me that cross-disciplinary studies do not mean talking at cross-purposes. Frances Rothstein, also in the anthropology department at Towson State, provided materials at the very beginning of my research.

The chapter on cannibalism in many ways exemplifies one of the threads running throughout *Gaiety Transfigured.* In it, I demonstrate the genealogy of transformation that occurs as successive generations of gay writers work through each others' material, transfiguring a homophobic trope into a somewhat celebratory one. The genealogy of transformation is dialectical, the product of the interaction between the dominant society and the gay subculture. The end result is *not* a pure gay discourse (no such thing can exist) but a discourse made more sympathetic to the lives of gay men. That this genealogy of transformation is not accidental can be seen in Tennessee Williams's rather self-conscious references to Melville at the beginning of *Sud-denly Last Summer.* Indeed Williams is a writer who constantly posi-tions his work within the tradition of gay writing using Melville and Hart Crane as repeated touchstones. The study on cannibalism and homosexuality also illustrates another project of gay literature that repeats itself through this book: the search for an earlier or more ar-chaic society which would validate and authorize the social role of homosexuals in contemporary culture.

Writing the chapter on cannibalism made me particularly aware that I needed to strengthen my case on the way that gay writers often established a gay canon for themselves and worked to propagate that canon. The trope of calling upon the gay worthies for help against the arguments of the homophobic goes back as far as Marlowe, who argued Edward II's case by reminding his audience:

> The mightiest kings have had their minions:
> Great Alexander loved Hephestion;
> The conquering Hercules for Hylas wept;
> And for Patroclus stern Achilles drooped
> And not kings only, but the wisest men:
> The Roman Tully loved Octavius;
> Grave Socrates wild Alcibiades.
>
> (*Edward II*, 287)

In Wallace Thurman's novel of Harlem life in the twenties, *Infants of the Spring,* Stephen asks the flamboyant gay painter Paul about his drawings, which are described as "nothing but highly colored phalli" (12). Paul answers: "That's easy. I'm a genius. I've never had a drawing lesson in my life, and I never intend to take one. I think that Oscar Wilde is the greatest man that ever lived. Huysmans' Des Esseintes is the greatest character in literature, and Baudelaire is the greatest poet. I also like Blake, Dowson, Verlaine, Rimbaud, Poe and Whitman" (24). When Stephen answers, "That's not telling me anything about your drawings," Paul tartly retorts, "Unless you're dumber than I think, I've told you all you need to know" (24). Clearly Paul believes he is communicating not just his artistic affinity with the decadent aesthetic of the fin de siècle, but his sexual orientation. A statement of these influences is all the key one should need, Paul asserts, to decode the homosexual subtext of his work. Thurman alerts his readers to the homosexuality of his character and of his book in general by calling up this genealogy.

I can think of no figure who better illustrates gay involvement in canon formation than F. O. Matthiessen. In his letters to Russell Cheney—starting with those from his early twenties—we can trace Matthiessen's reading through what, at that time, consisted of the small line of works explicitly about homosexuality: Whitman, Gide, Proust, and Edward Carpenter. In the chapter devoted to him I also show how later in his career Matthiessen elevated gay writers in his revision of the American literary canon and implicitly provided grounds for a gay aesthetic. As a gay man, Matthiessen sought a usable past in the works of other gay men just as a poet and critic I filiate my work with the gay writers of previous generations. Here I should generally acknowledge my debt to Richard Howard, who has been both a sponsor and an exemplar for many years. Few people are as learned and as generous with their learning as Richard. I must also thank Richard Poirier for his support to me as both a critic and poet, and for publishing the essay on Matthiessen in *Raritan*.

The chapters on families, cannibalism, and F. O. Matthiessen all trace how gay literature has articulated alternative roles that gay people can play in society. One role is as intermediary between the living and the dead, a role made more challenging by the AIDS epidemic. By following the work of AIDS activist Larry Kramer, who sees society as a dysfunctional family—and its response to the AIDS epidemic as the logical result of that dysfunction—I am able to show the difficulty gay writers have in using the model of the nuclear family. Kramer's vision tells us more, perhaps, about his personal mythos than it does about the epidemiology of AIDS. Nevertheless, I find Kramer a very useful figure to study in examining not only the gay response to AIDS, but the gay response to itself in society.

My essay on Larry Kramer caught the attention of Frank Lentricchia and resulted in his asking to see the manuscript for this book. I want to thank Frank Lentricchia for his support and enthusiasm; Allen Fitchen, the director of the University of Wisconsin Press, for his help and expert advice; and Robert K. Martin of Concordia University for his excellent suggestions, including, adding a chapter on race and homosexuality. I would also like to thank Lydia Howarth, who has been the best copy editor I have worked with in over a decade of publishing, and Raphael Kadushin, my supportive and understanding editor.

Some people contributed to the book in ways I have not been able to weave into this narrative, such as it is. The essay on camp, though it began as a project with Karl Keller, took a very different and better shape when Amitai Avi-Ram asked me to speak on the subject as part of a Modern Language Association panel he led on constituting the gay and lesbian reader. Phil Willkie published the text of that talk in *The James White Review*. Ken Smith gave me valuable leads in my study of black gay literature. Wayne Koestenbaum, Richard Katz, Jim Hubbard, John Lessner, and Christopher Craft have been sounding boards for my ideas for many years and helped in their diplomatic ways to strengthen my understanding. Susan Stewart helped me get a handle on certain Lacanian notions, and George Stambolian encouraged me at an important moment of the book's development. Peter Baker and Ted Sweitzer provided forums for testing my ideas. Ross

Posnock, in particular, has given me valuable help with and direction to my work. I must also thank Diana Collecott, who has been an enormously helpful colleague and supportive friend. Michael Borchardt was an excellent typist. In an age when the independent bookseller is hard pressed by the chains, I must single out thanks to Jack Garman at Lambda Rising who has gone to great trouble to find books I needed for this study and to suggest many titles I would have overlooked. The librarians of the Albert Cook Library at Towson State have also been extremely attentive to my esoteric needs.

If more than other writers I emphasize the book's development and the role others have played in its composition, I have done so, first, because I have relied more than other authors on the community of scholars and friends in shaping this book; second, because gay studies as a discipline is still more vulnerable than other disciplines to political and historical pressures; third, because I see my own work as part of a far-from-established cultural practice and, thus, more dependent on the insight and energies of individuals than on institutions; and finally, because as a gay artist and critic I am perhaps more aware than other scholars of the unfolding process of our culture, its perpetual weaving and unweaving of itself, and wish even here to register the power of that unfolding and its fascination.

2

The Structure of Homosexual Discourse

Robert Gluck could have been speaking for virtually all gay authors when he wrote, "Society wants its stories; I want to return to society the story it has made" (161). For gay writers have not generally tried to create their own mythology independent of the heterosexual world; rather in the last three hundred years, they have sought to modify the sexual terms they have received, inscribing less a "reverse discourse" of homosexuality, than a subdominant one, a transcription of the original into a distant, unrelated key. As Foucault acknowledged, "There is not, on the one side, a discourse of power, and opposite, another discourse that runs counter to it. Discourses are tactical elements or blocks operating in the field of force relations" (101–2). Since homosexuals have fashioned their sense of themselves out of and in response to the heterosexual discourse about them, homosexuality —even as conceived by homosexuals—cannot be viewed outside of the constructs of heterosexuality.

Jonathan Dollimore has identified the two major strategies homosexual men and women use to fashion their sense of what homosexuality is and who homosexuals are. The first strategy is fitting homosexuality within categories valorized by heterosexuality. For example, since heterosexuality approves of sex that is "natural," gay writers showed that homosexuality is "natural," and, thus, worthy of approval. Discussing *The Well of Loneliness,* Dollimore writes, "Radclyffe Hall not only appropriates the 'authority' of the medical discourse currently transferring homosexuality from the realm of crime to that of nature; she also brilliantly merges and so transforms the medical model with other positive identifications usurped from the dominant culture" (182). Yet Dollimore finds this strategy ultimately unsatisfying because "it authenticates both the dominant and the subordinate, unable to acknowledge fully the extent to which the former negates the latter. . . . it seeks legitimacy for its deviant hero / ine in the categories of the very order which denies her legitimacy" (184).

Instead Dollimore prefers a more radical strategy, one perfected by Oscar Wilde, who changed the categories of approval while accepting the dominant assessment of homosexuality. Wilde's method, according to Dollimore "is inversion and hierarchical reversal, especially the substitution of surface for depth and the superficial for the essential" (187). Wilde finds unnaturalness as the chief virtue of homosexuality; for him "artificial" is a term of approbation. Yet this second strategy also has its weakness: dependence on the categories it attempts to invert and subvert. No matter what means radically gay writers have used in their attempts to break from the discourse of the heterosexual, they have remained tied to it, according to Dollimore, in a "violent dialectic."

Because homosexuality in Euro-American culture is so tied to the dominant culture from which it emerges, and because its terms and values are generated out of the "violent dialectic" with that discourse, it is mistaken to connect the structure of current, western homosexuality with the male-male sexual activity of other times or cultures. The modern Euro-American homosexual views him- or herself in vastly different ways than the Greek pederast or the Melanesian pubescent. Though both progay and antigay forces have linked Euro-American homosexuality to institutional male sex in other cultures—especially the Greeks—such linkage only further distorts and obscures the nature of homosexuality in Europe and North America.

One must, I believe, distinguish sexual relations between men generally—what we may call "intramale sexuality"—from the sexual relations between men that has occurred in Euro-American society since the eighteenth century, what is generally termed "homosexuality." Homosexuality is the specific form of intramale sexuality that has developed within the framework of institutionalized heterosexuality, an antithesis, which gives heterosexuality its particular force and focus and has acted to alter and enrich—as Edward Carpenter and others have noted so long ago—the structure of Euro-American culture.

Homosexuality and other forms of sex between males get confused because they occur simultaneously in this society. According to the Kinsey Institute intramale sexual relations are a common (if undiscussed) part of American life. In the original study, Kinsey and his colleagues found that 60 percent of all males had had at least one sexual experience to orgasm with another male (651). Yet Kinsey indicated that only 10 percent of all males were "more or less exclusively homosexual" for three years or more, and a certain percentage of these numbers had engaged in such relations only during adolescence. Such individuals do not in the main regard themselves or their actions as homosexual nor does society regard them as such. Instead, the activity falls under the rubric of "experimentation" or "sexual release," perfectly acceptable heterosexual outlets of libido. The discourse of heterosexuality allows for a large number of contingencies in which the ostensibly heterosexual male may engage in sexual relations with other males. As James Baldwin has remarked, "Straight cats invented faggots so they can sleep with them without becoming faggots themselves" (Baldwin and Giovanni, 89). Prisoners engaged in intramale sexual acts, for example, may avoid the label of homosexual, provided that they are confined to single-sex institutions and that upon release they revert to heterosexual relations. Male prostitutes, especially "street hustlers," do not have to regard themselves as homosexuals—though many do—if they engage in such practices *only* for money.

The complexity of society's rules governing who must and who cannot be considered homosexual is epitomized in the population Bruce Jackson studies in "Deviance as Success: The Double Inversion of Stigmatized Roles." Male prisoners divide themselves sexually into three groups: queens, those who are homosexual outside of prison; studs, those who while in prison play the inserter role with other men; punks, those who while in prison play the receptor. If asked, studs and punks, in this system, say they played their roles because they are denied access to women. Jackson argues, however, that many of "those argot-role actors . . . would very much like to be homosexual outside, but they just *did not know how*" (260, Jackson's italics). According to Jackson, "prison was the only place they had a moral structure that permitted them to be acting-out homosexuals, a place where there was a grand body of folk culture that legitimized their behavior"

(261). Consequently, these men often commit crimes immediately after their release so that they can be returned to prison where they may reenter their desired sexual roles. "By adopting the convict stigma they were enabled to act out the homosexual roles without any of the attendant stigma they would have suffered (and self-applied) in the free world" (261). Their male egos can better accept being criminal than being gay.

Sexual identity and sexual practice are frequently separate in the discourse of both homo- and heterosexuality. In both discourses, the way you feel about what you do is far more important than what you do, and your experience of the sexual act is more determinate of its nature than the identity of the person with whom it is performed. Under the code of heterosexuality, some sexual roles are taboo for those men who wish to retain their heterosexual identity. Often the conditions under which an act is performed determine its acceptability. But the most important factor in determining the nature of a particular act is the kind of emotional and psychological awareness involved in its performance. People recognize themselves as homosexual without ever having sexual relations; similarly the vast majority of males who have had sex with other males regard themselves as heterosexuals. Individuals seem to hold within themselves a subtle, graduated scale which determines the spectrum lying between hetero- and homosexual experience. David Leavitt's novel *The Lost Language of Cranes* chronicles the evolution of awareness as a man moves from exclusive heterosexuality to intramale sexual activity, and ultimately, to homosexual consciousness. His is the classic progression found in "the coming-out story," the homosexual *Bildungsroman.*

David M. Halperin argues in *One Hundred Years of Homosexuality,* his study of "Greek love," what is more important to the Greeks in establishing sexuality is the style of one's desires. The Greeks, according to Halperin, "constructed male desire as wide-ranging, acquisitive, and object-directed, while constructing feminine desire . . . as objectless, passive, and entirely determined by the female body's need for regular phallic irrigation" (36). Since boys and male slaves possessed a feminine desire, they could service male desire just as satisfactorily as women. Halperin believes this emphasis on the style of desire rather than on the sex of the object of desire is a central contrast between Greek sexuality and modern American sexuality, but it seems to me that stylistics of desire is exactly what distinguishes the homosexual from the heterosexual male who engages in periodic sex with other men, what distinguishes in James Baldwin's terms, the "faggot" from the "straight cats" who "sleep with them." The stylistics of desire remains a determining factor in sexual identity.

What then is the structure of the discourse of homosexual experience? How does it differ from the discourse of intramale sexuality? And how is it related to heterosexuality? There are, I believe, several axes around which one can distinguish the homosexual from other sexual discourses.

1. The most significant term and the one from which the other differences derive is otherness. Although a sense of otherness affects us all, the otherness that affects the homosexual—or effects his sense of homosexuality—is more profound. For while otherness is an unavoidable part of any self's awareness of its own subjectivity and its difference to other persons around it, the homosexual suffers a categorical, perhaps even ontological, otherness since he is made to feel his "unlikeness" to the heterosexual acts and persons who gave him being. The otherness of the homosexual is not merely a heightening of the separateness which is a central feature of the ego structure of the heterosexual male, a separateness created by the hard and fixed boundaries heterosexual males erect both to protect their egos from the dangers of castration and to further their identifications with their fathers. The homosexual's separateness occurs with neither firm boundaries nor with heightened identification with the father. He is distanced without definition. Herbert Blau has spoken eloquently of the "egolessness in the diplomacy of the anus" which characterizes the site of homosexual desire. The very object world of the homosexual differs from that of the heterosexual so that he is constantly inscribing himself in Blau's phrase, in the "heraldic sign . . . which presupposes no first person, no ego, no *face* of power" (124). This negativity of self mirrors the sociological fact that no homosexual is raised as such; he finds no likeness in the family circle. Thus, the homosexual misses the bonding and identification which for the heterosexual bridges the gap between himself and others. Indeed the family reminds the homosexual of his own "unlikeness."

2. Homosexuality, unlike other intramale sexual states, is a lifelong condition. It is not a "phase" that one goes through, as heterosexual males go through a "phase" of homoeroticism. Nor is it a ritualized period of behavior as it was in the culture of the ancient Greeks or as it is in the Melanesian society which Gilbert Herdt has so exhaustively studied in *Guardians of the Flute*. In these cultures specific sexual roles

are determined by age. The male passes from one intrasexual role to another, at the end of which in Sambian society he becomes exclusively heterosexual. In contrast Euro-American homosexuality is for all ages.

3. A corollary of the lifelong condition of homosexuality is its genuineness of experience. Homosexuality is not a passing fancy or a substitute for heterosexual contact. The "heterosexual" male prisoner who has repeated sex with another man claims that his sexual activity is merely a substitute for his real desire which is for a woman. The homosexual, however, experiences his desire for men as genuine and often characterizes heterosexual activities in contrast as "shallow" or "false" or "pretended."

4. Finally, homosexuality differs from other intramale sexual relations and heterosexual relations by the equality of its relations. By equality I do not mean that in individual relationships the partners are equal—clearly, such is not the case—but rather that the institution of homosexuality does not assign specific roles to specific individuals. In Sambia, ancient Greece, or in parts of Africa, roles are rigidly polarized. Older, dominant, or ostensibly heterosexual males may—if they wish—play the inserter role in anal or oral intercourse. But they must *not* play the receptor role without being stigmatized. Younger, subordinate, and ostensibly homosexual males can *only* play the receptor roles. In Euro-American homosexuality these roles are not proscribed; indeed, homosexuality has developed a remarkable fluidity of roles and role-playing that cuts across racial, social, and cultural boundaries. No doubt, hierarchical forces come to play their part in homosexual relations—homosexuality exists only within the patriarchy—but homosexuality is more notable in the way it resists hierarchies than in the way it bends to them.

These may not be the only four terms that differentiate homosexual from either intramale sexual or heterosexual discourse, but they are significant terms and in combination give homosexuality and the homosexual their distinctive idiom of expression.

Otherness was not a homosexual invention; the term was applied to gay men by the discourse of heterosexuality. Indeed, heterosexual discourse calculated and labeled the homosexual with all the permutations of otherness. He was *not* Christian, *not* natural, *not* manly, *not* a woman, *not* of the heterosexual's country or region or continent, *not* human, *not* animal, *not* even to be named. An anonymous editor wrote in 1699 as preface to the proceeding of the trial against Lord Castlehaven for various sexual offenses, that the abomination

> shocks our natures and puts our modesty to blush so commonly perpetrated . . . the devilish and unnatural sin of buggery, a crime that sinks a man below the basest epithet, is so foul it admits of no aggravation and cannot be expressed in its horror, but by the doleful shrieks and groans of the damned. . . . The sin [is] now being translated from sodomitical original, or from the Turkish and Italian copies into English. (quoted in H. Montgomery Hyde, 63)

The editor would like to believe that no Englishman, by himself, could have sunk to buggery without foreign and demonic influence. The very term "buggery"—a corruption of "Bulgarian," a nationality in which heresy and perversion were thought to flourish—suggests the foreign nature of the vice. The editor has used virtually all the categories of negation to assert the otherness of sodomy, but the otherness of homosexuality is perhaps most dramatically presented by the failure of language to give it a name. It can be known, according to the editor, only by being "translated" or through "copies," which are less horrible than its native tongue.

Yet one must question whether the feeling of otherness proceeds from the recognition (even subconscious) of being homosexual, or whether it precedes and lays the groundwork for homosexuality. In their memoirs, gay men repeatedly speak of feeling "different" before they have any sense of their sexual orientation. Richard Isay, a psychoanalyst, claims that "almost all the gay men" he has treated "report that, starting from the age of four, they felt that they were 'different' from their peers" (23). This sense of being "different" begins long before any conscious awareness of their sexual orientation. In *If It Die* Gide recalls how at the age of ten and for no apparent reason he broke into uncontrollable sobs at the dining room table. Without understanding the cause of his enormous sorrow, he wailed to his mother, "I am not like other people. I am not like other people . . ." For Gide, "It was as though the special sluice-gate of some unknown, unbounded, mystic sea had suddenly been opened and an overwhelming flood poured into my heart" (111).

But not just people like Gide, whose extraordinary sensibility might account for such perceptions of otherness, record such experiences; ordinary gay men have reported the same feelings. One of the most striking accounts appears in Claude Hartland's autobiography *The*

Story of a Life published in St. Louis in 1901. Hartland "offers to the medical world the strange story of [his] own life, hoping that it may be a means by which other similar sufferers may be reached and relieved" (xii). At the age of nine, Hartland is sent with two or three brothers to school; "the first day," he recalls, "brought me to realize how different I was from other boys of my own age" (11). Many children, affected by the fear and anxiety of leaving home and starting school, are made self-consciously aware of their differences. But Hartland's sense of difference is, compared with his brothers', beyond the normal discomfort and self-consciousness. It is a force that separates him. This was not the first time Hartland had felt different, but the first time he could *judge* the difference.

At four, which is "as far back as [his] memory extends," he comes to feel "I was not like other children," wording remarkably similar to Gide's formulation (6). His recognition comes after burning three of his fingers and having them bandaged in splints. One may wonder whether the burnt fingers represent some subconscious desire for castration or whether the "stalls" in which they are wrapped represent erections, yet such symbols are far beyond Hartland's conscious awareness, for what is particularly striking about his memoir is its innocence of any other published work on sexual inversion. Although by 1901, Havelock Ellis had published *Sexual Inversion* and Oscar Wilde had stood for his highly publicized trial, Hartland seems completely unaware of such events. His expressions of otherness have all the painful genuineness of the naive. His is no self-conscious trope, but the guileless—if lachrymose and pietistic—confessions of a sufferer.

The homosexual's otherness is particularly distinguished from the difference or alienation we might expect in all persons brought up in Euro-American culture in the last three or four hundred years, a separateness in which each in the cell of himself is aware of others in their cells. Under such conditions, one's particular sense of otherness is at least partially ameliorated by the awareness of one's likeness to others in a similar state of isolation. Adorno, for example, writes of the necessary epistemological separation of subject and object, in which subjectivity must constitute itself as other in order to regard itself at all. Yet, according to Adorno, that split is almost immediately mediated by ideology, which—he states in language that already anticipates the triumph of heterosexism—"is indeed its normal form." In the "normal form," "the sense of identity of mind . . . repressively shapes its Other in its own image" ("Subject," 499). The dominance of the social order operates to mediate through narcissistic reflexivity the breach between subject and object. But the homosexual is not open to the normal forms of mediation; since he does not identify with the dominant father, the ideology of dominance cannot perform the same assuagement of the epistemological rupture that it can perform for the heterosexual. At best he is left with the sublime onrush of the undifferentiated that Gide describes as the "overwhelming flood" of "some unknown, unbounded, mystic sea." Rather than bridge the epistemological split by narcissism, the homosexual fills the gap with his unlikeness. For the rigid boundedness of the heterosexual male's ego structure, he posits unbounded, undifferentiated otherness.

The homosexual is made to feel the weight of his otherness in yet another manner that distinguishes it from the general alienation of society, for the homosexual is made to bear the onus of the heterosexual's homophobic paranoia. "Freud's famous 'persecutory paranoia,'" Guy Hocquenghem reminds us, "is in actual fact a paranoia that *seeks to persecute*" (42, Hocquenghem's italics). The homosexual's sense of persecution is *not* a fantasy, but a social reality, and yet he is made to feel his anxiety as his own distortion. Indeed, for Hocquenghem, the official discourse of homosexuality is produced by the homosexual panic of ostensibly heterosexual institutions. "Society's discourse," he argues "is the fruit of the paranoia through which a dominant sexual mode [heterosexuality] . . . manifests its anxiety at the suppressed but constantly recurring sexual modes [homosexuality]" (42).

But not all homosexuals find their otherness to be the stigma heterosexual discourse has labeled it. As Mary McIntosh observed in the sixties, homosexuals "welcome and support the notion of their otherness because it "appears to justify the deviant behavior as being appropriate for [them]" (32). Indeed, many transform otherness from a mark of shame into the very sign of their superiority. As Dollimore has pointed out, no one has done more to invert the categories of heterosexual discourse than Oscar Wilde. In his *De Profundis,* a work inscribed by the abyss of otherness, Wilde seeks to overturn the language that has dominated him. Despite his imprisonment, he proudly declares: "I am far more of an individualist that I ever was. My nature is seeking a fresh mode of self-realization. That is all I am concerned with" (289). And later he asserts, "I am one of those who are made for exceptions, not for laws" (291).

Usually, however, gay writers have not attempted to overturn the category of otherness so directly or so personally. One of the forms that gay writers have particularly favored is the ethnographic account or essay. Melville in *Typee* and *Mardi,* Charles Warren Stoddard in *South-Sea Idylls* and *The Island of Tranquil Delights,* Gide in his *Travels in the Congo,* Edward Carpenter in his *Intermediate Types Among Primitive Folk* and *Iolaus: Anthology of Friendship,* Edward Karsch-Haack in *The Same-Sex Life of Primitive Peoples,* Edward Westermarck in "Homosexual Love," and Tobias Schneebaum in *Keep the River on Your Right,* all have sought to legitimize otherness by finding other cultures that have accepted intramale sex. Indeed no literary form was more congenial to gay writers of the nineteenth and early twentieth centuries than the ethnographic study, and it was in ethnographic discourse that homosexual writers often found the terms for their own attacks on heterosexuality. As I explore in the chapter on the conjunction of homosexuality and cannibalism, ethnography provides the gay writer with the opportunity to subvert several types of otherness. The foreign, attacked by xenophobic heterosexual discourse, is elevated, and the pagan (non-Christian) is extolled for its honesty, vision, and humanity. But the most important effect of gay ethnography is its assertion of the naturalness of homosexuality. Gay writers are at pains to show that exclusive heterosexuality is an artificial barrier erected against the polymorphous perversity of nature.

Though we cannot doubt the power of heterosexual discourses to affect consciousness and to make their own reality, nevertheless, they do not explain why the four-year-old Hartland—who has yet to be labeled by society, feel its stigmatization, or even be aware of his sexual orientation—should conceive of himself as other. Some other force must come into play that affects, not so much his sexual orientation, as his ego development at the early stages of object-relations. Though one can imagine a number of scenarios that might lead to a homosexual orientation, the evidence of gay writing suggests that one's identity as other precedes and prepares for the later development of a homosexual identity.

Though children who will become homosexual have strong feelings toward their fathers—often warm, loving feelings toward them—they rarely identify with them. Nor do many identify with their mothers. Indeed, this early sense of otherness seems to reflect alienation from both parents, a vague, amorphous, and potentially empty selfhood. But though the child does not identify with his father, he is repeatedly encouraged to admire and emulate the father, and what the son cannot be he wishes to love and be loved by. His failed identification charges the father with additional desirableness.

The crisis for the gay child is in the tension between other people's views and expectations of him, and the views and expectations he has of himself. "The conscious feeling of having a personal identity is based on two simultaneous observations," according to Erik Erikson, "the perception of selfsameness and continuity of one's existence in time and space and the perception of the fact that others recognize one's sameness and continuity" (50). The son who will be gay learns early that how he is perceived differs sharply from how he perceives himself. But to the loss of "personal identity" is added the loss of what Erikson calls "ego identity" when the *style of one's individuality* does not coincide with "one's *meaning for significant others* in the immediate community" (50, Erikson's italics). Erikson's analysis permits us to view the modes of homosexual transformation of heterosexual otherness. The homosexual child experiences a sense of limitlessness, an otherness unbounded by the forms and shapes of his parents. But being free of any specific form, the child is free to put on any number of masks, or, as I develop further in the following chapter, in some Whitmanesque expansion, absorb within himself the various styles around him. Insofar as the feelings of otherness stem from the structure of the bourgeois family, such feelings are part of a historical constellation and not a necessary part of intramale sexual relations.

These ways of dealing with otherness develop early in children and may, in fact, determine the success with which they deal with their sexual orientation later in life. John Addington Symonds's *Memoirs,* which was expressly written to provide a picture of the development and life of a homosexual, grants us the opportunity to examine the style of his individuality. "It is significant," he insists,

> that two tales made a deep impression. . . . One was Andersen's story of the ugly duckling. I sympathized passionately with the poor bird swimming round and round the duck-puddle. I cried convulsively when he flew away to join the beautiful wide-winged white brethren. . . . Thousands of children have undoubtedly done the same, for it is a note of childhood, in souls destined for expansion, to feel solitary and disbarred from privileges due to them. The other [was] called "The Story Without End." . . . The mystical, dreamy communion with nature in wild woods and leafy places took my fancy. (37)

In his passionate sympathy for the duckling, Symonds identified with what was "solitary and disbarred from privileges," but such loss prepared him for the communion with all of nature. Later Symonds could throw himself into a state of "gradual but swiftly progressive obliteration of space, time and sensation" in which he achieved "a pure, absolute, abstract self" and "the apprehension of coming dissolution" (58).

In defending itself against homosexuality, patriarchal discourse has tried to deny both its permanence and its genuineness. All three of the ways in which patriarchy has conceived of homosexuality—as sin, crime, and disease—place it within frameworks that deny it permanence since sins may be overcome, crimes avoided, and diseases cured.

On the two occasions in western history when society has bothered to recognize intramale sexuality—as part of Greek culture and as a biblical abomination—the focus has been on those relations that were phaseal or fashionable. The Greek model of pederastia—which has largely been ignored but cannot be forgotten—assigns sexual and emotional roles by age. In the *Symposium* Socrates envisions a hierarchy of erotic states which culminates in a purely spiritual love. The Bible conceives of intramale sexual relations as a foreign import—a fashion adopted from outside of the tribe. In 1 Maccabees is an account of how Hebrew men "made themselves prepuces . . . and joined themselves to [Romans]" (1:15) whom they admired in the bathhouses and gymnasiums, and Paul is particularly upset by early Christians adopting the Roman sexual fashion of homosexuality. Heterosexual discourse has sought to limit homosexuality to the passing fad or a certain phase of development. As horrible as sodomy is in heterosexual discourse, it can have no permanent hold.

Patriarchal insistence on the impermanence of homosexual desire reappears in psychoanalytic theory which hypothesizes homosexuality as "arrested sexual development." For Freud every male (or female) goes through a period of bisexuality in which both mother and father are cathected objects. Homosexuality, thus, is "normally" a temporary and transitional stage; its prolongation in some people constitutes its abnormality. What the psychoanalyst attempts to do—though Freud *never* believes that it is possible—is to alleviate this infantile fixation and lead the homosexual toward a permanent heterosexual adjustment. In so doing, most psychoanalytic theory reinscribes even lifelong homosexuality within the transitional.

Popular gay literature, however, systematically distinguishes between phasic intramale sexual acts (which are accepted within the discourse of heterosexuality because they are empty of significance) and the "genuine" homosexual act. Aaron Fricke's *Reflections of a Rock Lobster,* written while Fricke was still a teenager, distinguishes the boundaries between accepted and unacceptable same-sex activities. Though once a participant in the sexual play that occurred in his grade school boys' bathroom, he drops out of such games in the fourth grade from fear of discovery (16). Explains Fricke: "At this point, I was already conscious that I was a homosexual" (18). As a homosexual he can no longer freely and unselfconsciously join in the fun. What he discovered, and what he fears others will discover, is his genuine pleasure in these activities. Such pleasures can be enjoyed only if they are not desired. In Fricke's case, desire terminates pleasure.

Fricke reverses the entire category of permanence: for him heterosexuality seems vague, impermanent, unfixed, and unreal. His father's anxious explanation of "the raw truth about heterosexuality" did not elicit in the twelve-year-old Aaron the desired shock of recognition:

> The concept of heterosexuality did not immediately sink in. I didn't reject it, I just found it difficult to swallow. *This* was the alternative that had somehow eluded me through childhood years. *This* was the thing that separated me from the beasts. . . . Surely it didn't have anything to do with me; I had no desire to try any of these heterosexual techniques. It all seemed like just conjecture; I didn't believe it could ever effect *me*. (22, Fricke's italics).

The "genuine" is the homosexual, for Fricke; the heterosexual is mere illusion, the *Arabian Nights* tale of patriarchal authority.

If Fricke's uncertainty places in question the "naturalness" of heterosexuality, Oscar Wilde subverts the approved categories even more radically. As Dollimore has shown, Wilde questions the very categories of patriarchal approval, subverting Max Nordau and Cesare Lombroso's concept of degeneration in which certain moral habits disintegrate through overuse or interbreeding. Wilde begins with the seemingly humble confession that he is a victim of his own excess. "I let myself be lured into long spells of senseless and sensual ease. . . . I became the spendthrift of my own genius, and to waste an eternal youth gave me a curious joy. Tired of being on the heights, I deliberately went to the depths in search of new sensations" (*De Profundis,* 288). He would have us believe that his homosexuality results from boredom with the common and "healthier" forms of sexuality. His pleasure in normal sexual acts exhausted, where else could he turn but to the arms of men? "People thought it dreadful," he wrote, "to have entertained at dinner the evil things of life." But Wilde is not to be ruled by what others think. "From the point of view through which I, as an artist in life, approach them they were delightfully suggestive and stimulating. It was like feasting with panthers" (*De Profundis,* 327). Since desire, for Wilde, gains its allure from being transitory and from its ability to both construct and deconstruct the desirer and the object of his desire, heterosexuality is no more permanent to the artist than homosexuality. Desire and its objects—if worth the desiring—are valuable *because* they are mutable. Wilde believes that nothing worth having should last forever.

To argue that homosexuality is, on the one hand, historically contingent and, on the other hand, lifelong and permanent may appear contradictory. Permanence seems to place homosexuality into an essentialist frame of reference at odds with the historicism of the rest of the analysis. But though homosexuality is permanent for those reared at a certain historical moment, it is not transhistorical or universal. What makes it difficult to separate the permanence of homosexuality from essentialism is that the very discourse of sexuality is itself grounded in humanistic and essentialist terms. But like class awareness—which is a historical contingency, but an inescapable component of our psyches—so, too, does homosexuality insist upon its permanence even as it dreams of a time when people and acts are no longer differentiated into sexual categories.

The most radical innovation of modern homosexuality is the egalitarian ideal to which it aspires. The discourse of equality between sexual partners distinguished Euro-American homosexuality from many forms of intramale sexual activity. Alan Bray, who has studied the emergence of a distinctly homosexual lifestyle and its beginning in England at the end of the seventeenth century, links the construction of homosexuality to changes in heterosexuality. Homosexuality, according to Bray, is a product of what Lawrence Stone has called "affective individualism," the more private domestic and affectional relationships which replaced the kinship, client-oriented, community-based relationships as the cement of the family (112–13). Homosexuality could not develop until men began to look at their own affections as the reason for intimate relations.

Although hysterically stigmatized by clerical and judicial authority in the early seventeenth century, sodomy was punished only when the perpetrator violated patriarchal order. In general, according to Bray, homosexuality was invisible because it developed no subculture and, more important, it respected and imitated the hierarchical structures of patriarchy. "Despite the contrary impression given by legal theorists," writes Bray, "so long as homosexual activity did not disturb the peace or the social order, and in particular so long as it was consistent with patriarchal mores, it was largely in practice ignored" (74). As evidence, Bray cites the noticeable absence of prosecutions between master and servant, teacher and student, guildman and apprentice.

With the advent of molly houses—places of homosexual assignation—come the first mass arrests of homosexuals in England. For Bray, the reason is clear: "The society of the molly houses did not follow class lines but rather tended to dissolve them. It did so because it was not mediated by existing social forms, of class, or otherwise: it was set alongside them, a social institution in its own right" (86). Molly houses were symbolic of, indeed, seemed to be the only structure in the homosexual subculture. In the tendency to dissolve class lines—the hierarchy of the patriarchy—homosexuality challenged the basic categories of patriarchal discourse and found itself immediately oppressed.

I do not mean to say that homosexuality achieves the democratic vista to which it aspires. Michael Moon, for example, sees in the homoerotic world of Horatio Alger's novels "an encapsulation of corporate/capitalist America's long-cherished myth" (10). Michael Pollak has argued that "of all the different types of masculine sexual behavior, homosexuality is undoubtedly the one whose functioning is most strongly suggestive of a market" (44). Patriarchal structures often reestablish themselves in their most nakedly oppressive forms within the gay community, but we must remember that Alger represents homosexuality in what Moon calls its most "fiercely repressed" form and Pollack discusses a limited historical and urban condition. Since gay men are raised within the patriarchy, they understandably import its features into their construction of homosexuality. What is notable is the degree to which they have resisted patriarchal hierarchies.

Against the patriarchal reinscriptions Moon and Pollack find in the fictions and mores of homosexuals, Joseph Allen Boone places the American quest romance whose "socially subversive content [is] . . . filtered first through the private realm of individual desire" (235). Boone finds three countertraditional possibilities in the "questing hero's escape from a marriage-oriented culture." Among those "possibilities" is "the elevation of mutuality—rather than polarity—in the male bond [which] presents a conceptual alternative to the gender inequality institutionalized by marriage in heterosexual relations" (272).

"Eros is a great leveler," declares Edward Carpenter, "perhaps the true Democracy rests, more firmly than anywhere else, on sentiment which easily passes the bounds of class and caste, and unites in the closest affection the most estranged ranks of society," those who fall into what Carpenter called "the intermediate sex" (*Intermediate Sex,* 114–15). Like his hero Walt Whitman, Carpenter believed that homosexuals were in the vanguard of a new social order that would do away with class and sexual hierarchies and promote a true democracy. He was not alone. Goldsworthy Lowes Dickinson, C. R. Ashbee, John Addington Symonds, and Carpenter all tried to restructure their lives in ways which may not meet with our approval today, for as Jeffrey Weeks has commented, their encounters with working-class men could trail off into "avidly exploitive sexual colonialism" (44). Nevertheless, they sought "the dream of class reconciliation" (44). Homosexuality was one of the most important avenues by which generations of Englishmen broke through the barriers of class, privilege, and rank.

If this is true for the English, it is especially true for Americans. *Democratic Vistas* is based in large measure on the sexual politics of male adhesiveness. According to Robert K. Martin, Melville went even further than Whitman. "The homosexual relationship is invested by Melville with radical social potential," Martin argues; "it is through the affirmation of the values of nonaggressive male-bonded couples that the power of the patriarchy can be contested and even defeated" (*Hero,* 70). The marriage of Queequeg and Ishmael constitutes a primal transgression against patriarchal rules; within the American racist and sexist ethos, no union could be more iconoclastic.

Despite formidable obstacles, the discourse of equality seems to have been translated widely into the lives of gay men. In *The Social Organization of Gay Males,* Joseph Harry and William B. DeVall have examined how gay men look at their relationships with their domestic partners. Their conclusion is that "rather than utilizing the conventional heterosexual marriage as a model for relationships, it seems that [gay] relationships are patterned after the nonexclusive conventional best friends model" (99). When they examined the specific connection between income and decision-making roles, Harry and DeVall discovered that though "those who made more money reported that they made more decisions," such inequalities in gay relationships still did not "come near to approximating the inequalities of heterosexual marriages" (99). In short, they conclude that "the marital relationships of gays tend to be modeled on the egalitarian friendship model" (98). In fact, the egalitarianism of the relationship translated into the bedroom where gay couples tended to exchange in reciprocal manner the various erotic positions.

However, lower-class gays tended to prefer less egalitarian relationships and more frequently used such inequalities to determine roles in sexual intercourse. Harry and DeVall infer that lower-class gays, just as their heterosexual counterparts, have much stronger tendencies to polarize roles. Inequalities seem to reflect social class, rather than sexual orientation (118–19).

Eve Kosofsky Sedgwick argues in *Between Men* that although the present society is both sexist and homophobic, "it has yet to be demonstrated that because most patriarchies structurally include homophobia, therefore patriarchy structurally *requires* homophobia" (4). She continues: "the example of the Greeks demonstrates, I think, that while heterosexuality is necessary for the maintenance of a patriarchy, homophobia, against males at any rate, is not. In fact, for the Greeks, the continuum between "men loving men" and "men promoting the interests of men" appears to have been quite seamless." (4). Sedgwick presents a telling argument for seeing all male behavior as existing on a continuum and viewing homosexuality as merely an extreme form of male bonding. Yet I believe a closer examination of the various structures of these same-sex relationships would reveal the distinction between intramale sexuality, which can be countenanced by the patriarchy, and homosexuality, which cannot be.

Sedgwick is mistaken when she says that the Greeks approved of "men loving men." Pederastia was approved only between men and boys, and the hierarchical relations were analogous—though not identical to—the relationship between men and women (Dover, 101). To the Greeks a hairy bottom was a decided obstacle no masculine freeman would surmount. Alkaios writes:

> Nicander, ooh, your leg's got hairs!
> Watch they don't creep up into your arse.
> Because, darling, if they do, you'll soon know
> How the lovers flee you, and years go.
>
> (Coote, 58)

Strato is no less explicit about the relationship between age and sexual acceptability:

> I delight in the prime of a boy of twelve,
> but a thirteen-year-old's better yet.

At fourteen he's Love's even sweeter flower,
& one going on fifteen's even more delightful.
Sixteen belongs to the gods, & seventeen . . .
it's not for me, but Zeus to seek.
If you want the older ones, you don't play
any more, but seek & answer back.

(Coote, 66)

Not only was there an acceptable limit to the boy's age, but as mentioned earlier, the sex roles were strictly apportioned. The older man had to be the inserter; the younger the receiver. Thus, Greek pederastia differed from Euro-American homosexuality by being phaseal and unequal, and by having pederasts experience no sense of otherness. It mirrored the patriarchal hierarchies of Athenian life and, therefore, did not threaten the structure of the patriarchy. Euro-American homosexuality, however, in its discourse of otherness, permanence, and equality, challenges the hierarchies of patriarchal structure.

Homosexuality has assumed a shape, a form, a language, which though borrowed from patriarchy, finds itself in a "violent dialectic" with it. It does not—by and large—comfortably rest in a continuum with other forms of male bonding or homosocial desire. Unlike other intramale sexual activities, it does not require the forcible exclusion of the feminine or triangulation through the feminine. By being based on terms of otherness, permanence, genuineness, and equality, homosexuality stands apart from the patriarchal terms that it has co-opted or inverted and will continue to remain structurally separate from the heterosexual discourse that gave it birth.

The four terms I have developed—otherness, equality, permanence, and genuineness—are not systematically analyzed in the chapters that follow. Although these terms would form a neat structure for the book, an analysis of American gay literature requires something more spacious, and their extended use would rob the texts of their fluidity, historicity, and ultimately their literary value. I have introduced these terms as the basic vocabulary from which and toward which gay writers have moved and as a general grounding for my own analysis. The value of these terms will be found not in how well they pigeonhole the literature, but in how usefully they serve us in revealing the complexity of what gay writers have done.

3

Choosing Our Fathers: Gender and Identity in Whitman, Ashbery, and Richard Howard

IN his preface to the volume *Homosexualities and French Literature,* Richard Howard divides authors into two groups: "homosexual writers" and "writers who are homosexual." These groups are not in competition, but in historic succession, for the former—whose number include Gide, Genet, and Proust, to name but the three most important—have given way some time around 1968, according to Howard's cultural calendar, to the Barthes and Tourniers of the next generation. Unlike the homosexual writers of the past, today's writer who is homosexual need not become "a sacred monster perpetrating those vast destructions . . . upon himself which enable him to survive" (20). Yet if the younger writer escapes the fate of his "glorious or scandalous progenitors," he suffers "a certain invisibility," the price exacted "to escape being no more than a *monstre sacré*" (21). The choice is between two limited options: either invisibility or demonology, either objectification as a gargoyle of sexual perversity or obliteration as the ghost of self-abasement. Such choices are caused, no doubt, in part by the highly charged reception that meets gay writing, but more significantly by what Herbert Blau calls the "egolessness" of the gay writer (124).

If we look for the source of this "egolessness," we must search not in

44

the vicissitudes of the Oedipal crisis, but in the sociohistorical constellation from which the child develops his object world. Blau reminds us that "whatever identity now being claimed or seized, no
homosexual is raised *as* a homosexual," (119) and thus gay men grow
up without the support, recognition, or modeling of others, all of
which are needed for consonance of signification. The child who will
grow up to be gay gazes at himself through a cracked mirror. In the
preceding chapter I discuss this crisis of gay signification in Eriksonian
terms. Since for Erikson "ego identity is the awareness . . . of selfsameness and continuity," and since the homosexual's sense of himself
does not "coincide with the sameness and continuity of one's *meaning
for significant others*" (50, Erikson's italics), the result is a "negative
identity" (88).

This negative identity is *not* merely an inversion of selfhood—being
the opposite of what others expect one to be—but rather an absence of
identity—no one can point the gay child toward a model of who he is.
Gay selfhood is constantly being lost in the opacity of the parental
gaze. It is no accident, it seems to me, that vampires who are not
reflected in mirrors have increasingly become encoded as homosexual,
and explicitly identified as such in Anne Rice's voluminous and popular novels. Later I will discuss how cannibalism and homosexuality
become intertwined, and no doubt vampirism feeds, so to speak, into
that imaginative current. But here I would like to emphasize how the
vampire's unreflectiveness is a sign of his homosexuality. The vampire
and the homosexual possess a narcissism without a reflection. They
fall into the abyss, not to embrace themselves, but in a vain search to
grab hold of any image.

Yet even homosexuals have difficulty accepting such egolessness.
One sees in Alfred Chester, whose apparent suicide followed a long
bout of paranoia, the case of a gay writer tortured by his self-acknowl-
edged lack of selfhood. He writes of his MacDowell Colony friends in
a style that blends panic and hilarity: "Nobody's queer, not even me
anymore. Besides I hate myself too. I can't stand it anymore not having a stable I. It is too much. Thrust into a totally new situation, here,
I don't know who I am. . . . I just want to scream fuck I am alfred
chester who? But no one will believe me, not even me. . . . As there is
no me except situationally, I have to have mental conversations in
order to be" (*Sad Angel,* 322). Chester's situation is, indeed, atypically
severe. It represents the extreme problem that the gay writer faces in a
hostile heterosexual environment. Chester remarks on his lost homo-

sexual libido as though his desire for men is one of only two reliable clues to his identity. Without a suitable object of desire, he has only his authorial voice to rely on and must maintain ongoing "mental conversations in order to be."

Joseph Brodsky has in "Less than One," his essay about growing up in Leningrad, described the heterosexual male ego in a metaphor that provides a useful model for our examination. "I guess there was always some 'me' inside that small, and later, somewhat bigger shell around which 'everything' moved," he writes. "Inside that shell the entity which one calls 'I' never changed and never stopped watching what was going on outside" (17). Brodsky's hard, self-enclosed, well-defended selfhood corresponds to Nancy Chodorow's description of the heterosexual male who possesses a "more emphatic individuation and a more defensive firming of experienced ego boundaries" and an object-world that is "more fixed and simpler" and that leads to "denial of . . . connectedness and isolation of affect" (167–69). To be sure, many heterosexual male poets have wished to transcend the encasement of their rigid ego structures and "break / into flower" as James Wright has put it in "A Blessing," but they can rarely risk the narcissistic wound such a transformation would require, and typically they run away from it in homosexual panic.

Gay writers rarely connect their weak sense of selfhood explicitly to issues of gender; each tends to view it as a personal quirk, but the mere frequency with which gay authors, especially gay poets, raise the issue lends credence to Blau's claims. John Ashbery, for instance, candidly admits to a weak selfhood, a weakness that leads to his characteristic ambiguity of pronoun reference. "I guess I don't have a very strong sense of my own identity . . .," he reported in an interview, "I find it very easy to move from one person in the sense of a pronoun to another" (Packard, 4). Similarly Thom Gunn has stated that he has never been interested in developing, "a unique poetic personality" and rejoices "in Eliot's lovely remark that art is the escape from personality." Gunn, however, acknowledges that in so doing he has made necessity a virtue since the impersonality of his work originally stemmed not from any aesthetic doctrine he might have embraced, but rather from a "lack in me" (196). Finally Robert Duncan in his *H.D. Book* speaks eloquently about the poet who "'daring to discard his personality' not only follows a tradition but is created in it" (86). Duncan alone explicitly traces this loss of personality to the erotic, and particularly the homoerotic. By following the figure of "Eros . . . developing from stone to the winged Homoeros to the divine Bridegroom," Duncan began "to find [his] identity not in the personality but in the concept of Man" (85).

Some gay writers have successfully projected a strong and unmistakable selfhood into their work. Despite his obvious camping, Frank O'Hara accurately describes his practice of writing as a matter of placing "the poem squarely between the poet and [his beloved] Lucky Pierre style," a position that leaves "the poem correspondingly gratified." Similarly he dislikes "Abstraction (in poetry, not in painting)" because it "involves removal by the poet" (xiv). Perhaps by so completely eroticizing the poem, O'Hara has made himself a palpable presence erupting from it, but his immediacy is just one of the factors that makes his work both so attractive and so difficult for gay poets to follow; typically, gay poets are far less present in their work.

The egolessness of the gay male poet is all the more noticeable when it is compared to the egocentricism of his heterosexual counterpart. It is not merely that Robert Lowell, W. C. Williams, or James Wright are more explicitly autobiographical than Crane, Duncan, or Edward Field. The difference goes to the heart of how their presence is manifested in their works. Lowell's *History,* for example, is on the surface less autobiographical than Merrill's *Changing Light at Sandover,* the recent poem most similar in both scope and ambition, but whereas history is a mirror in which Lowell finds pieces of his ever more fragmented but omnipresent face, Merrill's mirror is a history that takes him further and further from himself. Lowell is an artist of refiguring in which people "are poor passing facts / warned by that to give / each figure in the photograph / his living name" (127). Merrill is an artist of transfiguration; his bats become peacocks, and male prostitutes, angels. Everyone is subordinated to the larger Work. Merrill becomes the instrument through which history is articulated, whereas Lowell is the figure to whom History has come to be enacted.

The egolessness of the gay writer is not a recent phenomenon. As Jonathan Dollimore has shown, Wilde inverted the codes of heterosexuality especially in regard to the value of the ego, and "his defenses of lying, the unauthentic, masks and role playing . . . point to a notion of self as superficial, non-existent even" (187). Dorian Gray, for example, finds insincerity "merely a method by which we can multiply our personalities," and he wonders "at the shallow psychology of those who conceive the Ego of man as a thing simple, permanent, reliable, and of one essence" (158). What Dollimore makes clear is that the egolessness of gay poetry is not merely a result of gay writers' attempts to suppress the fact of their homosexuality, though clearly a writer who is compelled to suppress his sexual orientation will tend to hide other manifestations of the self and his emotions. Nor is such egolessness a result of the deep encoding of homosexuality which historically has taken place in the writings of homosexuals. Rather it is both one of the results of the homosexual's relationship to society and one of his tools for dealing with it. Yet two additional points must be made about gay egolessness. First, such an absence of selfhood is felt under the conditions of advanced capitalism across all sectors of society, but perhaps first and most intensely by homosexuals. Second, such an absence is not necessarily useful in correcting the problems that gave rise to it. In *Minima Moralia* Theodor Adorno, perhaps among the most phallocentric of thinkers, has warned, "Narcissism, deprived of its libidinal object by the decay of the self, is replaced by the masochistic satisfaction of no longer being a self, and the rising generation guards few of its goods so jealously as its selflessness, its communal and lasting possession" ("Subject," 65). One may see in the iconographic elevation of St. Sebastian, whom Richard Ellman calls "the favorite saint among homosexuals" (71), the masochism of selfless devotion to an absent father. Starting with Whitman, we will see that the egolessness of gay poets is felt both as a challenge and a burden, a source of discomfort and an opportunity for liberation.

Whitman invites us to view him as the supreme egoist, a kosmos through which the afflatus is surging and around which no orbit can be swept by a carpenter's compass. Yet to be everything is to be nothing, and if in "Song of Myself" Whitman is forever puffing himself up, he is also always in jeopardy of being atomized into nothingness. The poem concludes with his diffusion into the world:

> The last scud of day holds back for me,
> It flings my likeness after the rest and true as any on the
>   shadow'd wilds,
> It coaxes me to the vapor and the dusk.
> I depart as air, I shake my locks at the runaway sun,
> I effuse my flesh into eddies, and drift it in lacy jags.
>   (*Manuscripts,* sec. 52, ll. 4–8)

Whitman is too much a lover of the corporeal to be satisfied with this disembodied presence, and gathering his scattered remains together, he warns us in the final line that he has stopped waiting for us and merged himself into nature where he retains some substance, albeit unrecognizable. He left to other portions of *Leaves of Grass* the task of presenting an integrated, unified poetic selfhood, what he could not evoke despite its title in "Song of Myself."

The early drafts of *Calamus* indicate that Whitman still felt inhibited in expressing his sexuality directly and, therefore, fabricated a persona that obscured his true nature. In his previous poetry he was "held by the life that exhibits itself," the life permissable "in company," but now he wishes to "celebrate that concealed but substantial life," which is to be found in "the need of the love of comrades" (*Manuscripts,* 67–68). Whitman wishes us to know that in *Calamus* the mask of Everyman is to be dropped for his real face, a selfhood that, although less all-encompassing, is human-scaled and clearer. *Calamus* was to be the poetic sequence in which Whitman established—to use Thom Gunn's phrase—"a unique poetic personality" (196). As Robert K. Martin has noted, in *Calamus* Whitman attempts to learn "not survival but self-expression," withdrawing from society so that "he can find his own voice" (55).

Whitman clearly fails in this aim, for *Calamus* is only marginally more particularized than "Song of Myself." As Mark Bauerlein has noted, "While Whitman longed to exteriorize his self, to signify his desire in a medium that would preserve the ego's primacy and integrity, the opposite occurred" (146). Several factors are responsible for his failure. Identity is not self-generating; it demands a culture, a history, a society in which to develop. Although before the Civil War Whitman might have enjoyed in New York a large and mainly unmolested homosexual society, as recent scholarship suggests, by the time he finished *Calamus* that society had disappeared.

Moreover, in antebellum New York, homosexual society was allowed to exist only because it never asserted an identity. Yet it was this condition of anonymity that Whitman wished to end. Whitman's difficulties had more personal roots as well; his love affair with Fred Vaughn—which Charley Shively maintains is the basis for *Calamus*—ended in 1859, leaving Whitman with no working model of lasting love (38). Finally, as Bauerlein argues, Whitman's problem of selfhood may exist "at the linguistic level rather than the social level," because the very enterprise of encoding any selfhood is misguided; language can never embody the self (131). Consequently, Whitman had no social, poetic, or personal mirror in which to gain a view of himself, and no identity can be formed in such a void.

Of all these reasons, Whitman seems to have felt most acutely the absence of a lover. In "The Base of All Metaphysics," a section added in 1860, he alludes to the Socratic notion of love which celebrates the "attraction of friend to friend" (*Prose and Poetry,* 275). In the *Symposium* Aristophanes argues that our sense of identity, of wholeness, is to be found in love, "the desire and pursuit of the whole." Elsewhere, Whitman gives that conception a democratic turn. In "Among the Multitude" he speaks of his "lover and perfect equal" who shall be discovered "by the like in you," namely from being parts of some former whole (*Prose and Poetry,* 286). In the original ninth section of *Calamus,* significantly dropped from later editions, Whitman speaks of the "hours of torment" when "his friend, his lover [is] lost to him." Whitman particularly feels the isolation having no one in which to "see himself reflected," since without such a mirror, he loses his integrity, his sense of being, his identity (*Prose and Poetry,* 83).

Indeed, one may read *Calamus* as a quest for a substitute who would provide the lost mirror of selfhood his former lover held up to him. Originally Whitman intended the live-oak to be such an emblem of selfhood, but the poem that should have established its centrality fails on close scrutiny to serve its purpose. "It [the live-oak] remains," for Whitman "a curious token . . . of manly love," because although it can joyously exist "without a friend a lover near," Whitman knew "very well" that he could not (*Prose and Poetry,* 280). Even the calamus root, which Whitman ultimately selected as the emblem of the manly love of comrades, is unable to establish a stable relationship between Whitman and those around him. It is merely a token of exchange between those who love—not Whitman himself—but as he is "capable of loving."

Michael Moon in his brilliant recent study, *Disseminating Whitman,* reads "Calamus" as an unstable lyric sequence, although its instability is not the celebration of the "fluid" self that could be found in the first edition of *Leaves of Grass.* According to Moon, the fluidity of the first edition was "designed to accommodate the reader as well as the author, to bring them into affectionate contact with each other" (80), but the instability of the later editions comes from Whitman's "characteristic" practice of representing "subjectivity simultaneously *in the grip of* a deforming cultural formation . . . and *in the act of,* or perhaps more precisely, *in the act of imagining,* subverting the formation" (163, Moon's italics). Consequently, "Calamus," for Moon, dramatizes Whitman's "paranoid subject-positions" (163).

The general movement of *Calamus* is downward to loneliness, fragmentation, and loss, yet Whitman's rhetoric is always upward, expansive, and embracing. Whitman refuses to admit his basic estrangement and solitariness even as he calls attention to it. We may see this process of denial and exposure perhaps more clearly in "Out of the Cradle Endlessly Rocking" than in *Calamus* because in "Out of the Cradle" the process takes place within a single poem rather than across a sequence of small lyrics. In "Out of the Cradle" he addresses the widowed bird:

> O you singer solitary, singing by yourself, projecting me,
> O solitary me listening, never more shall I cease
>   perpetuating you,
> Never more shall I escape, never more the reverberations,
> Never more the cries of unsatisfied love be absent from me,
> Never again leave me to be the peaceful child I was
>   before. . . .
>
> *(Prose and Poetry, 393)*

The self-confessed isolation appears as a binding and abiding force, and the poem's rhetoric merges bird and boy in an everlasting amatory embrace even as its logic establishes their essential isolation, distance, and dissatisfaction. Whitman conflates the language of sexual awakening with the language of unrequited love without bothering to note that this empathic union is essentially empty. The same pattern is reiterated in the *Calamus* sequence. For example, "When I Heard at Close of Day," perhaps the most sustained personal love poem of the group, ends with what seems to be a rapturous declaration, "And that night I was happy," but its raptures quickly fade once we recognize Whitman's specificity in singling out "that night" (*Prose and Poetry*, 277). For if he is happy "that night," how does he feel on other nights? The line resonates not with joy—as seems to be intended—but against the pathos of his general unhappiness. Similarly in "That Shadow My Likeness," the penultimate poem of the sequence, and in "Full of Life Now," the same tension appears between Whitman's sad condition and the cheerful rhetoric he uses ostensibly to convince the reader of his happiness. As the title of "That Shadow My Likeness" (*Prose and Poetry*, 286) suggests, Whitman has been reduced to seeking for himself in shadows, wondering whether the shadow "is really me;" however, when he is among lovers, he "never doubts whether that is really" he. The ironies are multiple. In the last line he doesn't assert that he's *not* a shadow; he merely assures us that he has no doubts, and since that assurance only occurs when he is "among my lovers"—a rarity since he is fundamentally alone—it follows logically that he is almost entirely in doubt about his likeness. Similarly in "Full of Life Now" (*Prose and Poetry*, 287), Whitman tells us that he will meet his intended comrade who will "realize" his poems only after his death, and he roguishly warns him: "Be it as if I were with you. (Be not too certain but I am now with you.)" The mood is intended to be upbeat, but Whitman must use both the subjunctive mood and a double negative to achieve that air of natural nonchalance.

In *Calamus* Whitman had hoped to create a reasonable image of selfhood, derived not from the grandiose appropriation of all around him, but from the self-affirming contact with manly love, yet he is unable to sustain any clear or positive image of himself. He begins in isolation and ends a ghost. He starts off with a lover of flesh and blood, but ends with dream figures of the still-as-yet-unborn. He totters from the indefinite everything to the clearly nothing without ever passing through a midpoint of some personal, limited sense of self. Whitman's genius is not that he was able to establish a gay identity—would we expect such a thing of him?—but that he points out the difficulties so clearly. *Calamus* is ultimately a moving portrait of psychosexual isolation against which his grandiosity is clearly a strategy to prevent the most profound depression. Even so, Whitman does not evade the hardest truths: his love of men and the impossibility of sustaining such a love within the context of the 1860s. Of these desires and frustrations, he writes with a frankness, a tenderness, and an unaffected passion never expressed before.

Since Whitman, gay poets have moved in two different directions, often simultaneously, in their attempts to resolve the problem of the social construction of a gay poetic selfhood. The first direction is to resolve to go without a poetic identity—to regard the unitary and limited construct of the ego as a seductive, but ultimately unnecessary piece of poetic baggage. The other direction is to construct a self out of the growing tradition of gay literary presence. Neither of these directions could exist without Whitman, whose heroic failure constitutes a bulwark upon which so much of American poetics is situated. Indeed, both of these strategies are reinforced by—as well as form a significant part of—the project of postmodernism by creating a self-conscious critique of the egoism of romantic assumption and the supposed impersonality of high modernist practice. Perhaps the most imposing example of the first strategy—the rejection of the heterosexual male ego—is to be found in John Ashbery's work, of which "Self-Portrait in a Convex Mirror" constitutes by its mingling of unfulfilled longing and belated disenchantment one of the central texts of American literature. The second strategy is best typified by Richard Howard whose erudition and dramatic sense make not only his individual monologues an encounter and reincorporation of the past, but his entire corpus a comic enactment of self-construction.

As Charles Berger has noted, Whitman meets Ashbery at that visionary juncture where the marginality of selfhood becomes the central stance of the poem (174). Whitman becomes for Ashbery the *genius locus* of that territory of imaginative fullness and prelapsarian innocence, the meadow—to use Robert Duncan's phrase—that Ashbery is often permitted to return to. This psychic space takes on several forms: the prospect of flowers in which little J. A. is painted, the Holy Land of Western New York State, the divine sepulchre which at some point Ashbery will be forced to vacate, the North Farm in which "The sacks of meal [are] piled to the rafters," and "The streams run with sweetness, fattening fish" (*Wave,* 1). Whitman guards a "holy land" compounded of the American past, Ashbery's own idyllic childhood, the Eden of metaphysical poetry, the pastoral of Romanticism, and the paradise of Genesis. The world is threatened not by the loss of *unselfconsciousness*—since Ashbery does not have a clear enough self to become conscious of—but by *nonselfconsciousness,* the awareness that his lack of selfhood is itself the fall from grace, a recognition brought about most commonly by the emergence of the homoerotic.

In Ashbery's earliest attempt at self-portraiture, "The Picture of Little J. A. in a Prospect of Flowers," the garden imagery only highlights his grotesque lack of definition even as it betokens his fall into awareness of the sexual. This prototypic emblem of Ashberian selfhood is both highly charged and densely ambiguous:

> Yet I cannot escape the picture
> Of my small self in that bank of flowers:
> My head among the blazing phlox
> Seemed a pale and gigantic fungus.
>
> (*Some Trees,* 28)

Ashbery would like to "escape" the picture, to hide himself in the foliage or simply forget his humiliating exposure, but he cannot run away from the vision of himself as a "pale and gigantic fungus."

Marvell's "little T. C.," who is also discovered in a "Prospect of Flowers," presents a striking contrast to J. A., for where he wishes to elude our sight, she claims our attention, issuing one "command severe" after another, in a heroic desire to "Reform the errors of the spring" (1:38). Moreover, whereas Ashbery can "imagine our rewards" only "in the light of lost words" (*Some Trees,* 29), little T. C. gives all the flowers names, usurping Adam's mythic role as poet laureate of creation. Though he wishes to present himself in the timeless world of the prelapsarian garden, he is painfully aware of his belatedness; whereas T. C. confidently assumes her role as scourge of earthly corruption. Yet despite these differences, little J. A. joins little T. C. in violating the erotic order. In her tyrannical obedience to "chaster laws," T. C. battles "wanton Love" and risks angering Flora by committing the crime of "kill[ing] her infants in their prime." While J. A. commits nothing so aggressive as infanticide, his fungal appearance transforms him into a sexless blob "accepting / Everything, taking nothing," (*Some Trees,* 28–29) reproducing by asexual spores, narcissistic eruptions. He stands in contrast to the "blazing phlox." To the flux of the mutable world, he appears cold and inert, another kind of violator of Flora's fecundity, or perhaps already burning in the hell of overbreeding.

Any crossing of the boundary into the mythic Eden of Ashbery's imagination involves anxiety, particularly sexual anxiety, for such transgressions expose Ashbery's weak, amorphous, homosexual sense of selfhood. The sojourn from the holy land of western New York, for example, excites "a note of panic / because the old man had peed in his pants again" (*Self-Portrait,* 6). In "Farm Implements and Rutabagas in a Landscape," Popeye is forced "to flee the country" because according to Olive "his wizened, duplicate father" is in an Oedipal rage and "jealous of the apartment / And all that it contains, myself and spinach / In particular, heaves bolts of loving thunder" (*Double Dream,* 47–48). Finally in "Vetiver," a poem named for the East Indian grass that grows by asexual reproduction and means literally in Tamil, "root that is dug up," we learn that though "the gates / Had been left open intentionally," we are not to follow for "in some room someone examines his youth / Finds it dry and hollow, porous to the touch" (*April Galleons,* 1). The poem concludes with the Whitmanesque lament:

> O keep me with you, unless the outdoors
> Embrace both of us, unites us, unless

The birdcatchers put away their twigs,
The fishermen haul in their sleek empty nets
. . . and the crying
In the leaves is saved, the last silver drops.

(*April Galleons*, 1)

Yet I think we will have missed an important part of Ashbery's achievement if we note only the anxiety and unhappiness that so often accompanies his confrontation with the heterosexual world represented in "Vetiver" by those two archetypes of heterosexual male pursuits: hunting and fishing. For Ashbery's desire is not to become a hunter and fisherman, to join in the sorrowful acts of death and destruction. Rather, he enjoins us to give up these practices which are regarded as normal and acceptable. "Normalcy" can be a highly self-destructive desire to follow, as Ashbery makes clear in "Qualm," his homage to the term's inventor, Warren G. Harding. In the poem, Ashbery has the "hysterical" public "follow [Harding] to the edge / Of the inferno," but luckily "the fall is deliciously, only his." We can avoid the "agony" that "normalcy" would bring us to, an agony that has no transcendent value since it is "permanent / Rather than eternal," of this, not of the other, world. In "Self-Portrait in a Convex Mirror," Ashbery finally confronts the heterosexual ego, which he first feels drawn to and later distances himself from, for in it he sees not only the emblem of psychological rigidity, but also of artistic stagnation.

In "Self-Portrait in a Convex Mirror" Ashbery goes to unusual pains to describe Parmigianino's picture, quoting Vasari's account at length. The self-portrait is painted on a hemisphere of wood covered with canvas; thus, the painting does not strictly imitate the three-dimensional barber's mirror from which Parmigianino worked, but it *is* three-dimensional. The illusion of the portrait is the way it depicts a three-dimensional world behind or, more properly, before it. The illusion is of a sphere, when the painting is only hemispherical. I mention this configuration because it so perfectly echoes Brodsky's metaphor of the male ego as a seed inside a shell in which the ego can grow without leaving. The convex self-portrait is, as well, a fitting metaphor for Chodorow's account of the heterosexual male ego since it is hard, fixed, and self-enclosed.

"Self-Portrait in a Convex Mirror" is driven by Ashbery's ambivalent attitude toward the perfect icon of straight male selfhood. Ashbery is unquestionably attracted to Parmigianino's self-portrait because it presents a model of such aggressive masterliness and sexual assertion, and even Parmigianino's vulnerability is alluring. Parmigianino's face strikes Ashbery as "an unfamiliar stereotype" that fits Vasari's description of him as "'rather angel than human'" (*Self-Portrait,* 73). "There is in the gaze," Ashbery notes, "a combination / Of tenderness, amusement and regret, so powerful / In its restraint that one cannot look for long" (*Self-Portrait,* 69). Yet if Ashbery must turn away from the portrait, he is also pulled back to it by the magnetism of its gaze, or rather by the force of Parmigianino's hand, which with phallic assertiveness is "thrust at the viewer" even as it swerves away "to protect / What it advertises" (*Self-Portrait,* 68).

The hand's gesture, which opens the poem, is emblematic of the contrary forces at work in Parmigianino—the aggressive and the self-protective—forces Ashbery understands, needs to elude, and finally recognizes as necessary for Parmigianino's survival. For it is his aggressive, self-protectiveness that saves Parmigianino during the sack of Rome when "soldiers . . . burst in on him" and "amazed . . . decided to spare his life" (*Self-Portrait,* 75). The hand dominates the picture in what Ashbery recognizes only at the end of the poem as "the shield of greeting," a welcoming that is also a barrier (*Self-Portrait,* 82). Yet the hand, though it separates Parmigianino from the outside and fends off attack from his enemies, is not the typical barrier, as Ashbery makes clear from the outset:

> One would like to stick one's hand
> Out of the globe, but its dimensions,
> What carries it, will not allow it.
> No doubt it is this, not the reflex
> To hide something, which makes the hand loom large
> As it retreats slightly. There is no way
> To build it flat like a section of wall:
> It must join the segment of a circle,
> Roving back to the body of which it seems
> So unlikely a part, to fence in and shore up the face
> On which the effort of this condition reads
> Like a pinpoint of a smile.
>
> (*Self-Portrait,* 69–70)

The hand's curvature creates a wholeness that is in jeopardy of being lost in the very manner of its presentation. It invites us to enter the picture, beckoning to the viewer, even as it seals the face off and completes it. Christopher Craft has noted how the hand in Tennyson's *In*

Memoriam is "at once an overdetermined *and* unstable signifier," including both "the sexually innocent gestures of Victorian male homosociality" and under "a slightly altered social context, only too [ready to] take on the heat and pressure of the sexual" (91). The hand carries much of the same instability and overdetermination for Ashbery, who wishes to reach across the globe of the portrait and out for Parmigianino, but the hand that extends through what Ashbery later terms a "magma of interiors" "must join" and "shore up the face" and "perpetuate the enchantment of self with self" (*Self-Portrait,* 72). Ashbery feels both drawn to and rebuffed by the narcissism of the painting which is both flirtatious and aloof, inviting and distant.

Parmigianino's pose and manner constantly endanger his self-portrait as well as its viewer, for not only is the harmony and wholeness of the face always risking a grotesque dismemberment should its boundaries be violated, but the viewer risks being consumed within the portrait by the very perspective that seeks to close the picture off. Because of Parmigianino's "extreme care in rendering / The velleities of the rounded reflected surface," Ashbery believes that "you could be fooled for a moment / Before you realize the reflection / Isn't yours" (*Self-Portrait,* 74). The viewer could mistakenly project himself into the picture, but the result for Ashbery is not to replace Parmigianino; to the contrary, with Ashbery's weak sense of ego identity, the concern is that he might become one of "Hoffman characters who have been deprived / Of a reflection" and that Ashbery would be "supplanted by the strict / Otherness of the painter in his / Other room" (*Self-Portrait,* 74). Indeed, Ashbery argues, since the global self-portrait is "a metaphor / Made to include us, we are part of it and / Can live in it as in fact we have done" (*Self-Portrait,* 76). Ashbery's shift into the past tense is significant, indicating that the self-enclosed selfhood of Parmigianino's self-portrait is not a condition to aspire to, but a stage to outgrow. It has included him; he has lived it. But as the only metaphor of life, it is unsatisfactory.

Ashbery does not find fault with Parmigianino's fragile condition; indeed, that vulnerability continues to be part of his allure. Rather Ashbery faults Parmigianino for his rigidity, remoteness, and unresponsiveness. When we envision ourselves in such a shell, Ashbery argues:

> The soul is held captive, treated humanely, kept
> In suspense, unable to advance much farther . . .

> The soul has to stay where it is
> Even though restless, hearing raindrops at the pane . . .
> Longing to be free, outside, but it must stay
> Posing in this place. It must move
> As little as possible.
>
> (*Self-Portrait,* 68–69)

Such a position, Ashbery willingly admits, will allow one to "stay on
. . . serene in / [a] gesture which is neither embrace nor warning /
But which holds something of both," yet such a "pure / Affirmation"
in the end "doesn't affirm anything" and soon "the balloon pops" leaving one nothing at all (*Self-Portrait,* 70).

As the poem progresses, Ashbery comes to regard such portrait-
making as Parmigianino's with its depiction of an assertive but remote
selfhood as a "life-obstructing task" rather than a psychic or artistic
goal. For Parmigianino's strategy for self-construction is not good for
either Ashbery's personal growth or his artistic development. "Aping
naturalism," Ashbery argues, "may be the first step / Toward achieving an inner calm, / But it is the first step only, and often / Remains a
frozen gesture" (*Self-Portrait,* 82). Such criticism of Parmigianino
should be placed against his praise of Courbet in his 1966 article "The
Romance of Reality," in which Ashbery locates Courbet's "modern-
ism" specifically in the "unvisual qualities he incorporates into realistic
landscapes and portraits" (30). Of particular note is *Roe-deer in
Snow,* in which Courbet appeared to continue "to paint *after* he had
obtained a satisfactorily realistic image" (30, Ashbery's italics).
Though "Self-Portrait in a Convex Mirror" does not lack depth—the
perspective is brilliantly recreated—it does lack density because it has
only one layer. "Everything," Ashbery complains, "is surface. The surface is what's there / And nothing can exist except what's there" (*Self-
Portrait,* 70). Parmigianino's art remains stunted in its own bravura,
its masterliness, in an egoism so self-sufficient it is content to "ape
naturalism."

Like Virginia Woolf, who must kill the Angel in the House, whose
image of submissive heterosexual femininity becomes an obstacle to
her artistic and personal development, so too must Ashbery do away
with the grinning, handsome, smug face of Parmigianino and the aping naturalism of the heterosexual male ego. At the end of the poem,
Ashbery lifts the revolver with "one bullet in the chamber" to smash
this icon that has both tempted and intimidated him as an artist and a
person. Not that Parmigianino is a bad artist—to the contrary, Ash-

bery is perhaps inordinately sensible to the portrait's allure—but his direction is not one that Ashbery can further himself in, and though he regrets rejecting the portrait, he recognizes it as necessary for his own development. If one were to ask how Ashbery regards his weak sense of ego identity, one might find no better phrase than one he uses in an earlier poem on his melting sense of selfhood. "A Blessing in Disguise," a poem in which the desire "to sing of me / Which are you"—a "you" he prefers in the plural—results in "this feeling of exaltation" (*Rivers and Mountains*, 26).

Ashbery's resolve to accept his weak ego identity has allowed him to produce a body of work perhaps unrivaled in American poetry in its power to explore the workings of consciousness stripped of personality, yet this is only one resolution to the problems gay poets have inherited from Whitman or find themselves confronting on their own. Richard Howard suggests another way of resolving the artistic and psychological problems that beset the American gay poet and of situating selfhood in his work. Howard's way is to construct a cultural and historical matrix in which his own depersonalized work may be located and against which it can resonate. The construction of such a matrix and the establishment of such a tradition have been projects not unlike the ones feminist poets such as Adrienne Rich, Sandra M. Gilbert, and Marilyn Hacker have set for themselves. Yet the dramatic forms that Howard so often employs to evoke, reconstruct, and explore this continuity make the dialogue between himself and his tradition more problematic and vivid, for it is as though he must be possessed by that tradition so that he might be created through it. At nearly every step of the way, Howard makes problematic the historicism that is central to his construction of the imaginative space of his poems.

Howard's dramatic monologues and dialogues, like the paintings Ashbery admires, are not involved, as they are sometimes naively assumed to be, in "aping naturalism." As vivid as some of his characters appear to be, the poems are not particularly concerned with depicting an essential selfhood nor in the presentation of depth psychology. Unlike Browning, whose works often take as their subject madness, jealously, or fear in a serious attempt to explore personality at key moments of revelation, Howard generally avoids situations that make the psychology of his figures the pivot on which the poems turn. His preferred form is the letter, the epistolary poem, in which he particularly emphasizes the social self, a selfhood not stripped away to some core of being, but a selfhood that has been invested (in the many senses of the word) in all the draperies culture will allow it. In the two poems that deal most specifically with the nude, "Howard's Way" and "Move Still, Still So," the central characters are traumatized by exposure and seek to cover themselves either in the objectifying gaze or by their removal from the scene. J. D. McClatchy may find in such poems the disfiguring tic of the "grotesque" because they represent "those areas of life most emphatically themselves," (299), but it is this flirtation with the grotesque which is always the source of tension in the dramatic monologue. In either case, selfhood in Howard's poetry cannot bear unmediated exposure, for it excites both the anxiety that under such investigation selfhood disappears and the horror of transgressions against the sacred, that merely looking is a profanation. Consequently, Howard's poetry is concerned far less than might at first appear with revelation of character than with the exploration of mentality.

So urgent, in fact, appears Howard's need to establish a cultural, artistic, and sexual matrix for himself that his books unfold themselves in a seemingly programmatic way, integrating his personal history with the larger history of the past. Indeed, from the first poem of his first book, "Advice from the Cocoon," Howard establishes identity as his major theme. At such an early stage of development, Howard is concerned simply with preserving the most rudimentary presence through the exigencies of the mask; "survival" required that you "seal yourself in layers of yourself, / . . . for the hungriest winter and beyond" (*Quantities,* 11). But by the end of *Quantities,* Howard is prepared to move out of this shell-like posture and accept intercourse with the world. In the concluding poem of that volume, "Sandusky-New York," Howard—though aware that "Ohio from a train / Looked always other . . . / unfinished, unfulfilled / And frankly alien"—hopes that arriving in a "capital city" where "the landscape lived in him / As he might live in it" will give him knowledge of "the shore of all his history" since as the epigram to the poem promises, "If you have received well / you are what you have received" (*Quantities,* 77–80).

In the volumes that have followed, Howard has perfected his reception of the cosmopolitan world in which he would be a citizen even at the expense perhaps of his own faltering provincial voice, a voice that must have struck him as being like the landscape of Ohio, essentially alien. He stated in an interview with Sanford Friedman, "I soon began to hear [dramatic] voices much more readily than I had ever heard the voice of my own poems before" (23). At first the voices that appear to channel through Howard are ancestral voices who coordinate various axes of Howard's *mentalities*. In *Untitled Subjects,* his third book of poetry, we find characters such as Ruskin, Tennyson, and Mrs. William Morris, all of whose sexual irregularities in part mirror his own; Sir Moses Montefiore, a co-religionist; and a host of other characters who possess aesthetic affinities.

The construction or translation of such voices whose concerns are deflections of his own could not alone have sustained Howard's need to erect a suitably rich matrix in which to work. As Claude Summers and Ted-Larry Pebworth have noted, more than nostalgia, the voices are "a way of bridging past, present and future" (19–20). At best they could constitute a foundation on which to build further; as Howard told Friedman, the characters of *Two-Part Inventions* were meant to fill in the gaps left by the portraits in *Untitled Subjects.*

> The dialogues [in *Two-Part Inventions*] occur mostly in relation to the figures who represented for my parents' generation the great men and women, the sacred monsters—either in reality or as I might invent them —of the arts. No longer Victorians but the figures who were not only popular but even luminous for my mother and her friends . . . so I've moved in the poems up toward 1926, when I was born. (23)

Just as Ashbery must construct the "sacred monster" of Parmigianino, so must Howard resurrect the figures of his parents' cultural past whose patterns have inscribed themselves on Howard's own consciousness. But whereas Howard uses these figures to create a "luminous" framework out of which he may construct his own personal tradition, Ashbery uses Parmigianino as a core against which to react, or from which to radiate his own unbounded selfhood.

One might speculate that Howard's sense of the generative powers of language is a consequence of his being quite literally an adopted child, his parentage as much a result of speech acts as biological ones. For Howard, who is one of the finest translators of French (itself in gay slang the term for oral sex), English is very much a "mother tongue" which can give birth to something new. Howard told Friedman, "What I'm interested in is that two people can be speaking to each other about a third thing which is there—which can be brought into existence without either of them even acknowledging it, and brought into existence for the use of readers and listeners" (25). The dialogic interactions of speech can produce something beyond and removed from that speech, a presence, a being whose existence is not predicated on its acknowledgment. Like Jack in *The Importance of Being Ernest,* who traces his line back to Victoria Station and would produce a handbag in lieu of a parent, Howard in "Discarded" finds kinship with *References for Literary Workers,* a book discarded by the Central Falls Public Library. According to the records in the book's cover, a page that had been missing was located on the day of Howard's birth. In the process of the poem, he becomes the missing page and his birth the book's reintegration if not into life, at least into literary reference. He writes:

> Adoption is that human act which alloys
> Accident and intention. Hence my saying
> I was "found," come upon, invented—found in
> nature and not yet imitated by man,
> as the old poets used to speak of *invention.*
>
> (*Fellow Feelings,* 48)

Howard is the third part of his two-part inventions, the thing that comes into being without acknowledgment. But Howard not only is adopted by the language, he also adopts the language as his own; he chooses his literary references even as he is invented by them. In *Two-Part Inventions* he gives birth to himself out of the intercourse of Walt Whitman and Oscar Wilde, Rodin and an anonymous sodomite, Edith Wharton and a Mr. Roseman, among others, and it is no mistake that the last two dialogues occur in transit, for it is as though he, too, were traveling in utero or propelled out of their "moving" discourse.

Yet the poem that links back to the promise of "Sandusky—New York," in which Howard dedicates himself to a program of linguistic self-creation, is "Decades," a work that traces his relation—his own bridge—with Hart Crane, fellow traveler, homosexual, and Ohioan. "Decades," a poem in five parts, traces the Howard / Crane connection at intervals of ten years, starting when Howard is four. It opens with Howard's adopted parents dining out with Hart Crane's parents. There they sit, four distinguished adults and one respectful child, on the eve of Crane's suicide. The poem continues through Howard's first purchase of Crane's poetry (age 14), Howard's residence in France (age 24), a visit to the Brooklyn Bridge (age 34), and concludes with Howard's visit (at age 44) to Garretsville, Ohio. Only then Crane's spirit—or language—at his side can Howard assume a place and his linguistic identity in the literary line of gay American poets. "We suffer from / the same fabled disease," he tells Crane,

> and only hope
> of dying of it keeps a man alive. Keeps!
> I press your poems as if they were Wild Flowers
> for a sidelong grammar of paternity.
> We join the Fathers after all, Hart, rejoin
> not to repel or repeal or destroy, but to fuse,
> as Walt declared it: wisdom of the shores,
> easy to conceive of, hard to come by, to choose
> our fathers and to make our history.
>
> *(Fellow Feelings, 5)*

For Howard literary adoptions and references are not, however, acts simply of choice; they are a compulsion against the very emptiness which is the "diplomacy" of the homosexual as he ministers among the "alien" lands of the heterosexual. Yet the danger, as Howard recognizes, is that the "invention against the void, the silence—leaves you very often with the void, and the void masters you, the void wins" (Friedman, "Interview," 28). The emptiness, the lack of bounded presences is not necessarily secured by deriving one's self from the language of others, for such a conjugation as James Merrill has noted in a poem dedicated to Howard, can leave the gay poet "lost in translation." Invention alone cannot guarantee the presence of gay identity in poetry, but without such invention—which as Howard notes is a quality "found" not "imitated"—there is no hope for identity of any sort, even the chameleon selfhood which Dollimore suggests is the particular province of gay postmodernism.

Howard and Ashbery are linked not necessarily by the directions they take toward selfhood or sexuality, but in two foci of their work: (1) the construction of a cosmopolitan linguistic community which though not denying the localism of their backgrounds, locates that provincialism within a larger and less alienating matrix; and (2) in finding in Whitman, not a father that must be rejected in the Oedipal drama Pound, for instance, enacted, but a companion whose hand can be grasped, whose affection can be accepted, and whose promises of comradeship can be—if not fulfilled—satisfied at least for the moment. In so doing they have prepared in their own way lines of invention that will in turn be reinvented by those they will engender.

4

The Inadmissable and Inevitable Francis Grierson

I F Francis Grierson's *The Valley of Shadows,* first published in 1909, remains today a little-known book, it is not for want of advocates. During the late forties and early fifties, critics of such stature as Edmund Wilson, Bernard De Voto, and Van Wyck Brooks made a concerted effort to find a niche for his chief work in the edifice of American literature by writing about him, editing his books, and including him in memoirs. They failed, at least in part, because of the critical context in which they placed the book, but also in part because the book is such a strange amalgam of genres that it would never win a wide or popular audience. By presenting *The Valley of Shadows* as an example of local color, as a part of Lincoln hagiography, or as a specimen of turn-of-the-century American spiritualism, its admirers doomed the book to obscurity. They could not state that the book was perhaps the most radical critique of the relationship between homosexuality and bourgeois capitalism that had yet been developed in America, one which suggested that the country faced a succession of wars because of its unwillingness to learn from the homosexual and follow his spiritual and economic lead. *The Valley of Shadows* is steeped in the Whitmanian ethos of male adhesiveness. But whereas Whitman sees those democratic vistas as a goal to which the country should move, Grierson sees them as an origin from which we are moving further away.

To be sure, Grierson obscured the thrust of his book by adapting a narrative strategy that could render his theme innocuous. He wrote *Valley of Shadows* so that it could be read as merely a colorful memoir of antebellum Illinois, as a chronicle of life on the plains. He presents scenes of camp-meetings in which settlers whip themselves into religious frenzies and thrilling accounts of runaway slaves and the underground railroad, climaxed by a slave hunter's house bursting into flames as if through divine intercession. He pictures the last Lincoln-Douglas debate in Alton, Illinois, where Grierson's family moves, and he paints vignettes of life on the Mississippi à la Mark Twain. These scenes draw attention away from the critique of America's sexual-political economy which Grierson develops in passages that break the narrative's headlong rush toward the Civil War. The interpolated passages locate the points when the country placed itself on the track of inevitable carnage, and they build a critique of the evils of captalism and of the bourgeois family, which is capitalism's most powerful instrument of maintenance.

The collective failure of the admirers of *Valley of Shadows* would not have surprised Grierson, who had accepted his marginality with an equanimity that he claimed was the hallmark of all productive geniuses. In *The Celtic Temperament, and Other Essays,* he placed himself among those rare writers who achieve only a small following because they "treat of the inadmissable and the inevitable" (83). Grierson's subjects are the inevitable (but unforseen) consequences of cultural failures and the "inadmissable" topic of homosexuality. Like Landor, whom he quoted approvingly, Grierson asked only for "ten competent minds as readers" (*Celtic,* 160). Yet one feels beneath his general aloofness an impatience with his coterie status and a yearning for a wider audience.

As one might imagine, Grierson maintained an ambivalent attitude toward his audience. As a performer and a theater lover who wrote intelligently about the musical hall, opera, and the stage, Grierson was a student of audiences, asserting that "No true lover of the playhouse ever ignores the size, the quality, and the condition of the audience. . . . Indeed, the most interesting thing connected with a theatre is the people who witness the plays." Yet he immediately adds, "for the theatre is a veritable battle-field of conflicting emotions, opinions, and sentiments. The playwright who knows his business attacks the public by the antithesis of tears and laughter" (*Celtic,* 97). For Grierson, the artist is involved in a struggle with his audience even when the audience is unaware of it. In this battle, the artist must be careful of his allies. Grierson wrote in *Modern Mysticism,* another of his books of essays, that the genius reveals himself "only to those who are intimate with its language," for he has "learned the futility of frank speech on such occasions. . . . Reticence is the only refuge for a competent mind in a crowd" (156). Grierson's reticence is not merely the consequence of his contempt for the man of the masses, but also the defense that any homosexual writer of his time used in a hostile society. "Words are always more or less dangerous," he warns, and "spoken sentiments are seldom just what the soul would say" (*Celtic,* 167). Furthermore, his reticence is an important part of his aesthetics, for he finds few blemishes more serious to a work of art than a descent into polemic. Beauty "lies in the neutrality of repose—a perfect conception of an idea without a suggestion of intellectual antagonism. The moment we begin to sermonize, we sever the delicate thread that binds the sense of beauty to that of passive harmony" (*Modern,* 172). Although Grierson allows conflict to exist between the characters within his memoir, the narrator generally avoids polemics. What ideas Grierson allows himself in the work must be presented in a mode that allows the work as a whole to exist in "passive harmony."

Like Wilde, Whitman, or Henry James, Grierson was torn in both his life and art between competing desires to reveal and to conceal his more subversive sexual self, subversive if, for no other reason, than because as a homosexual he placed himself outside of and in opposition to the law. Yet in celebrating the American quest into the frontier without women, Grierson invited what Joseph Allen Boone has described as "a *potentially* radical critique of the marital norms, restrictive sexual roles, and imbalances of power underlying nineteenth-century American familial and social life" (227). As a consequence, according to Harold Simonson (40), Grierson gave the impression of being a charlatan to more than one observer. His struggle with the problem of how much to reveal about his sexuality also evinced itself in contradictory behavior toward Lawrence Waldemar Tonner, the man whom Theodore Spencer tactfully refers to as Grierson's "devoted . . . secretary, friend and companion" (Grierson, *Valley,* xxviii).

Not much is known about Tonner. In 1885, he met Grierson in Chicago, and they lived together for the rest of Grierson's life. A Polish tailor, he was at Grierson's death running a dry cleaning store in Los Angeles. On the basis of Grierson's writing, Edmund Wilson speculates that Tonner may have been Jewish (83). Tonner wrote prefaces to several of Grierson's books, answered his correspondence, and assisted Grierson in the creation of Villa Montezuma, the pleasure palace, public relations ploy, and occult center they built in San Diego (Wilson, 72). Yet despite their intimate connection, Grierson seems to have balked at appearing, even privately, as a couple. Van Wyck Brooks reports of entertaining Grierson at his house for dinner. At the end of the evening, Brooks escorted his guest to the door and found a "strange man sitting on the steps." It was Tonner "who had been waiting there all evening through" (Simonson, 49). In an age when few men dared live openly with one another, Grierson's ménage with Tonner was daring, and yet, as if in concession to prejudice or perhaps to hide what was tacitly recognized, Grierson kept Tonner waiting outside while he dined comfortably within.

Grierson's literary persona mirrored the contradictions of his personal behavior. Edmund Wilson, for example, describes Grierson's essayistic voice as "combining a very Scottish common sense with the aloofness of a disembodied spirit" (75). From *Valley of Shadows* and its tales of log cabins and marauding Indians, one might think Grierson was a sort of primitive, the kind of rough-hewn genius he celebrates in Abraham Lincoln. Yet in person he presented an entirely different picture. "I had never seen a man with lips and cheeks rouged and eyes darkened," Theodore Rousseau wrote. "His hair was arranged in careful disorder over his brow, his hands elaborately manicured and with many rings on his fingers; he wore a softly tinted, flowing cravat" (Wilson, 78). Theodore Spencer quotes Arnold Bennett, whose *Journal* paints Grierson as an aging queen. "He still looked astoundingly young," Bennett notes. "His wig was curiously long, his moustache of course dyed. But he has not the skin, wrinkles, nor above all the gestures of a very old man" (Grierson, *Valley,* xxxiv). What emerges from these descriptions is not the rugged mien of a frontiersman, but the picture of a fin de siècle dandy—an Oscar Wilde, or an Eric, Count Stenbock, or the tall, elegant figure of Mark André Raffalovich, the author of *Uranisme et Unisexualité.*

Yet ascribing all the contradictions in Grierson's literary and public images to the need for subterfuge would be mistaken. Often the apparent contradictions are the result of Grierson's twin desires to escape provincialism and to cultivate what we might call today a "decentered subjectivity." The evils of provincialism were often on his mind. "The greatest thinkers," Grierson tells us, no doubt including himself, "never concern themselves with local conditions and interests" (*Celtic,* 157). He repeatedly inveighed against "provincialism":

> Emerson is wrong when he said that a man could learn as much by staying at home as by going abroad. The man who expects to rise above mediocrity in this age must not only become familiar with the characteristics of his own people, but must acquaint himself with the virtues and vanities of other nations in order to wear off the provincial veneer which adheres to all individuals without practical experience, and mocks one in a too conscious security of contentment or indifference. (*Modern,* 83–84).

Grierson is pleased to acknowledge his rather cosmopolitan background; for example, in a rare aside in *Valley of Shadows,* he says of Alton, Illinois, that he sees no "difference between it and Boston or London," (192) a comment sufficient to alert the reader that the author is in a position to make the comparison. At such moments Grierson appears defensive, protecting himself against the very criticism he levels at others. Yet his antiprovincialism is energized not merely by snobbery, but by political concerns. As a homosexual, he certainly felt the smug self-righteousness of bigots whose views were reenforced by the narrowness of their experience. One of Grierson's chief terms of approbation is "cosmopolitan," by which he means more than city dweller or man of the world, but a person who has expanded his perspective beyond his original limited viewpoint, a person who has cultivated a "decentered subjectivity."

Grierson did more than write about the cosmopolitan, he became one. One of the central events of his life was the changing of his name from Jesse Shepard to Francis Grierson, a change that corresponds to his desire to live a myriad of lives. By changing his name, Grierson placed himself in the tradition of homosexual writers who affected noms de plume, writers such as Baron Corvo who was born Frederick Rolfe or "Bertram Lawrence" who was John Francis Bloxam. From the age of twenty, when he first went to Paris, to forty-one, Grierson presented himself to the world as Jesse Shepard, musician, mystic, and architect; in 1889, with the publication of his first book, he became Francis Grierson so that his "serious" work as a writer would not be confused with the "mere work" of a musician. His upbringing contributed to his decenteredness. Born Benjamin Henry Jesse Francis Shepard in 1848, he was given enough names for at least four people.

His father kept the family moving so that Jesse lacked any firm bonds to either land or friends. When Grierson was only six months old, the family moved from England to settle in Sangamon County, Illinois. In 1858, they moved to Alton, Illinois, and a year later to St. Louis. In 1863, they moved to Niagara Falls, at which point *Valley of Shadows* ends. At the age of twenty, he arrived penniless in Paris, where in a matter of months he was playing his piano improvisations in the most fashionable salons of that most fashionable of cities. Alexandre Dumas *père* is reported to have told him, "With your gifts you will find all doors open before you" (Simonson, 27). And for a while, he did. He triumphed throughout Germany and in Russia playing before the relatives of the Czar. In England, he found less support, but when he returned to France his improvisations brought him the recognition of Stéphane Mallarmé, whose Tuesday evening salons he frequented with Verlaine and Sully-Prudhomme among others. Grierson's first book, the work to bear his new name, *La Révolte Idéaliste,* was written in French as if to signify that he was not only international, but bilingual, and paid allegiance to no nationality or language. The name he chose as his nom de plume is equally significant, jettisoning his patronymic and combining his mother's maiden name with the Teutonic word for "free." Jesse Shepard finds freedom for himself in the matrilineal descent, the form of descent believed at the time to be prior to patriarchy and more conducive to creativity. In short, Grierson, by changing his name, writing in two languages, maintaining residences in several countries, cultivating several different artistic and intellectual careers, put into practice the "decentered subjectivity" found in the narrative voice of *Valley of Shadows.*

In *Valley of Shadows* the figure who is allowed to speak, if not *for* Grierson at least with Grierson's permission, is Zack Caverly, nicknamed Socrates, a name that signals both his intellectual authority and erotic orientation. Caverly appears early, and then progressively disappears from the book. He is the only one of the book's early male characters to disappear, for at the memoir's conclusion the other important ones—Azariah James and Elihu Gest—reappear as Union soldiers.

Socrates' failure to show up at the end of the novel as a Union soldier signals his pacifism and his estrangement from the political divisions of the community. On a visit to Socrates' cabin, the narrator finds him "sitting at his cabin door, smoking, dreaming and listening to whatever strange sounds might reach him from the woods. As he sat there he felt himself detached from the world, yet near enough to human beings to have all the society he desired. He thought of the new settlers, their troubles and vexations, and he wondered how many of them were as free from care as himself" (59). If Socrates is detached from the community's concerns, it is not because he is a misanthrope, but rather because he cannot ease the new settlers' "troubles and vexations." He prefers to remain at the margins of society. We are told that "he loved everything wild, regarding his solitary mode of life as the most natural thing in the world" (61) and possessed a "naive irony and unconscious satire," (61) which made him a figure both vexing and desirable to the others. Socrates' bachelorhood separates him from the rest of the community and makes him a social deviant. As Joseph Boone has noted, "in the eyes of a culture that valued marriage as its highest good, [the solitary quester-figure] was foreordained to enact a role . . . counter-traditional." Boone quotes from a fiction-alized tract entitled *Married and Single*, dated 1845, in which a bach-elor is warned that by remaining single he has "acted the strange, unnatural, criminal part" (233).

I have said that Socrates disappears from *Valley of Shadows*, but perhaps it is more accurate to say that he becomes absorbed into it and overtaken by it. He is an old man when we first meet him, "the last of his peculiar mode of life in this part of the country, and towns and railroads would soon put an end to such a mode of living" (60). As a resident of Sangamon County for twenty-five years, he is one of its original pioneers, living as a backwoodsman who has little use for the so-called "improvements" of society. Time has passed him by, and the memoir soon becomes absorbed in the current of events.

I want to draw attention to Grierson's emphasis on Socrates' "pecu-liar mode of living," especially the term "peculiar." Again and again, in various ways, the language around Socrates will take on an opacity absent from the rest of the book, an opacity that indicates more is meant than is said. Socrates is the genius who reveals information "only to those who are intimate with its language and gestures." Grier-son describes their first meeting this way:

> I slipped out again just in time to see a man come loping along on a small, shaggy horse, man and animal looking as if they had both grown up on the prairie together. It was Zack Caverly, nicknamed Socrates. Zack was indeed a Socrates of the prairie as well in looks as in speech, and the per-son who first called him after the immortal sage had one of those flashes

of inspiration that come now and then to the cosmopolitan whose experience permits him to judge men by a single phrase or a gesture. (7)

Grierson seems to refer arbitrarily to "the cosmopolitan" who alone could have had the flash of inspiration to have nicknamed Caverly as Socrates. No doubt this is another instance of Grierson's contempt for provincialism. Yet the comment suggests more than Grierson's satisfaction with being "a man of the world," for the cosmopolitan catches more than the allusion to Socrates. He is able "by a single phrase and gesture" to decode a person's sexual type. Grierson is trading on the notion that homosexuals—those preeminent cosmopolitans—have the ability to spot each other by some secret intuition, some peculiar capacity for mutual recognition not granted to everyone. As Proust notes in *Cities of the Plain,* sodomites, as he calls them, not only take "pleasure in recalling that Socrates was one of themselves," but also have the power to "recognize one another immediately by . . . signs . . . which the rest of humanity does not suspect" (14–15). Grierson's mother, for example, though a cosmopolitan of sorts, is unable "to fathom the secret of [Caverly's] strange originality" (*Valley,* 43). Of all the characters in *Valley of Shadows,* only young Grierson has an intuitive understanding of Socrates whose every word the boy "devoured" (40).

Socrates' homosexuality is marked in various ways, by his name, his bachelorhood, his exclusively male companions, and by references to his "peculiar mode of life." Yet imbedded in the text are more subtle forms of sexual encoding, one of which is worth mentioning. Socrates is generally associated with the rough, the natural, and the simple. He argues against modern technology, including farming techniques and store-bought clothes (42). Yet when his friends come to visit him, he serves them coffee in "big blue china cups" (76), a rather Wildean touch in the wilderness. It recalls Oscar's famous quip that he found it "harder and harder every day to live up to [his] blue china" (Ellmann, 45). Socrates' concern for his crockery lends to the shaggy backwoodsman a touch of the London aesthete, the sort of gesture the cosmopolitan could read in an instant.

Grierson has Socrates voice a rather full critique of bourgeois society and the patriarchal structure of capitalism, and part of what makes his "mode of life" appear so peculiar to those around him is his general refusal to take part in the economic system. One of Socrates' first pronouncements in the book, a statement that causes general uneasiness among his listeners, "a shuffling of feet and spitting," is his belief that "the niggers are a sight better off 'n we uns air. They ain't got no stakes in the groun'" (9). For Socrates, freedom and the ownership of property are antithetical. Indeed, it is the maintenance of property that leads to slavery. In a chapter entitled "Socrates Gives Advice," he returns to this subject:

> The world air a sorrowin' vale, kase folks hez too many stakes in the groun'. Ez fer me, I kin shoot en trap all I kin eat, jes' plantin' 'nough corn fer hoe-cakes en a leetle fodder, en some taters en turnips en pumpkins; en I hev a sight more smoked venison en b'ar meat in winter than I kin eat ez a single man with on'y one stommick; en I 'low I kin give a traveller hoe-cakes en fried chicken all he wants to fill up on. (41)

Socrates advocates a subsistence economy that requires little property and labor, and in which agriculture—minimal, varied—leaves the land fertile and plentiful. He raises few animals and only as supplements to those he hunts in the wild. Only when a man has the "ability to take care of himself without the slightest trouble or worry" is he truly free (41).

Socrates goes on to compare his subsistence economy to the capitalist farms springing up in Sangamon County:

> Thar be folks that air trampin' over these prairies a-spadin' up trouble like thar warn't none to be hed by settin' down in the city en lettin' other folks bring it to 'em. Thar's a heap too much corn en wheat, a durned sight too many kyows en hosses; en the four-legged critters chaws up what the two-legged critters gathers in. It air wus nor dog eat dog, seein' ez how the four-legged critters air livin' on the fat o' the land while the pore planters air livin' on spar' ribs en hens with sinoos ez tough ez b'iled owels. (42)

The land is laid waste by overproduction in order to create surplus wealth. Instead of improving the quality of their life, the planters have reduced it, for their labor is increased while their food declines. The objections to Socrates' position come quickly enough. The narrator's mother objects that Socrates' regime, though fine for a single man, is not applicable to family life in which parents have the responsibility to care for and educate their children, responsibilities that require a cushion of excess production. "But [having surplus goods to sell] makes a great difference when a man has a family to support and educate"

(42), she says, arguing the parental concern that has given bourgeois capitalism its moral urgency. Socrates makes no direct reply except to suggest that the educational system itself has been created to serve an economic system which, in turn, justifies itself by being the means for providing the education. Grierson could have learned the argument from William Morris: one wouldn't need to learn how to keep accounts if capitalism did not require account keeping. Yet Socrates does not gloat over his intellectual triumph; to the contrary, he is filled with pity "when he thought of all the hard work [Grierson's mother] would have to do" (43) to maintain the system which had unnecessarily imprisoned her. Pity aside, he is unable or unwilling to let the subject rest: "Thar's skasely a settler amoung the new uns but what'll tell ye they air workin' to live. It air workin' te die, that's what *I* call it" (43–44).

Socrates may insist on the subject because he sees the economics of the bourgeois family as the source of the political conflicts which will culminate in the Civil War. The surplus wealth necessitated by the family farm requires "hirin' extry hands" (45), and for Socrates it is but a short step from hired labor to slave labor, the cheapest form of labor needed to amass surplus wealth. In fact, he sees no difference between the farmer who buys labor and the farmer who owns slaves, and he questions the bourgeois abolitionists around him, "What difference does it make to you whether they work ez slaves or work ez we uns work?" (47). Socrates is no agrarian trying to return America to a nation of small family farms. He believes that agrarianism already contains the seeds of corruption, particularly the need for capital formation and wage labor. For Grierson, America lost its pristine virtue when it ceased to be a land of hunters and gatherers and its settlers took more than a casual interest in sowing the land.

Socrates presents the conception of American history which controls the book's development. For Socrates, the American West was a land in which man, nature, and spiritual forces existed in harmony. During this harmonious time the land was inhabited by Native Americans and only male backwoodsmen, both of which groups were predominately hunters and gatherers living in a subsistence economy. The harmony was broken by settlers who brought their families to secure homesteads and develop the land. Once that harmony was broken, American society inevitably was fated to lose itself in materialism and the subjugation of others, or to put it another way, the

Civil War was the inevitable result of the bourgeois family and its need for surplus wealth and hired labor.

In presenting this critique of the relationship between the family, property, and freedom, Grierson is hardly breaking new ground. Much of his argument might be found in Engels's *The Origin of the Family, Private Property, and the State* in which the introduction of cattle breeding and agriculture is seen both as creating the patriarchal, monogamous family and as stimulated by it, where the need for excess labor for managing herds and crops robs women of their rights as well as creates slavery (65–69). But Grierson's critique—at least as articulated through Socrates—differs from Engels's argument in several ways, all of which make his position more radical than any I know of that had been proposed up to that time. First, Engels insists that the early stages of development were dominated by "mother right" and that matrilineal descent is the norm for the primitive communistic world that predates the bourgeois family. Engels is indebted to Bachofen and especially to Lewis Henry Morgan for his belief in "mother right" as the original form of sexual organization. Grierson makes no mention and allows no provisions in *Valley of Shadows* for such a form of organization. For Socrates, and I believe for Grierson, neither the Indian culture—on which Morgan and Engels based their beliefs —nor the society of original hunters and gatherers give women a higher right. Indeed, for Socrates the society that possessed natural harmony was one that celebrated androgyny and avoided the polarities of heterosexism. This brings us to the second difference—Engels's treatment of homosexuality. Upon such matters, Engels entertained the most conservatively bourgeois notions. For Engels, homosexuality is a further degeneration of the sexuality inherent in patriarchal families. Writing about the ancient Athenian family, he insists that "the degradation of the women recoiled on the men themselves and degraded them too, until they sank into the perversion of boy-love, degrading both themselves and their gods by the myth of Ganymede" (74). Later Engels speaks sneeringly of Germans who migrated to the Black Sea and "suffered considerable moral degeneration and, apart from their horsemanship, acquired serious unnatural vices" from the local residents (73). For Grierson, homosexual relations are not the result of degeneration, but rather constitute a mode of social organization that escapes the economic forces that will finally corrupt heterosexual relations and societies built upon such relationships.

Engels was not, however, the only source of these ideas. Whitman in "Democratic Vistas" also points to the "crudeness, vice, caprices" of a people who have not cultivated "manly love" (363). Whitman argues: "The depravity of the business classes of our country is not less than has been supposed, but infinitely greater. . . . In business . . . the one sole object is, by any means, pecuniary gain. . . . The best class we show is but a mob of fashionably dressed speculators and vulgarians" (370). To counteract the depravity of capitalist competition, Whitman advocates "intense and loving comradship, the personal and passionate attachment of man to man" which "when thoroughly develop'd, cultivated and recognized in manners and literature [is] the most substantial hope and safety of the future of these States" (414). Yet nowhere in "Democratic Vistas" does Whitman explain how "loving comradship" will correct the depravity of market capitalism, except for offering the rather weak explanation that such fellowship promotes altruism. Manly love, for Whitman, is a condition that neither preexisted capitalism, nor is structurally incompatible with capitalism, as it is for Grierson. Manly love is Whitman's utopian hope for a future that will moderate, not substantially question, the basis of capital excess.

Edward Carpenter, Whitman's protégé in England, provides a more detailed understanding of the relationship between the "intermediate sexes" and society. Although he followed Engels in the belief that societies originally evolved through a stage of "mother right," Carpenter also believed that "intermediate types" coexisted with these primitive folk (*Coming of Age*, 161–64). Carpenter completely rejected Engels's belief in the degeneracy of homosexuals, and in fact saw "urnings" as people who might lead society away from the patriarchal family that institutionalized so much suffering (*Intermediate Sex*, 136). In *Intermediate Types Among Primitive Folk,* Carpenter, like Grierson, proposes a social evolutionary pattern in which homosexuals have an important part. He states rather straightforwardly that "if it had not been for the emergence of intermediate types—the more or less feminine man and similarly the more or less masculine woman—social life might never have advanced beyond . . . primitive phases" (58). In his essay "The Place of the Uranian in Society," the final chapter to *The Intermediate Sex,* his book published in 1908, a year before *Valley of Shadows,* Carpenter argues that, "underneath the surface of general Society," an urning society exists in which love is placed before everything, "postponing to it the motives like money-making, business success, fame" (123). Carpenter strikes me as closest to Grierson of any author, and the man against whom Grierson appears not as some strange creature, but as a recognizable, even typical figure of his time and place. Yet, again, we must point to several important differences. Carpenter sees the "intermediate man or woman" as advancing the material culture of society by developing the arts and crafts which hunters and gatherers are uninterested in developing. They are, thus, placed as the creators of the bourgeois comforts that surplus wealth is supposed to achieve. Instead of being inimical to capital formation, they tend to be the instruments by which society escapes a subsistence economy. "Intermediate types," Carpenter argues, "have penetrated into the framework of normal society and made themselves useful if not indispensable" (*Intermediate Types,* 11). Homosexuals, however, are useful in reforming the excess of capitalism because they are possessed of greater spiritual awareness than heterosexuals and because they are more willing to fight for ideals. Carpenter believed that "there *is* an organic connection between the homosexual temperament and unusual psychic or divinatory powers" (*Intermediate Types,* 49, Carpenter's italics). Because homosexuals do not view love as merely a way of propagating the species, they are more aware of the spiritual aspects that bind person to person (*Intermediate Sex,* 72–73). Carpenter also argues that only those "free from the responsibilities and impedimenta of family life" will have the force and energy to protect democratic ideals (*Intermediate Sex,* 74).

Another of the chief differences between Carpenter and Grierson is that as a socialist, Carpenter is committed to a specific program of social action that includes cooperative businesses and farms and the equality of both sexes. In none of his works does Grierson suggest a program of action except to argue the need for an alliance between England and the United States against the military threat of China and Japan. In general Grierson is content to provide a critique of the economic and social forces that could bring Western society to disaster. If Socrates' behavior is a model, Grierson's program is one of nonparticipation, of personal refusal to join the machinery of capital formation or patriarchal domination. In this regard his position may be less subversive in practical terms than Carpenter's Fabianism. We see in Socrates' and Grierson's abstention from capitalism a working out on a personal level of the equality that is, as I argued earlier, one of the distinguishing features of homosexuality in Euro-American culture.

Men engaged in subsistence economies must stand in near, if not in absolute, equality with one another since they do not have the resources for accumulating wealth.

Although Socrates as a character fades from the book, his ideas permeate the work, and the structure of *Valley of Shadows* supports his critique of bourgeois society. Most critics of the book have faulted its structure, believing as Edmund Wilson did that the book falters after the narrator leaves Sangamon County (Wilson, 82). Clearly, the book's organization is unusual. It progresses in two directions: the main narrative moves inexorably toward the outbreak of the Civil War, but interpolated stories that interrupt the synchronic narration travel back in time. The memoir moves alternatively between a search for the causes of social conflict and exposure of their inevitable consequences. The two most important of these interpolated narratives are accounts of the first white death in Sangamon County and of General John Charles Frémont's ill-fated first expedition to locate an easy southern passage across the Rockies. These interpolated stories illustrate the destruction of the original harmony of the land, and in so doing support Socrates' view of American history.

The first and longest of these two episodes is the story of a love triangle: Vicky Roberts is a beautiful, proud West Virginian who is courted by Hank Cutler and Jack Stone. Stone finally marries her under dubious circumstances—the justice of the peace who conducts the ceremony is no longer in office—but Cutler convinces Vicky of the marriage's irregularities and persuades her to run off with him. Moving restlessly for many years, Cutler and Roberts finally settle in Sangamon County where Cutler leads a band of robbers that terrorize the area. After much debate the farmers decide to form a posse to stop the gang, but they cannot find anyone willing to lead them. When all seems lost, a stranger appears. He agrees to be their chief. The stranger, of course, is Stone, who has searched nine years for Vicky. In the shootout between Cutler's gang and the posse, Cutler is killed, and his burial place is "the first grave of a white man in these parts" (184). Vicky returns to West Virginia, her beauty gone, her life shattered.

Although the story has all the earmarks of a cheap romance, Grierson wants us to take it seriously, at least as a parable. There is something classical in the way the story illustrates "death even in arcadia" or in Stone's nine-year odyssey. Biblical allusions abound. The visitor narrating the story comments that "for [Vicky] the beautiful rolling prairies an' the rich bottoms of the Illinois River was not a paradise but a valley o' shadows" (164) and later that "providence was kind of settin' of [Cutler] up right in the new Garden of Eden to tempt him in the right way, for there was no forbidden apples here in those days—" (166).

We are also invited to read this account from Zack "Socrates" Caverly's prospective, for Caverly, accompanied by a male friend, is part of the audience of this story. We note the arbitrariness of the marriage rules and see how heterosexual competition over a female leads to unrest, thievery, and finally murder. In the end, death comes to this fallen Garden of Eden not by the murder of Abel by his brother, but through heterosexual competition for a woman. Without women there has been harmony and, by suggestion, eternal life.

Clearly, Grierson's position is misogynistic, associating the appearance of white women with the corruption of capitalism. But it is not women per se who are the corrupting force, but rather the effect women have on men whose construction of gender tends to become dualistic once women are introduced into their presence. Vicky Roberts is a passive object of competition—a Helen of Troy—who sets in motion the drives of dominance and possession in the men around her. Women do not spoil the harmony of nature—both male and female Indians remain attuned to nature—rather it is the white man's response to the women in his midst that disturbs the balance of nature. All the runaway slaves in *Valley of Shadows* are either women or children who seek escape from a patriarchy that imagines itself to be acting on their behalf. In the end, women are the most immediate victims of the economic forces men set in motion for the supposed benefit of women.

The second major interpolated tale is somewhat harder to interpret than the tale of Vicky Roberts. It breaks into the narrative following Grierson's account of the first skirmish of the Civil War to take place in St. Louis. Instead of continuing with the story of the Civil War, Grierson recounts what he considers was the last chance the country had to avoid the War; that last opportunity was stopping General Frémont from finding an easy passage across the Rocky Mountains. Once the passage was discovered, white families would inevitably populate the entire continent, drive Native Americans from their hunting and foraging lands, require more and more slaves to labor on their territories, and acquire more and more excess wealth, which would aid them in further plundering the land and defending their "rights" to such usurpation. For Grierson, General Frémont is the linchpin, and his expedition is the beginning of a rapid process of deterioration that will inevitably end in war.

The only people who might be able to stop Frémont and the final disruption of the primal harmony of North America are the Indians themselves, and in the chapter fittingly entitled "The Dance of Death," virtually all the Southwestern tribes gather to destroy Frémont (240). Ultimately the effort is placed on two men, "the much dreaded Arappa-Honta, a grand enchanter of the Navahoes, and Umbaha-Tan, a great medicine-man and 'weaver of spells' of the Utahs" (241). They lead the tribes in a great dance designed to doom Frémont's expedition by subjecting it to the destructive forces of nature.

Although modern anthropologists such as Walter L. Williams argue that shamanism is *not* necessarily part of being a *berdache*—the homosexual, intermediate-gendered figure in Native American society —turn-of-the-century ethnographers emphasized the connection (35). Among the most important of these thinkers was Edward Westermarck, whose *The Origin and Development of Moral Ideas* contained an entire chapter on "Homosexual Love." Published in 1908, a year before Grierson completed and published *Valley of Shadows*, Westermarck's book, even if it was not Grierson's source, establishes the contemporary view of the medicine man and shaman in Native American society. In fact Westermarck begins his international survey of homosexuality by looking at "American homosexual customs . . . among a great number of the native tribes" and lists references to no less than thirty sources in Latin, Spanish, French, German, and English (456–57). From the sources, Westermarck concludes that there was a strong "connection between homosexual practice and shamanism" among North American Indians (472). Thus in Grierson's time the presumption was that medicine men were *berdache*. Indeed Edward Carpenter believed that homosexuals were predisposed to two sorts of roles in society—to be its warriors and its religious figures—and made "this connection of homosexuality with divination and religion" a special area of analysis (*Intermediate Types*, 12). Let me quote Westermarck's relevant passage at some length:

> There is no indication that the North American aborigines attached any opprobrium to men who had intercourse with those members of their own sex who had assumed the dress and habits of women. In Kadiak such a companion was on the contrary regarded as a great acquisition;

and the effeminate men themselves, far from being despised, were held in repute by the people, most of them being wizards. We have previously noticed the connection between homosexual practice and shamanism. . . . it is said that such shamans as had changed their sex were greatly feared by the people as very powerful. Among the Illinois and Naudowessies the effeminate men assist in all the juggleries and the solemn dance in honor of the *calumet,* or sacred tobacco pipe, for which the Indians have such a deference that one may call it "the god of peace and war, and the arbiter of life and death" but they are not permitted either to dance or sing. They are called into the councils of the Indians, and nothing can be decided upon without their advice; for because of their extraordinary manner of living they are looked upon as *manitous,* or supernatural beings and persons of consequence. (472–73)

Though Arappa-Honta and Umbaha-Tan are from the Navaho and Utah tribes, their position is not unlike the one Westermarck discusses for the Illinois and Naudowessies. For example, Arappa-Honta leads the community in a tobacco ceremony (244), and though he organizes the dance and acts as a kind of master of ceremonies, he does not dance in it or sing. Finally, according to Grierson even "the white visitors" to Arappa-Honta's tent "immediately became conscious of something wonderful in the influence he threw about him of length and distance" (243).

According to Walter L. Williams, the *berdache* had a significant role in many important Native American ceremonies. For the Cheyenne, the *berdache* "were closely associated with the warfare complex" and were essential for forming war parties and for performing the victorious Scalp Dance (69). *Berdache* cut down the tree that was the central object in the Sun Dance, "the chief religious rite of Plains culture" (36). The Navaho called their *berdache* figures *nadle,* and they were "considered particularly excellent as chanters" and shamans (35).

Although shamans were generally thought of as *berdache,* Grierson goes further and marks Arappa-Honta as homosexual (or a *berdache*) in two subtle ways. One way is in his physical description:

Everything about his features was long and thin: long, narrow head, rising far above his eyebrows; long, narrow eyes, veiled and absent; long, thin nose . . . and a neck that might have grown in a night, like a mushroom-stalk. The marvelous head was capped with a circle of feathers, and from the center of the crown rose three huge ostrich-plumes, which must have been brought from St. Louis or Mexico, or stolen from emigrants. (243)

The long, thin physiognomy of Arappa-Honta recalls strangely enough Grierson's vision of Lincoln (who, for Grierson, is a type of shaman), but Arappa-Honta's gaunt face lacks the masculinity of Lincoln's; the neck, particularly, seems weak. What most effectively feminizes the "savage" are the three "ostrich-plumes," which are so clearly foreign, alien, queer, and perhaps stolen from emigrant women's hats. Arappa-Honta's tent, filled with "thick cushions of bear and buffalo skins," recalls Socrates' cabin whose rafters are hung with "pelt of fox and wildcat," whose couch "was covered with a buffalo robe" and on whose floor "were some old skins of the black bear" (60). Socrates and Arappa-Honta are linked by their fur-lined accommodations, which seem to suggest both their fierce natural power and their luxuriant sensuality. In short, the all-man community of white backwoodsmen and the world of Native American tribes are united by their subsistence economies, their harmony with the natural world, their avoidance of the bourgeois family, and their tacit acceptance of homosexuality.

The spell that Arappa-Honta casts on Frémont's expedition is only partially successful, for while it dooms his first expedition to failure, it is ineffective in preventing Frémont from undertaking a second expedition, one that succeeds. Consequently, the "Dance of Death," which is directed as much to the Native Americans themselves as against Frémont, signals the last hold they have over their native lands. *Valley of Shadows* does not allow itself regret over this loss; one senses that a greater destiny, a more powerful force, is at work.

Grierson's sense of destiny demands to be examined. Edmund Wilson wrote of Grierson that he "regarded himself as a mystic, but his mysticism was queerly limited," in that he "appears to assure that the human world which we know has behind it invisible forces whose impulses and aims can be read" (75–76). It seems to me that rather than being "queerly limited" Grierson's sense of "invisible forces" is gaily inclusive, for the forces at work in Grierson's universe are diverse. Though Grierson rarely speaks of God, he seems to have a sense of telos, but that telos is reached by a confluence of economic factors, cultural materialist elements, genetic predispositions (that enter his work as racial "characteristics"), and psychological capacities, all of which together form a forcefield, what he calls in *The Humour of the Underman,* "phenomenal relativity" (85–86). Grierson at no point argues for trying to regain the lost primal world of the original settlers. He invokes that primal world to locate within it the moment of its inevitable fall before the forces of capitalism and the bourgeois family, to expose the corruption that capitalism and bourgeois values brought, and to suggest what might occur in the future. "Systems, like men, wear themselves out, not by sudden friction, nor by fits in starts, but by stages as definitely marked on the map of time as the stages of a desert route of the marching caravans," he wrote in *Modern Mysticism* (116). He went on to predict, "Socialism will strip society of its false aristocracy. Socialism, in turn, will be conquered and governed by the aristocracy of intellect, the only unconquerable thing in the world" (125). Though Grierson remained a believer in idealist subjectivity, he believed that its preeminence would come about through a materialist dialectic that would leave the mind free to see things as in fact they really are.

The failure of Arappa-Honta and Zack "Socrates" Caverly to stop the invading forces of Frémont's expedition or family settlers is part of the larger process of "phenomenal relativity" which has brought crisis to America. In his preface to *Valley of Shadows,* Grierson characterizes his memoir as a record "of the passing of the old democracy and the old social system in the United States," which he compares to Paris in 1869 to 1870, recollections of which he hopes to publish in the future (viii). In *Modern Mysticism,* he explains further: "We have witnessed not only the decadence, but the death of individual authority" (118), but "liberty of conscience," which is one of the sources of "individual authority," will return vested in "one man or a single group of men" (122). It seems to me that by implication that "group of men," who are by definition marginal, will be predominately homosexual or objects of homosexual longing, since Socrates, Arappa-Honta, and Lincoln are its only three representatives in *Valley of Shadows.*

Valley of Shadows contains a central tension: the "individual authority" of the mind is, like all prophetic modes, arrived at either by emptying itself or by making room for other consciousness. Arappa-Honta, for example, goes through a dream-journey before he prepares his spell; Socrates keeps his mind on the present, emptied of past fears and future anxieties; Lincoln was "the prophetic man of the present" in part because a person "so ungainly, so natural, so earnest . . . had no place in his mental economy for the thing called vanity" (198). The authority, then, of the narrator rests on his ability to receive the forces that are around him by cultivating the "neutrality of repose." *Valley of Shadows* then presents without comment the various scenes that appear in the process of "phenomenal relativity," but the aggregate arrangement of those impressions constitutes a map, so to speak, of the forces of that destiny.

As narrator, Grierson remains in a peculiar relationship to his own material. As a homosexual, Grierson is outside of the bourgeois family that comes to represent in the memoir the most corrupting force within early capitalism, yet as a son in such a family, he is part of that force.

Grierson's homosexuality acts as a decentering force; as a child he learns how heterosexuals think even as he retains his own sexual orientation. His memoir contains a subtle and moving scene which shows his youthful adjustment to the dominance of heterosexuality. Responding to his shock that a character is married, his mother replies: "Why, of course, he's married, like all good Christians . . . and you'll be married too, some day, when the proper time comes." Instead of replying, young Grierson meditates: "I had pictured him as a kind of hermit, living somewhere all alone, perhaps fed by ravens, like Elijah the prophet; and even now I could hardly believe that he had a regular, fixed abode" (85). The unmarried male is not "fixed," not "regular;" instead he is a prophet living in harmony with nature, which comes and feeds him. Grierson does not settle for one vision over another, but juggles the two at once. This shifting doubleness creates his depth of vision like the two images converged by the stereopticon.

Valley of Shadows employs two strategies typical of gay literature and thought. It seeks to authorize homosexuality by asserting its naturalness and its cultural superiority. Its naturalness may be observed, as I've shown, in the invocation of aboriginal peoples—in this case Native Americans—who become a model for the social, political, and economic integration of homosexuals. By invoking the authority of primitive societies, Grierson makes a move that will be repeated in Melville's accounts of the Pacific Islanders, Tobias Schneebaum's tale of life among the Amazonians, and Alain Locke's theorizing on Africans. By invoking the name of Socrates, Grierson also calls on the authority of Hellenism. Grierson finds the homosexual approved by both ends of the cultural spectrum: he is as at home among the noble savages as he is among the ancient philosophers. In subsequent chapters we will see gay writers searching in both cultural directions for form and tradition, function and acceptance, a cultural destiny and a social place.

Grierson's vision is not stable or complete. Homosexuality pushes

Grierson, as it does Socrates and Arappa-Honta, to the invisible margins of society. When these three subjectivities are brought into relationship, we can see the depth of *Valley of Shadows*. Socrates shows how the bourgeois family and capitalism are inimical to the homosexual and his harmony with nature. Even if bourgeois society never becomes overtly homophobic, it cannot tolerate the freedom necessary for people like Socrates or Arappa-Honta to flourish. Arappa-Honta shows that, although the homosexual possesses spiritual power, this power cannot resist the material forces of capitalism. Grierson himself is witness to the violence, corruption, and waste that occur in America. Though he would like to join Carpenter and Whitman in believing that "intense and loving comradeship [is] the most substantial hope and safety of the future of these States," he believes that "Whitman [is] too jubilant and expectant" (*Celtic,* 85). Bourgeois society will not give a role to the homosexual because, in his own sexual economy, the homosexual rejects the surplus wealth that is the justification for—as well as the aim of—the bourgeois family. By combining the spiritual critique of homosexuality with the economic-political critique of heterosexuality, Grierson has developed a far more radical and, in the short run, a more pessimistic analysis of both society and the homosexual's role in it. But, as he wrote, a pessimist is "one who prepares for the exigencies of the future by every means devisable by the ingenuity of human imagination" (*Celtic,* 81).

5

F. O. Matthiessen: The Critic as Homosexual

DESPITE the publicity that attended F. O. Matthiessen's suicide in 1950, and the books that were subsequently written about him, including May Sarton's 1955 novel *Faithful are the Wounds,* it was not until a quarter of a century later that his homosexuality became public knowledge. During his life, Matthiessen had not tried to hide the fact, but neither had he made it a public issue. Friends, colleagues, and even students widely understood that Matthiessen was gay, but they felt in large measure what William E. Cain has recently said, that the "facts of Matthiessen's sexual . . . life . . . do not have much direct bearing at all" on his work (*Matthiessen,* 48).

Matthiessen would have disagreed. He kept his sexual identity and his scholarly reputation separate only because the social atmosphere in which he worked necessitated such a division. Any attempt to bring them together would have given a rare opportunity to those who wished to discredit him and his work. He understood quite clearly how dear a price he paid for his discretion and how it distorted what he said and how he spoke. "My sex bothers me," he wrote, "sometimes when it makes me aware of the falseness of my position in the world. . . . But damn it! I hate to have to hide when what I thrive on is absolute directness" (Hyde, *Rat and the Devil* [hereafter cited as *RD*], 200). Matthiessen, who prized honesty and plain speech, understood that he had to be discreet and evasive if he wished to survive.

His discretion succeeded. Today he is regarded as the most influential writer on American culture of the 1930s and 1940s. As a teacher at Harvard, he personally influenced an entire generation of students and scholars, and through his writing and especially *American Renaissance,* his masterpiece, he continues to exert an important presence. Moreover, by keeping his sexual life relatively quiet he was able to play a role in the politics of his era as president and founder of the Harvard Teachers' Union and as a campaigner for Henry Wallace, the Progressive Party's 1948 candidate for president. In these public roles he did not deny his homosexuality; he merely performed them without any reference to sexuality. No doubt, it was a difficult line to walk, and his repeated bouts of depression were likely deepened by his precarious position.

Matthiessen felt that sexuality always plays a part in a writer's work. Although he rejected crude biographical procedures, he advocated the use of psychoanalytic insights that would uncover basic structures in a writer's sensibility or development. Since Matthiessen advocated what today would be called a "holistic" approach to literary studies, an approach in which critics should "make use of what we inevitably bring from our own lives" (*Renaissance,* xiii), the absence of a careful examination of the relationship between Matthiessen's sexuality and his criticism is a gap that, despite Leo Marx's admirable attempt, cries out to be filled. Unlike most critics whose private lives remain obscure, Matthiessen's life and his sexuality were opened to our inspection through the publication of *Rat and the Devil,* a selection of the approximately three thousand letters he exchanged with his lover, Russell Cheney. We have, therefore, both the motive and the opportunity to examine Cheney's impact on Matthiessen's conception of himself as a homosexual and the impact of Matthiessen's sexuality on his writing. By examining these issues, I hope to be answering Thomas Yingling's call "to acknowledge [the] use of gay texts for gay readers and to investigate the function of writers such as Whitman, Crane and Matthiessen to the production of a homosexual culture within an American culture" (23).

F. O. Matthiessen met Russell Cheney in 1924, aboard the *Paris,* the newest, largest, and most luxurious of the French Line's fleet (Newell, 87). What began as a shipboard romance became the central emotional attachment of their lives, a relationship that ended a quarter of a century later with Cheney's death from heart disease.

When they met, Cheney was a painter of some reputation, while Matthiessen was a promising student of English. Cheney came from a close-knit, old New England family who had settled one of the Connecticut valleys in colonial days. Matthiessen's family was far-flung and had relatively recently arrived, though his mother was a distant relation to Sarah Orne Jewett. While both were the children of privilege, Matthiessen had seen his father fritter away the fortune he inherited from his own father, the founder of what became Westclox. Cheney, in contrast, was part of a family that carefully husbanded its wealth through many generations and filled positions of civic and religious responsibility. In many ways, Cheney had the background that Matthiessen dreamed of having, and for all Matthiessen's belief in the goodness of the masses and the need for social justice, his writing contains more than a little of the patrician concern for social form as well as social obligation.

The most striking difference between them was their ages. When they met, Matthiessen was twenty-two, Cheney forty-two. This difference in generation affected many of the experiences that bound them together. For example, although both men were Yale graduates and were proud of their connection with their alma mater, they went to very different schools. Matthiessen was only two years old when Cheney was graduated, and consequently the faculty had largely changed by the time Matty (as he was called by his friends) was matriculated. Their attitudes toward homosexuality were also a source of occasional conflict. Born in 1881, Cheney was raised with Victorian notions of sexuality while Matthiessen, a child of the twentieth century, had studied the matter, in his words, "scientifically" and felt much freer.

Cheney entered Matthiessen's life at a time when Matthiessen was especially receptive to such a relationship. They met as Matthiessen was returning to England to complete his second and last year as a Rhodes Scholar. His mother had recently died and, with her, whatever plans he had of a home after Oxford. Having lost his own mother, Cheney could empathize with Matthiessen, and within weeks of their meeting, he sent Matthiessen his mother's photograph. Matthiessen replied:

How I loved that picture of your mother's birthday. Except for my quick impatience I think we must have had exactly the same sort of relationships with our mothers. And then just when it gets to the point that after I return from Oxford she is to make a home for me in New Haven and I can maybe give her some culture and some of the love she has always been denied, the poor devoted little woman dies. Never did she have anyone to look after her. When I was five, my father sent my two brothers away to boarding school. My mother, my sister, and I went to California, presumably just for the winter for my sister's health. Of course, any one with any worldliness . . . would have seen that my father never intended to give her a home again. . . . She wouldn't listen to the mention of divorce, for in spite of his being absolutely worthless—God pity her—she loved him to the end. Finally when I was thirteen he practically forced her into a divorce for he wanted to marry again. . . . How I remember the impotence of my thirteen year old rape. (RD, 48)

With the death of his mother, Matthiessen was without a person on whom he could bestow his love and caring attention and who might return his affection and provide a home. The letter makes clear how allied Matthiessen and his mother had been. Her unworldliness and homelessness merge with his own innocence and dispossession. He translates the imposition of his mother's divorce into a rape of his own impotent body, and the love his mother bears for her undeserving husband carries with it his own unrequited affection for his father. Cheney did not so much replace Mrs. Matthiessen as fill a vacuum that her death had created.

Cheney's most immediate effect on Matthiessen was to force Matty to reconsider what it meant to be gay. Before their meeting, Matthiessen's homosexual experiences seem to have been either brief anonymous contacts or those circumscribed by boarding school. Matthiessen had bravely discussed his sexual orientation with his closest friends, telling Russell Davenport that though he "didn't want to be an alarmist," he thought he "might very likely be altogether homosexual" (RD, 47). At the time of his conversation with Davenport, Matthiessen saw only three possible outcomes to his predicament: (1) "morbidity" by repressing all sexual expression, (2) "self-abuse," and (3) "the old business with men," namely, anonymous sexual contacts. But by falling in love with Cheney, Matthiessen becomes aware of a fourth option—"love between men"—and he writes Cheney of the "surprise" that realization has for him: "Was it possible? I had known lust. I had prided myself that it had never touched the purity of my friendships. Was it possible for love and friendship to be blended into one? But before I had time to even ask the question it was answered" (RD, 48).

His love for Cheney forces Matthiessen to reconsider the nature and social implications of homosexuality; it transforms an ugly truth into a glorious opportunity, "the old business with men" into "the advance guard of any hope for a spirit of brotherhood" (RD, 47).

Matthiessen was not, however, content to feel "this new sensitive tingling in the tips of my fingers, and on my lips" (RD, 48). As a firm believer in the Eliotic "unified sensibility," he had to blend an emotional apprehension of his sexuality with its intellectual comprehension. Matthiessen began to test his sexual response in the field and to research whatever was available in the library. Consequently, his letters provide one of the finest records now available of how a man formed his understanding of what it meant to be homosexual.

Some of his experiments sound boyishly comic. For example, after meeting Rudy Vallee, a fellow "son of Eli," in a London hotel, the two —at Vallee's suggestion—visit "the toughest dive in Europe." There Matthiessen "enter[s] upon a little study in the psychology of sex" by dancing with the "painted whores. . . . in a way that would ordinarily land [him] in jail," but he discovers "no female physical attraction" (RD, 34–35). In another letter to Cheney he discusses a plan to rent a room from a "homosexual fellow . . . who ran a lodging house" and "who might have been a way to gain added sex knowledge," but he rejects the idea in deference to Cheney (RD, 26).

Even before they met, Matthiessen had begun to read sexual psychology, particularly Havelock Ellis's *Sexual Inversion,* which had first "brought home to me that I was what I was by *nature*" (RD, 47, Matthiessen's italics). But meeting Cheney accelerates the reading process. Cheney inspires him to reread Whitman, whom Matthiessen had only begun to read for "an intellectual kick" the year before (RD, 26). Whitman becomes a regular topic of their early letters. Then Matthiessen begins reading Edward Carpenter, first *The Intermediate Sex* and then *Days with Walt Whitman.* He takes up John Addington Symonds, Shelley, and George Barnefield's essay on Shelley as a homosexual. Cheney makes reference to Proust and Raymond Radiguet, the Rimbaud-like boy genius who had died at age twenty in 1923. Largely cut off from a gay community, Matthiessen and Cheney construct much of their sexual identities from what they read.

Matthiessen's thoughts were spurred by opposition. He claimed that he learned the most from Irving Babbitt because, by disagreeing "at nearly every point," Matthiessen was forced "to fight for [his] tastes, which grew stronger by the exercise" (Cain, *Matthiessen,* 57).

Similarly, the changes in Matthiessen's attitudes toward his sexuality do not become clear until Cheney challenged them during one of his intermittent bouts of guilt, panic, and conventionality. Six months after their meeting, the relationship ripening, Matthiessen requested permission from Cheney to write his closest friends about their relationship, but the idea of exposing it to the scrutiny of outsiders drove Cheney into one of his periodic depressions. "You cannot conceive the intensity of emotion," Cheney wrote Matthiessen, "that hauled me right out of bed a couple of times night before last." The notion of public exposure of their sexual relations was "absolutely intolerable" (RD, 80). Cheney believed "it absolutely impossible for two fellers to get away with the situation . . . in society . . . as it is organized" (RD, 80). He sums it up: "for the outside world, you are outcast" (RD, 81).

Cheney at times appears to approve of society's condemnation of homosexuality. He sees himself as a man driven and degraded by "two indulgences, in drink and sex" which have destroyed "the simple sweet nature that was part of me in my teens" (RD, 80–81). He tells Matthiessen that his "character had steadily deteriorated in will power" over the last ten to fifteen years, and the only way to return to mental health and spiritual well-being is to stop indulging in both drink and sex. "I believe, that the base of our love is not physical but intense understanding of a mutual problem," (RD, 80) he tells Matthiessen and invites his young lover to help him abstain from alcohol and sexual contact.

Matthiessen's lengthy response strikes me as enormously sympathetic under the circumstances even as it strongly rejects both Cheney's proposition and assumptions. The tone is notably paternal, considering their differences in age, as though Matthiessen were comforting a scared, unhappy child. At the same time, he gives Cheney hardly an inch: "I've got to tell the truth, don't I? This is the essence of our life. And the truth is that from my point of view I don't agree with anything you said" (RD, 86).

Matthiessen rebuts Cheney's assertion that homosexuality is an acquired trait, a bad habit that willpower alone can eradicate:

Can you acknowledge the fact that you were born different from most people sexually and that consequently you react to different stimuli. . . .

That to me is the essence of it; we are born as we are. I am no longer the least ashamed of it. What is there to be ashamed of? It simply reveals the fact that sex is not mathematical and clear-cut, something to be separated definitely into male and female; but that just as there are energetic active women and sensitive delicate men, so also there are women who appear to be feminine but have a male sex element, and men, like us, who appear to be masculine but have a female sex element. Ashamed of it? Forty years ago, perhaps, when nothing was really known about it, I would have felt myself an outcast. But now that the matter has been studied scientifically, and the facts are there in black and white? (*RD*, 87)

Matthiessen bases his argument on Havelock Ellis, Edward Carpenter, and through them on Karl Heinrich Ulrich's theory of Uranian androgyny. Though his talk about "sex elements" seems quaint today and perhaps a bit homophobic compared with the current debate on hormonal factors that might lead to sexual predispositions, Matthiessen based his assertion on the best medical and psychoanalytic theories of his time in an attempt to remain objective.

Matthiessen also refutes Cheney's notions that they should abstain from sex and keep their relationship secret from their nearest friends. At the heart of Matthiessen's argument is the importance of human "completeness" and integrity, two conditions that cannot be achieved unless the individual not only integrates the various parts of his own self, but joins his integrated self to the society at large. Sixteen years later these values, as Jonathan Arac has pointed out, will be among the most important aesthetic criteria used in *American Renaissance*. "I'm striving for . . . the realization of a fully developed character," Matthiessen writes Cheney, and that full development can only occur when sexual desires are acted on. "Before meeting you I had known love only of the mind and of the soul. I was not a fully arrived personality. I was hesitant, and partially repressed in that I had furtive sexual desires that I refused to satisfy. You changed this" (*RD*, 86). Later Matthiessen admonishes Cheney that if they "no longer lived a *complete* life of truth together, we would both be unhappy" (*RD*, 87). Matthiessen admits that "law and public opinion are clear enough" in their disdain for homosexuals, but that if gay men give in to these pressures, they will be harming only themselves. Some people will regard his decision to "follow the deepest voice of [his] nature" as "egocentric and selfish," but Matthiessen believes that by acting on his homosexual desires he realizes "a force infinitely stronger and nobler than myself," a spirit of love that binds the world. Society will be harmed if they "deny the body" (*RD*, 88–89).

While Matthiessen never fully integrated his sexual self into his public world and kept knowledge of his gay identity within the private sphere of friends and relatives, still he was perfectly aware that this secrecy damaged himself, his work, and his relationship with Cheney. During his composition of his book on Elizabethan translation, he wrote that "the falseness [of his position in the world] seems to sap my confidence of power. Have I any right in a community that would so utterly disapprove of me if it knew the facts? I ask myself that, and then I laugh; for I know I would never ask it at all if isolation from you didn't make me search into myself" (RD, 200). Matthiessen deeply wished to come out of the closet, but he knew that Cheney and the public, even the relatively enlightened public of Harvard University, were not ready for such truth, preferring the comforting falseness of fragmentation. As Matthiessen's political activity grew more and more controversial, he must have been aware that colleagues who wished to get rid of him on political grounds, but couldn't because he held tenure, would be ready to challenge him on moral grounds—his one vulnerable flank—were he to make his sexuality a public issue.

The extremely homophobic atmosphere in which Matthiessen lived and worked probably contributed to his suicide on the morning of 1 April 1950. The events preceding his death paint a vivid, if ugly, picture of national intolerance. On 28 February 1950, Under Secretary of State John Peurifoy testified before the Senate Appropriations Committee that most of the ninety-one employees dismissed from his department on moral grounds were homosexuals. The Republicans immediately added "sexual perverts" to the issue of communists in high government positions. In March of 1950, stories about sexual deviants in government made the front page of the New York Times three times, and in June, the Senate authorized an investigation into the hiring of homosexuals (D'Emilio, 41–42). Between April and September of 1950, the number of homosexuals fired by the administration rose from an average of five to sixty a month, a twelvefold increase (D'Emilio, 44). As a gay man who had made very little effort to conceal his sexual identity, Matthiessen faced a world that seemed more hostile, if anything, than it had been when he first met Cheney.

It is ironic, to say the least, that critics today, by ignoring the very realities he so painfully was forced to consider, attack Matthiessen's efforts to be scientific about homosexuality and his discretion in handling the institutional and social homophobia that surrounded him. Kenneth S. Lynn in his portrait of Matthiessen writes:

> I was struck by Matthiessen's silence, in his lectures and tutorial conversations, on the subject of homosexuality in American literature. His

comments on Whitman's interest in young male beauty were singularly guarded and inadequate, while the blatant case of Hart Crane obviously made him uncomfortable. The conclusion I drew from this at the time, and have subsequently had no reason to doubt, was that Matthiessen's own sex life was a guilt-ridden horror to him. So full of revulsion was he that he could barely pronounce the word homosexuality, let alone release his feelings through candid discussions. (116)

Such a passage is a remarkable example of students' projections of "guilt-ridden horror" onto gay professors, for none of Lynn's examples of Matthiessen's "guarded" behavior warrant his extreme conclusion. Forty years after Matthiessen taught, I still find it difficult to broach such topics with students whose prejudices and misinformation are ugly, offensive, and well entrenched. One can only imagine how misunderstood Matthiessen's motives would have been had he "released his feelings" in "candid discussions" during private tutorials, as Lynn would have had him do. Lynn's analysis is not merely naive, it reinforces the double-bind in which gay teachers and scholars typically find themselves: if they comment on homosexuality, they are accused of projecting their personal issues into the classroom; if they remain silent, they are accused of self-loathing. In the guise of being sympathetic, Lynn reveals the attitude that keeps gay teachers from discussing homosexuality.

Lynn's belief in Matthiessen's "guilt-ridden horror" of homosexuality appears in more recent scholarship, perpetuating the distortion. James W. Tuttleton, for example, concludes that "Matthiessen's suicidal impulse probably had its origins in an emotional state of self-loathing, confusingly and inextricably connected with his homosexuality" (9). William E. Cain finds Matthiessen's letters to Cheney "sometimes embarrassing," an embarrassment he feels in reading all love letters, yet he concedes that despite the "gushes of sentiment . . . they are also tough-minded, persistent, and persevering" and "reveal an admirable strength and courage" (46). Cain's critical language is full of masculinist coding. When Matthiessen exhibits such "feminine" traits as being gushy and "sentimental," Cain finds him embarrassing, but when he exhibits such masculine traits as "strength," "courage," and tough-mindedness, Cain declares him "admirable." Although Cain recognizes that "Matthiessen is zealously determined to carry his and Cheney's love through hard times and tensions," he also finds evidence of "self-disapproval" in *American Renaissance* when Matthiessen argues that "the passivity of [Whitman's] body" in "Song of Myself" indicates that "there is a quality vaguely pathological and homosexual" (48). I will look at Matthiessen's attitude toward Whitman, and particularly at this passage, at greater length later; here it should suffice to say that Matthiessen is only repeating what in his day was the best clinical evaluation and psychoanalytic understanding of Whitman's condition. As the entire context will reveal, he is being descriptive rather than evaluative in calling Whitman's passivity pathological, and insofar as he appears to be disapproving, he is reflecting psychiatry's general disapproval of male passivity. Cain's nonhistorical approach to Matthiessen places Matthiessen in yet another double bind. Cain criticizes him for breaking out of masculine emotional restraints in his private letters, and for being too constrained by medical opinion in his public criticism.

American Renaissance is a long and complex book, over one thousand pages in manuscript, and it was intended to serve a number of functions. Among its many interrelated themes is a sexual one. Rather than "distanc[ing] himself from" homosexuality and wanting to show that he "spurned 'abnormal' homosexual attitudes in poetry," as Cain contends (*Matthiessen,* 48), I believe Matthiessen tacitly shows that the finest strain of expression in America culture is to be found in gay works, those derived from the homosexual's "divine gifts" as "the advance guard of any hope for a spirit of brotherhood" (*RD,* 47). In short, *American Renaissance* is Matthiessen's ultimate expression of his love for Cheney and a covert celebration of the homosexual artist.

Cheney was an explicit presence in many Matthiessen books. Matthiessen wrote *Russell Cheney, 1881–1945, A Record of His Work* as a memorial. *From the Heart of Europe* includes a discussion of Cheney, and in his first book, *Sarah Orne Jewett,* Matthiessen credits Cheney, who contributed illustrations, with suggesting the subject. The Jewett book is in other respects a covert celebration of the homosexual artist, for without ever overtly calling Jewett a lesbian, Matthiessen repeatedly insists that Jewett had a great deal of the "masculine element" that might be found even in otherwise feminine women. At one point, Matthiessen comments that "Miss Jewett could be, when she saw fit, masculine enough to equip three average male story-tellers" (95) and "had more need of a wife than a husband" since like one of her characters, she had other business than "a woman's natural work" (72–73). Moreover, by celebrating Jewett's relationship to Annie Fields, Matthiessen honors his relationship with Cheney. According to Matthiessen,

If [Jewett] thought of marriage at all, it was as a hinderance and complication that would step between her and her dreams. But the generous warmth of her nature demanded an outlet, and she found herself sustained in her devotion to Annie Fields. They were together constantly in Boston, or in Mrs. Fields' summer home . . . and when they were separated, daily letters sped between them, hardly letters, but jotted notes of love, plans of what they would do when they met, things they wanted to talk about, books they would read together. (73)

While Matthiessen taught most of the year in Cambridge, Cheney stayed in their home in Kittery Point, Maine, not far from Jewett's house. In their divided living arrangements and in their whirlwind of correspondence, the Jewett-Fields relationship provided a model for Matthiessen and Cheney, who complained in their early letters of knowing no "parallel case" that would steer them through the "uncharted, uninhabited country" of same-sex "marriages" (*RD,* 71).

Though *American Renaissance* more explicitly discusses homosexuality, like *Sarah Orne Jewett* its larger argument about the role of the gay writer in the canon of American literature remains implicit. Such self-censorship is perfectly understandable in the 1930s and 1940s when *American Renaissance* was written, and indeed it is one of the book's subjects. For example, taking issue with Richard Henry Stoddard's contention that popular audiences, "captivated by stories of maritime life," indulged Melville's penchant for gritty realism, Matthiessen counters that Melville was "actually . . . constrained by such genteel demands." He points out that Melville, though claiming in *White Jacket* to be "withholding nothing, inventing nothing," omits the captain's epithets because, in Melville's words, he "should not like to be the first person to introduce [such language] to the public" (422). Matthiessen goes on to comment:

His own modesty joined again with the taboos of his age when he came to probe the daily life of the men, for he skirted the subject with remote allusions to the *Oedipus* and to Shelley's *Cenci,* and with the remark that 'the sins for which the cities of the plain were overthrown still linger in some of these wooden-walled Gomorrahs of the deep.' (422)

Matthiessen's remarks on Melville should alert us to his own predicament. To get his book published, he, too, will have to skirt the subject of sexuality and especially homosexuality through remote allusions and other rhetorical diversions. In fact, in some ways, the taboos of

Matthiessen's age were more difficult to skirt than those of Melville's time because Freud had made readers so much more savvy about sexual subtexts. As Matthiessen notes: "the sexual element in Claggart's ambivalence" "may have been only latent for Melville," but it is "one of the passages where a writer today would be fully aware" (506). Freud had made the public more conscious of sex without breaking down its prejudices. Consequently, Matthiessen had to be far more inventive than Melville in eluding his readers' conventional morals and avoiding their censure.

A recurring theme of *American Renaissance* is the need of mid-nineteenth-century American authors to avoid arousing the moral righteousness of their genteel and provincial readers. Matthiessen quotes Emerson's dictum, "Everything in the universe goes by indirection," (57) and he examines Whitman's belief that the American poet must be "indirect" and cannot rely on finding a "voice through any of the conventional modes" (519). He notes Henry James's practice of presenting material with "unnamed sexual implications" (476). He recalls approvingly Thoreau's belief that "Poetry *implies* the whole truth. Philosophy *expresses* a particle of it" (85, Thoreau's italics) and cites Melville's pronouncement that "All that has been said but multiplies the avenues to what remains to be said" (414). Matthiessen's close attention to the text uncovers the silences that society and the unconscious impose upon it and language's devious ways for circumventing censorship.

Structure is one way to make a point tacitly, and the structure of *American Renaissance* clearly argues for the supremacy of gay writers. The book focuses on five authors: two optimistic essayists, two tragic novelists, and a poet, in that order. Of the essayists, Emerson and Thoreau, Matthiessen prefers Thoreau; between the two novelists, Hawthorne and Melville, Matthiessen chooses Melville. But it is Whitman, the poet, who is the model writer. In each case the homosexual writer (or the one whose works reveal the strongest homoerotic tendencies) is preferred over his ostensibly heterosexual rival. Matthiessen erected in *American Renaissance* virtually a gay canon of American literature. Just how gay can be judged by the writers he admittedly excludes from the study—Poe, Longfellow, Holmes, and by stopping before the Civil War, Twain. In addition, among the subjects of Matthiessen's monographs—Jewett, James, T. S. Eliot, Dreiser— Dreiser is the sole figure whose sexual orientation has not been a serious subject of speculation. Matthiessen's elevation of gay writers rests not merely on the specific figures he chose, but on the argument he makes for these figures. If not the greatest author of the five under discussion, Whitman, nevertheless, is the one who best exemplifies Matthiessen's conception of The Great American Writer.

Matthiessen's reasons were surely personal in part. Cheney introduced Matthiessen to Whitman, and Whitman became not only the first American author Matthiessen grew to love, but the touchstone for all his notions of homosexuality. Whitman's poetry voiced all Matthiessen's youthful expressions of affection and, as Cain has pointed out, Matthiessen unconsciously translated his verses into his love letters to Cheney (*Matthiessen,* 47). But such sentimental reasons alone would not have convinced Matthiessen to elevate Whitman to so honored a position as he occupies in *American Renaissance.* What fascinates Matthiessen about Whitman is that, though Whitman was no theorist, he nevertheless developed a process of writing that exemplifies for Matthiessen the ideal procedures of an American writer to achieve organic form; the procedures embody the belief that only through the acceptance of one's primordial homosexual feelings can an artist both penetrate to the deepest wellsprings of experience and fully express the democratic spirit.

Critics usually classify Matthiessen as a formalist, but as a Christian Socialist and a student of Marx and Ruskin, he refuses to split the work of art from the labor through which it came into being. He contends in *American Renaissance* that to judge a writer's contribution most adequately, one must "come to *what* he created through examining his own *process of creation*" (80, Matthiessen's italics). In his chapter "Method and Scope," Matthiessen insists that all of his authors believed "that there should be no split between art and the other functions of the community, that there should be an organic union between labor and culture" (xv). An aesthetic which attempts to split the creative process from the finished product ends up either in the fallacy of imitative form, an apology for gaseous speculation, or in an empty ornamentalism. By insisting on organic or functional formalism, Matthiessen incorporates process into considerations of form, but in so doing, he does not engage in a simplistic biographical criticism. He rejects "the vulgarization of Saint-Beuve's subtle method— the direct reading of an author's personal life into his works" (xii). Rather, through a particular sort of "cultural history," Matthiessen located larger patterns of relations "since a man can articulate only what he is, and what he has been made by the society of which he is a willing or an unwilling part" (xv). In creating this "cultural history," Matthiessen examined politics, economics, and the history of ideas, of art, of science. In particular, Matthiessen was interested in psychology, and he wrote, "What a critic can gain from Freudian theory is a very comprehensive kind of description of human norms and processes, an incalculably great asset in interpreting patterns of character and meaning" (479).

For Matthiessen, as for Freud, the creative process is directly related to specific psychic conditions which allow the individual access or propel the artist into the creative act. These psychic structures, however, are also related to social institutions which either encourage or discourage their existence. Matthiessen gains from Freudian theory an explanation of how the "cultural" environment in which a work is situated is shaped by such sociopsychological issues as the relationship between child-rearing practices and adult curiosity, daydreaming, and emotional expressiveness. As Freud had argued in his studies of Leonardo da Vinci (to which Matthiessen alludes [479]), great art emerges in cultures in which children are subjected to conditions that evoke their artistic capacities.

Throughout *American Renaissance,* Matthiessen accompanied his analysis of particularly moving passages with descriptions of the psychological state from which they arose. Whitman elicits Matthiessen's most comprehensive description and becomes the model for American authors in general:

> Readers with a distaste for loosely defined mysticism have plenty of grounds for objection in the way the poet's belief in divine inspiration is clothed in imagery that obscures all the distinctions between body and soul by portraying the soul as merely the sexual agent. Moreover, in the passivity of the poet's body there is a quality vaguely pathological and homosexual. This is in keeping with the regressive, infantile fluidity, imaginatively polyperverse, which breaks down all mature barriers, a little further on in "Song of Myself," to declare that he is "maternal as well as paternal, a child as well as a man." Nevertheless, this fluidity of sexual sympathy made possible Whitman's receptivity to life. The ability to live spontaneously on primitive levels, whose very existence was denied by the educated mind of his time, wiped out arbitrary conventions and yielded a broader experience than of any of his contemporaries. And he did not simply exhibit pathological symptoms; he created poetry. (535–36)

When William E. Cain quoted a portion of this passage to indicate Matthiessen's disapproval of homosexuality, he failed to acknowledge either the elaborate rhetorical context or the much larger and positive argument in which it occurred. Matthiessen adopts the debater's strategy of acknowledging opponents' objections, admitting that certain people would be understandably critical of Whitman for mystical vagueness, sexualizing the spiritual, and for passivity. But Matthiessen is not among those critics since, as he asserts at the end, Whitman "did not simply exhibit pathological symptoms; he created poetry." The passivity of Whitman's body is a precondition for poetic activity since "somnambulism . . . let him be swept into the currents of the unconscious mind, and so made it possible for him to plumb emotional forces far beyond the depths of most writers of his day" (574).

Matthiessen derived his notion of Whitman's creative state of mind from two sources. From Freud's essay on "Creative Writers and Daydreaming," Matthiessen learned that inspiration came from those moments when the ego could project its desires and feelings more fully into conscious life. From Edward Carpenter, Matthiessen gained the insight that these moments of revery were democratic in spirit when they derived from the desire to blur the distinctions of class and gender. Carpenter argued that the Uranian was twice as often possessed of an artistic temperament than was the general population because the Uranian's "dual nature and swift and constant interaction between its masculine and feminine elements. . . . [make] it easy or natural for the Uranian man to become an artist" (*Selected,* 234).

To be sure, Matthiessen does not explicitly associate Whitman's creativity or creativity in general to a homosexual orientation. He does, however, insist that sexual fluidity and an ability "to live spontaneously on primitive levels" away from the "arbitrary conventions" of bourgeois society *are* a component of the greatest moments of art and, furthermore, that the capacity to regress and become receptive is, in turn, linked to an acceptance of homosexuality or, at the very least, bodily passivity. But this experience is not limited to homosexuals alone. Even so ostensibly a heterosexual as Hawthorne experienced the same process: "A more certain sign of his creative temperament was the tenderness mixed in with strength, an almost feminine passivity, which many of his friends noted and Alcott expressed in his own way by asking: 'Was he some damsel imprisoned in that manly form pleading alway [sic] for release?'" (230).

Matthiessen, however, carefully distinguishes between two passive psychic states that look like daydreaming: the first is a vacant daze that leads to formless woolgathering; the second is an awakening to the objective world where arbitrary distinctions have been obliterated. The vacant daze is a sign of isolation from the material world and Matthiessen associates it with Emerson's narcissism, Clifford's attempted leap from the window in *House of the Seven Gables,* and White Jacket's fall from the yard arm. In each case, the individuals lose a sense of proportion, of definition, or of the connection between things, and, quite often, their balance. In Clifford's case, Matthiessen says daydreaming is "a childish pleasure in any passing attraction that can divert him from the confused memories of his terrible years of gloom" (328). But the second state of awakened receptivity is marked by a new appreciation of the concrete, objective, and real. Because Whitman obliterates the gender distinctions at such moments, he gains an increased receptivity to things and a greater awareness of their true form. According to Matthiessen, only if writers see the world with a concreteness that transcends the conventional categories that falsify reality can they produce works whose form possesses a coherence that is more than the arbitrary imposition of an empty design.

For example, in his discussion of Whitman's language, Matthiessen points out that the relationships between sign and signified are obscured in the nineteenth century partly because of that era's "tendency to divorce education of the mind from the body and to treat language as something to be learned from a dictionary." Matthiessen goes on to argue that "such division of the individual's wholeness, intensified by the specialization of a mechanized society, has become a chief cause of the neurotic strain oppressing present-day man" (518). The organism from which organic form was to grow was the psyche reunited on a primitive level to its polymorphous sexual self. Lacan, no doubt, would insist that language as well as the desire for wholeness already are symptoms of the "division of the individual's wholeness" (40–45). But Matthiessen maintains that in his finest work Whitman returned to that primordial relationship of psychic and social wholeness in which "poetic rhythm was an organic response to the centers of experience—to the internal pulsations of the body, to its external movements in work and in making love, to such sounds as the wind and the sea" (564). No artist can sustain such moments, and even Whitman was reared in a culture that imposed division. Nor can there be a society in which Evil does not force such division on the psyche. Yet through art and in moments of spiritual grace, we gain glimpses of the wholeness that ordinarily eludes us, and in those glimpses that convince us of the constancy of wholeness, we find "the strongest sign by which the Father—and he is mankind's as well as the child's—persuades that the soul endures beyond all natural phenomena" (577).

The homosexual artist and the heterosexual artist in touch with his primordial homosexual feelings are closer to such wholeness than the heterosexual who has split off his homosexual feelings and no longer can retrieve them. Those, like Claggart in "Billy Budd," who split off their erotic attachments to persons of the same sex or seek to deny such attachments ultimately foster racial, political, and sexual oppression. But those who learn to accept such feelings gain access to the democratic impulse. As Matthiessen wrote, Melville "gave his fullest presentation of the transforming power of [sympathy with another human being] in the relation between Ishmael and Queequeg. When Ishmael recognized that 'the man's a human being just as I am,' he was freed from the burden of his isolation, his heart no longer turned against society. . . . he rediscovered the sense of Christian brotherhood through companionship with a tattooed pagan" (445).

I do not want to give the impression that Matthiessen's sense of organic form was merely a spasmodic emoting. He clearly "recognized that it was not enough to proclaim the radiance of the vision he had had" (28) and this visionary apprehension must achieve concentrated form to be appreciated. But without the primal perception of the concrete shape of things, without the sense of the arbitrariness of conventional categories, writers could not create "the tension between form and liberation" (63), the hard, clear shape that Matthiessen so admired. Though Matthiessen insisted that "the conception of art as inspiration . . . is in sharp opposition to that of art as craftsmanship," he believed with Horatio Greenough that "the normal way for an American to begin to gain that mastery [over formal principles] is by the fullest acceptance of the possibility of democracy" (*Renaissance*, 146).

Three months after their meeting, Matthiessen sent Cheney a copy of Edward Carpenter's *The Intermediate Sex,* whose concluding chapter, "The Uranian in Society," Matthiessen had annotated. Matthiessen commented that the book "doesn't tell us anything we don't know already" (*RD*, 47). In it Carpenter asserts that Uranians are predisposed to become artists (*Selected*, 234), tend to participate in "the important social work of Education" (235), and that since "true Democracy rests . . . on a sentiment which easily passes the bounds of class and caste, and unites in the closest affection the most estranged ranks in society. . . . the nobler Uranians of today may be destined . . . to be pioneers and advanced guard" of "the Comradeship on which Whitman founds a large portion of his message" (237–38). In returning to those sentiments articulated in less dramatic and simplistic form, but with some of the same passionate intensity, Matthiessen makes *American Renaissance* not only a celebration of homosexuality but of his life with Cheney. "The crucial task of the American future," Matthiessen argues in relation to Whitman, "was some reconciliation of the contradictory needs of full personal development and for 'one's obligations to the State and Nation'" (591). Both the artistic and scholarly acts united these imperatives, for by "dealing with sex" Matthiessen was promoting a "'sanity of atmosphere'" that might heal the wounds of the world as well as Cheney's and his psychic pain. "Beyond the bright circle of man's educated consciousness lay unsuspected energies that were both magnificent and terrifying," wrote Matthiessen at the end of *American Renaissance;* it is his and our tragedy that the magnificent finally gave way to the terrifying on that midcentury night of fools, 1 April 1950, when he dove from the window of the Manger Hotel.

The Uranian, according to Carpenter, is important to society because by returning to the primal stage of gender undifferentiatedness, he can lead society beyond the duality of sexual relations. "Finding himself *different* from the great majority, sought after by some and despised by others, now an object of contumely and now an object of love and admiration," the Uranian, according to Carpenter, "was forced to *think*. His mind turned inwards on himself would be forced to tackle the problems of his own nature, and afterwards the problem of the world and of outer nature. He would become one of the first thinkers, dreamers, discoverers" (274). Similarly, Matthiessen's American Renaissance was a world in which thinkers, dreamers, and discoverers, by turning their minds inward, were forced to reexamine the world and its outer nature. His difference was a burden not simply because it placed him at odds with "the great majority," but because it laid on him a special burden to advance society toward the democratic vista which awaited it.

6

Strategic Camp: The Art of Gay Rhetoric

"Notes on Camp," Susan Sontag's groundbreaking essay, was meant to be only the first attempt to define a species of expression. Its numbered paragraphs were themselves a spoof of the canonical and definitive texts "camp" was set against. Sontag subordinated camp to her larger concern, the creation of "an erotics of art" (14), and if she emptied camp of content, she did so to heighten the significance of its style. Here was a mode, Sontag argued, that asked nothing but to give pleasure to each moment. Sontag linked camp to the homosexual subculture, but she did not indicate how the "erotics" of such a literature was related to the sexuality of its creators and audience. In the polymorphous perversity of Sontag's ideal readers, such concerns of gender would, I assume, have been shed like their clothing: when you get into bed with a campy book, it should not matter what sex you have on.

Yet, camp has not developed in such a utopian setting nor for such ideal readers. Indeed, camp probably would never have evolved in such a liberated or permissive atmosphere as Sontag postulates. Camp is an outgrowth of the particular historical and cultural environment in which gay artists and readers have had to function, and it has served as a means of giving gay people a larger space in which to move, loosened from the restraints of the dominant society. As Jack Babuscio has commented: "As a means to personal liberation through the exploration of experience, camp is an assertion of one's integrity—a temporary means of accommodation with society in which art becomes, at one and the same time, an intense mode of individualism and a form of spirited protest" (42).

Some critics, such as Andrew Ross, have confined camp to the twentieth century, and particularly to the 1950s and years after. Robert F. Kiernan argues that though "one can speak of a tradition of camping in the English novel . . . such a tradition is largely happenstantial . . . [and does] not constitute a tradition in the sense of designating an essential line of development" (148). I am uncertain of what Kiernan means by an "essential line of development," but I do think that certain gay writers have learned to camp from their friends and from what they have read and that such a line may be thought of as a tradition. The campiness that runs from Firbank to Compton-Burnett to Jane Bowles through to Alfred Chester does not seem to me to be purely as "accidental and . . . peripheral" as Kiernan claims (148).

In fact, the earliest records of a gay subculture in Euro-American society depict rather elaborate camp ceremonies. In 1709, the author of *The London Spy* investigated The Mollies Club, "a particular Gang of Wretches . . . degenerated from all Masculine Deportment or Manly exercises that they fancy themselves women." There he witnessed "a jointed Baby they had provided, which wooden Offspring was to be afterwards Christened, whilst one in a High Crowned Hat, I am old Beldam's Pinner, representing a Country Midwife, & another dizen'd up in a Huswife's Coif for a Nurse & all the rest of an impertinent *Decorum* of a Christening" (28). Although the author scorns this "unbecoming mirth," he does not seem particularly shocked by it and prefers to let the Reforming Society handle these "preternatural polotions." In fact, by allowing the voice of the old Beldam's Pinner to erupt into his text, he shows how willing he is to join in the festivities. He saves his most savage attacks in his *Secret History of the London Clubs* for the Quacks' Club. "Of all the Plagues with which our Land is cursed," he argues, "The Frauds of Physic seem to be the worst" (31). He believes that camp is clearly better than quackery and less dangerous to the body politic. Nor would the Mollies have tried to disabuse him of the thought since their survival depended on such tolerance; conviction on even lesser charges than sodomy meant, if not hanging, time in the pillory which many prisoners also did not survive.

The molly houses were only one eighteenth-century institution that gave opportunity for the emerging gay subculture to express its campy self. Terry Castle has written how the masquerade—the first public one held in 1717 by John James Heidegger at the Haymarket Theatre —became a venue for "cutting across historic lines of rank and privilege" (159) and presented oppressed groups, such as the lower classes, women, and sodomites, "unprecedented liberties" (168).

Camp is the extreme expression of what Thomas E. Yingling has described as the general problem of homosexual style. According to Yingling, merely because they were male, "gay men have historically had access" to the system of "culturally determined codes" and the means of literary production, but because these authors were gay, the codes "denied validity to their existence" (25). Consequently, "gay writers . . . have found literature less a matter of self-expression and more a matter of coding: from Byron through John Ashbery, the consistent locus of parody in gay texts suggests a self-consciousness about what texts may or may not do" (25). Camp is the mode in which coding is most self-consciously played with and where the apparent emptying of self-expression is most conspicuous. Of course, by making these "culturally determined codes" self-conscious and conspicuous, gay writers destabilize them and open them to analysis and criticism. Thus the avoidance of "self-expression" becomes paradoxically a powerful expression of gay selfhood. One might say that camp is the post-structuralist mode *par excellence*.

Oscar Wilde clarified how the foregrounding of style is a strategic move in a much larger battle with the forces of society. In "The Decay of Lying," Vivian articulates a genealogy of art.

> Art begins with abstract decoration, with purely imaginative and decorative work dealing with what is unreal and nonexistent. This is the first stage. Then Life becomes fascinated with this new wonder, and asks to be admitted into this charmed circle. Art takes Life as part of her rough material, recreates it and refashions it in fresh forms, is absolutely indifferent to fact, invents, imagines, dreams, and keeps between herself and reality the impenetrable barrier of beautiful style, of decorative and ideal, treatment. The third stage is when Life gets the upper hand and drives Art out of the wilderness. This is true decadence, and it is from this that we are now suffering. (*Artist as Critic*, 301)

Style, for Wilde, is not an end in itself, but a protective device which the imaginative, decorative, and—in his particular cultural genealogy —primitive world of art used to keep itself from being appropriated, corrupted, and destroyed by social controls and conformity. Unlike the Mollies, Wilde views style (and his own campy style in particular) as the buffer between the private erotic world and the public civil world. To those on the side of Life, Art consists only of its style. To those on the side of Art, style is the chameleon skin used to preserve the imaginative freedom against Life. One cannot speak about camp without evoking metaphors of inside and outside, flatness and depth, and such metaphors underscore the homosexual world from which camp arises. In her study of female impersonators completed a year after Sontag's essay, Esther Newton claims that "the gay world revolves" around images of masculinity and femininity which become the opposition between inside and out. "Ultimately," she writes, camp "opposes 'inner' or 'real' self (subjective self) to the 'outer' self (social self)" (100). Babuscio places "incongruity" at "the core" of camp in the way it challenges the very notions of deviance and normality (41). Yet if camp constantly plays with notions of inside and outside, masculine and feminine, it does not locate the truth at these polarities. Instead, as I argue later, camp constantly questions the dualisms of the dominant society. Wilde, for example, is satisfied with neither the face nor the mask as symbols of selfhood; he demands an unending production of identities.

To those looking in on camp, its style seems flat and extreme; consequently, the heterosexual readers' response to overtly gay literature is always problematical, especially when that literature is particularly campy. Usually the problem has been masked by denial of the homosexual or campy component (as in the case of Whitman), hostility, or avoidance. Several years ago Adam West, the star of the television version of *Batman,* provided *Gay Community News* with its "Quote of the Week" in his angry denial that the series was camp. "I detest the word," he is reported to have said. "I don't even know the definition. If you spoof and satirize something, if you make it bigger than life, if you make fun of it—I don't think that's camp. Camp to me, means *La Cage aux Folles,* if anything. If you're flouncing around as a cross-dresser, that says camp" (25 June 1988, p. 2). Rarely have straight critics—especially straight male critics—acknowledged that their difficulties with a work are related to issues of gender. At a conference I heard Charles Molesworth, Charles Altieri, and Cary Nelson complain that they could not locate the tone of several passages in James Merrill's poetry. At first, none of these ostensibly heterosexual readers was willing to admit his inability to recognize camp and shifted the blame for the "indeterminacy" of tone onto Merrill.

One of the few exceptions, an early one at that, is M. L. Rosenthal, who is willing to recognize—at least in the case of Robert Duncan— that his difficulties derive from gender differences. While Rosenthal's position is almost comically stuffy and heterosexist, he is also refreshingly honest. While praising Duncan in *The New Poets* as "probably the figure with the richest natural genius among the Black Mountain poets," he nevertheless concludes that Duncan's "art is to some degree self-defeating" because "in a number of poems an acceptance of homosexual love is taken for granted; that is, it assumed that everyone will share the poem's felt meanings" (183). Rosenthal implicitly assumes that only male heterosexual expressions of love can be shared by everyone. Rosenthal exposes his prejudice by choosing "A Sequence of Poems for H.D.'s Birthday" as his illustration of Duncan's "self-defeating" tendencies:

> The young Japanese son was in love with a servant boy.
> To be in love! Dont you remember how the whole world is
>   governd
> by a fact that embraces
>   everything that happens?
>
>   (183)

Rosenthal comments:

> I will not say that such a passage is an imposition on the heterosexual reader. It is only one instance among many in our modern literature of the freedom of sexual expression; one can find cognate passages in writers otherwise as unlike Duncan and each other as Ginsberg and Paul Goodman. But the shift from the literal statement of the first line to the girlish outcry and sentimental philosophizing of the ensuing lines is emptily facile. At best it will induce a certain depression in most of us at the exploitation of what is anyway a romantic cliche in such a context. (183)

Although Rosenthal situates the poem within the broader trend of sexual expression in modern literature, the poem contains nothing sexually explicit and is as chaste and, in its way, as old-fashioned as Spenser's January eclogue, which also speaks of youthful love and homosexual desire. Compared to the works of Lowell, Sexton, or Berryman, Duncan's poetry is hardly an example of modern sexual license.

Duncan takes the opportunity in his preface to *Caesar's Gate* to rebut Rosenthal's argument. Duncan comments that he intended this "pathetic exclamation . . . not as some affect of the writer's indisposition in need of expression, but as the content of the poem itself" (i). Duncan had all along intended "the pitch of the outcry" to be "questionable" (ii). In short, the very excessiveness in style cues the reader to the passage's camp, a cue Rosenthal failed to respond to appropriately. Duncan also could have noted that Rosenthal improperly analyzed the poem's audience. Duncan rightly assumed that as a birthday present for H.D. and for the enjoyment of her friends, the poem would have had readers who, in Rosenthal's words, shared "an acceptance of homosexual love" and "the poet's felt meanings." To be sure, Duncan never limits himself to a gay readership, and rejects a gay separatist position, yet he is not obliged artistically to write for readers hostile to homosexual love. In his essay "The Homosexual in Society," Duncan specifically rejects "the cultivation of a secret language, the *camp,* a tone and a vocabulary" when it is "loaded with contempt for the human" (320). He does not thereby commit himself, however, to write for a public that will not imagine the possibility of one man's love for another. Rosenthal expects all poets to write for heterosexual readers and is unwilling to make adjustments to homosexual writers. He does not like finding himself in the awkward position of being on the outside looking in, yet such uneasiness is the best evidence of the unconscious political dimensions of camp and its effectiveness.

Rosenthal's uneasiness with Duncan's sexual assumptions is telling in another respect: as a Jew, Rosenthal might have criticized Ezra Pound's anti-Semitic assumptions on the same grounds. But Rosenthal, who wrote an early and useful book on Pound, either ignores his exclusion from the gentile readership assumed by Pound or accepts it as part of the price Jews must pay to be readers of English literature. Duncan, in fact, draws the connection between the Jewish and the homosexual reader and writer when in "The Homosexual in Society" he explains: "In drawing rooms and in little magazines I celebrated the cult [of homosexuality] with a sense of sanctuary such as a Medieval Jew must have found in the ghetto" (322). The differences between the Jewish reader of Christian texts and the heterosexual reader of gay texts are that the Jewish reader is a minority and has centuries of practice reading hostile texts, but only in the twentieth century, and especially since the Second World War, have heterosexual readers had the chance to read overtly homosexual literature explicitly addressed to gay people.

Before the Second World War, gay writers went to extreme lengths to control their audience and avoid explicitly identifying themselves or their readers as homosexual. They did so, of course, to avoid blackmail, social stigma, and imprisonment. The police that D. A. Miller finds ubiquitous in Victorian novels also enforced more private communications (xii). Although not particularly good readers, they were persistent ones, searching for sexual texts they could interpret. In one of the many passages of *The Importance of Being Ernest* in which Wilde prefigures his own trial, we learn that the text of a cigarette case may be used in evidence (256–58). In fact, the authorities favor homosexual texts written inadvertently: the revealing gesture, the details of dreams, as well as the excremental scrawl of hotel sheets, the last of which Wilde saw used against him (Ellmann, 460). Though the prosecutor could not fathom the paradoxes of Wilde's "Phrases and Philosophies for the Use of the Very Young," he could read the writing on the bedroom linens.

Yet even where sodomy laws were overlooked or repealed, gay men had difficulty addressing each other directly as homosexuals. Though France had under Napoleon abolished laws against adult sodomy, Gide published the first two dialogues of *Corydon* in 1911 in an unsigned, private edition of twelve copies. In 1920, when he expanded the edition to twenty-four copies and added two more dialogues and the preface, he continued to publish the work privately and anonymously (Howard, "Note," xv). Similarly, John Addington Symonds composed *A Problem of Greek Ethics* in 1873, but not until 1883—a decade later—did he print it privately, and then in an edition of only ten copies. He took such care in limiting to whom he lent and gave copies that in 1892—nine years after the printing—he could give Edward Carpenter one. Despite such careful control, Symonds did not feel comfortable alluding to his own case and on the title page insists that his "inquiry into the phenomenon of sexual inversion" be "addressed especially to medical psychiatrists and jurists." In 1891, when Symonds printed *A Problem of Modern Ethics,* the edition of fifty copies still was addressed to doctors and judges.

Such precautions would seem protection enough for his readers, but apparently they did not reassure one famous admirer of Symonds's ideas: Henry James, who had acquired his copy through Edmund Gosse. During Oscar Wilde's trial for sodomy, James returned "the fond outpourings of poor J. A. S." in registered envelopes, noting: "These are days in which one's modesty is, in every direction, much exposed, and one should be thankful for every veil that one can hastily snatch up or that a friendly hand precipitately muffles one withal" (Edel, IV, 12). This picture of James as a demure Salome cloaking his seductive dance in as many veils as he could possibly gather suggests not only what James feared the book's discovery might reveal, but also the vulnerability at the time of any man with homosexual feelings. James had enormous sympathies for Symonds. On hearing of Symonds's death he wrote Gosse: "somehow I too can't help feeling the news as a pang—and with a personal emotion. It always seemed as if I *might* know him—and of few men whom I didn't know has the image so much come home to me. Poor much-living, much-doing, passionately out-giving man!" (Edel, III, 409).

James wrote several letters to Symonds, but only one has survived. Attempting to communicate what cannot be safely said, it is a study in the need for and employment of camp: "I did send you the *Century* more than a year ago with my paper on Venice," he reminds Symonds.

> I sent it to you because it was a constructive way of expressing the good will I felt for you in consequence of what you had written about the land of Italy—and of intimating to you, somewhat dumbly, that I am an attentive and sympathetic reader. I nourish for the said Italy an unspeakably tender passion, and your pages always seemed to say to me that you were one of the small number of people who love it as much as I do—in addition to your knowing it immeasurably better, I want to recognize this (to your knowledge); for it seemed to me that the victims of a common passion should exchange a look. (Edel, III 29–30)

I think one would be wrong to see in the circuity of the passage only the typical Jamesian evasiveness, for the sentence is a flirtation of quite a literal sort. James wants Symonds to recognize that he is more than "an attentive and sympathetic reader" of his histories, and that he, like Symonds, is "one of the small number of people" that share an "unspeakably tender passion," a passion that can be signaled by the style of text or in passing by the exchange of a look in the street. James is, to use a dated gay expression, "dropping his beads," defined by Bruce Rodgers as "leav[ing] broad hints about one's homosexuality," a singularly important disclosure between gay men (69).

Symonds seems to have brought out the camp in James in letters he exchanged with Gosse and Morton Fullerton which Leon Edel characterizes as "coy." On receipt of *A Problem of Modern Ethics,* James wrote Gosse:

J. A. S. is truly, I gather, a candid and consistant creature, and the exhibition is infinitely remarkable. It's on the whole, a queer place to plant the standard of duty, but he does it with extraordinary gallantry. If he has, or gathers, a band of emulous, we may look for capital sport. But I don't wonder that some of his friends and relations are haunted with a vague malaise. I think one ought to wish him more *humour*—it is really *the* saving salt. But the great reformers never have it—and he is the Gladstone of the affair. That perhaps is a reason the more for conveying him back to you one of these days. (Edel, III, 398)

The passage has all the elements of classic camping: (1) both the author and the reader wear disguises—the disguise of heterosexuality; (2) the masquerade enforces an intimacy even as it distances the participants in the masquerade; (3) it is maintained with a buoyant humor (lacking in Symonds), the "camp" laugh; (4) the entire affair is conducted in an elaborate style which while seemingly superficial, reveals to the initiated an unspoken subtext.

Camp shares many of the qualities of its now academically far more respectable condition, what Mikhail Bakhtin has dubbed, "the carnivalesque." Indeed in the English translation by Helene Iswolsky, one of the most common words to describe the "carnivalesque" is "gay": "The entire world is seen in its droll aspect, in its gay relativity. . . . it is gay, triumphant, and at the same time mocking and deriding" (11–12). To be sure, Iswolsky and Bakhtin mean "gay" in its more traditional sense of "lively," "carefree," "light-hearted." But since the carnivalesque enjoys punning especially in sexually provocative ways, and since the homosexual subculture has carried in its celebration of Mardi Gras and Halloween the very traditions of the carnivalesque, the two meanings blend in a form Bakhtin virtually licences.

The connection between camp and the carnivalesque is further suggested by Peter Stallybrass and Allon White who in their study of *The Politics and Poetics of Transgression* argue that the carnivalesque is best applied to works "where the political difference between the dominant and subordinate culture is particularly charged" (11). Although they use neocolonial and Soviet Yiddish literature as two examples, certainly camp gay literature would fall under this rubric quite as easily, for it, too, asks for "licenced release" (13) and develops an "inverted hierarchy" (2). Even more telling a comparison may be found in the "*grammatica jocosa*," an essential part of carnivalesque literature. According to Stallybrass and White, the *grammatica jocosa* is a style in which "grammatical order is transgressed to reveal erotic and obscene or merely materially, satisfying counter-meaning" (10). So, too, is camp a network of puns, innuendos, and allusions arrayed with bawdy abandon.

But before I explore further the connection between camp and the carnivalesque, I should point out that they are not synonymous. The carnivalesque is always visible, an open provocation of the dominant culture; while camp frequently separates gay culture from straight culture. Bakhtin also places stress on the literally reproductive aspects of the carnivalesque: "one of the fundamental tendencies of the grotesque image of the body is to show two bodies in one. . . . From one body a new body always emerges in some form or other" (26). Camp, however, often depicts reproduction as one of the aspects of heterosexual society that must be inverted, as in the "sacred parody" of christening performed by the Mollies. Finally, Bakhtin regards the folk grotesque as "a festival of spring, of sunrise, of morning," and while camp does not entirely reject these periods, it does not celebrate "the natural" with the abandon that the "carnivalesque" embraces it. It is in its critique of "the natural" that the camp grotesque may be said to offer a more radical posture of opposition than the carnivalesque. For if the folk grotesque pits the social against the natural, camp pits both nature and society against art. Camp, while nostalgic for the medieval festival, is self-consciously very modern in its questioning of categories. For example, Alfred Chester's *The Exquisite Corpse* plays repeatedly with the artifice of fatherhood:

> Mary Poorpoor was only a child herself when her son was conceived. She was unmarried and alone in the world. She was homeless, hungry and skinny. She had no idea who the father could be, but it came to pass that she hoped more and more it was the kindly fat social worker who befriended her a few months after she became pregnant. The social worker was named Emily. . . . a stately-looking sober yet playful woman with large breasts under either or both of which she was given to hiding one-dollar bills. (38)

The passage inverts and subverts one category after another. Mary's hope that Emily is the father shifts the word *conceived* from its biological to its aesthetic meaning. Chester's subtle introduction of the faintly biblical locution "it came to pass" further transforms this magical pregnancy into an immaculate conception. Moreover Emily's social work becomes the sexual exploitation of the poor. To this set of ironies is added one more: according to Ira Cohen, Mary Poorpoor is based on Susan Sontag's "to whom Alfred gave the secret of Camp" (364).

Another fine example of camp's self-conscious questioning of the categories embraced by the carnivalesque is Joel Peter Witkins's 1981 photograph, "Androgyny Breastfeeding a Fetus" (Weiermair, 174). In it a man with a sizable penis holds to his enlarged breast a doll whose waxy surface reflects the texture of the breast at which it nurses. The very title of the photograph mocks the maternity it might appear to celebrate, for fetuses do not breastfeed, just as this androgyne has no organ through which to deliver a baby. The photograph goes further than the mock christening in the Mollies Club to question the very categories of the natural.

Despite these serious differences, camp and the carnivalesque occupy many of the same cultural positions. For example, Bakhtin argues that the carnivalesque has three basic forms: the ritual spectacle, comic verbal composition, and various forms of abuse such as curses and oaths. Camp takes such equivalent forms as the drag show, the queeny repartee, and the gay put-down. Like the carnivalesque, it merges the sublimely grand with the earthily ridiculous. The Sisters of Perpetual Indulgence, the name of a San Francisco political awareness group, expresses the carnivalesque contempt for religious sanctimoniousness even as it asserts its own moral agenda.

Yet camp shows its greatest similarity to the carnivalesque, even as it questions the dualisms that structure the carnivalesque, in its depictions of the body. Bakhtin distinguishes two styles of depictions of the body, the classical and the grotesque:

> The Renaissance saw the body in quite a different light than the Middle Ages, in a different aspect of life, and a different relation to the exterior nonbodily world. As conceived by the canons, the body was first of all a strictly completed, finished product. Furthermore, it was isolated, alone, fenced off from all other bodies. All signs of its unfinished character, of its growth and proliferation were eliminated. . . . The ever unfinished nature of the body was hidden. . . . The age represented was as far removed from the mother's womb as from the grave, the age most distant from either threshold of individual life. The accent was placed on the completed, self-sufficient individuality of the given body. Corporeal acts were shown only when the borderlines dividing the body from the outside world were sharply defined. . . . Such were the fundamental tendencies of the classic canons. (29)

Commenting on this distinction, Stallybrass and White have written: "The classical statue has no openings or orifices whereas grotesque costume and masks emphasize the gaping mouth, the protuberant belly and buttocks, the feet and the genitals. In this way the grotesque body stands in opposition to the bourgeois individualist conception of the body, which finds its image and legitimization in the classical" (21–22). Camp plays with the categories of the classical and the grotesque particularly in drag shows and gay photography. By representing both the classical and the grotesque body as artifice, camp questions the "naturalness" which both claim as their own.

The drag queen is, I suppose, more closely associated with the grotesque than with the classical. The heavily glossed lips, rather than smoothing away the flesh, act to emphasize the gaping mouth. The rouge and facial powder draw our attention to the beard stubble below. We are reminded only too often that this is a man dressed up, and because the drag artist often imitates a famous woman—Marilyn Monroe, Bette Davis, Liza Minelli—we compare this representation with the larger, classical representation we know from film or television. By alluding to the classical—and camp is highly allusive—drag forces the classical to participate in the grotesque. Moreover, as Esther Newton has pointed out, the drag queen's "genitals must *never* be seen" (101) just as the classical nude had genitals stylized or concealed. The drag queen stands apart, nostalgic for a classicism it cannot lay claim to. In this sense, the drag queen does function as Andrew Ross's utterly humorless analysis suggests he does, by assuming "aristocratic affectations [as] a sign of his *disqualification,* or remoteness from power, because they comfortably symbolize, to the bourgeois, the decreased power of the aristocrat, while they are equally removed from the threatening, embryonic power of the masses" (11, Ross's italics). The drag artist is classical, a failed classicism, just as one of the cliches of Gothicism is the classical temple in ruins. The drag is the remains of classicism as is the overdeveloped weight lifter he often poses beside and against.

Heterosexuals accept the drag queen more readily than any other part of the homosexual world or any other aspect of the camp style, as witnessed by the popularity of *La Cage aux Folles* or *Torch Song Trilogy.* Consequently, drag has lost a good deal of its immediate transgressive power. Quentin Crisp, who aroused hostility in the Britain of the 1940s and 1950s, had become by his own admission an

"old homosexual institution" in the late 1960s. Yet the seemingly ineffectual should not be mistaken for the truly powerless. The limpidity
that Ross sees as one of the defects of camp disguises a cutting edge.
By projecting an image of powerlessness, Crisp exercised his considerable powers to avoid attack, successfully defending himself against
charges of homosexual solicitation by arguing that looking as he did,
no one would possibly engage him in broad daylight. The argument
seemed powerful enough to win release from the magistrate. Crisp's
case is not unique. In 1819 Jane Pirie and Marianne Woods, two mis-
tresses of a girls' boarding school, won libel damages against Dame
Helen Cumming Gordon when the House of Lords decided that mid-
dle-class women had no sexual desires and "that the crime here alleged
has no existence" (Federman, 147–49). The guise of absolute powerlessness provided at least some protection to generations of lesbian
women.

Drag camp has not lost all power to transgress and disturb the categories of bourgeois society. Jim Hubbard's film, *Homosexual Desire
in Minnesota,* for example, started a near riot before a gay audience
when it was first shown in part because it segues between gay rights
marches and drag queen performances. Among Hubbard's points is
that gay political activity originated in drag performance: the Stonewall riots of 1969—the three nights of confrontations between the gay
citizens of New York and the city's police, usually regarded as the beginning of the gay liberation movement—were touched off, not by
homophile organizations, but by boys in drag drowning their sorrow over the death of Judy Garland, who had been buried that day.
The controversies over Robert Mapplethorpe's retrospective, *The
Perfect Moment,* are perhaps the most potent of recent examples of
camp's power to offend.

Mapplethorpe is a good example of how an artist can modify camp
so that it retains its power to offend its audiences. His technically immaculate prints with their silvery, luminous lighting made his viewers
distinctly uneasy by presenting images that challenged their very con-
ceptions of themselves, which as Stallybrass and White have noted
are: "continuously defined and redefined . . . through the exclusion of
what [is] marked out as 'low'—as dirty, repulsive, noisy, contaminating" (191). I have in mind two self-portraits that Mapplethorpe executed in 1980. In the first, he is naked from the waist up, so that from
the outset the viewer is aware of his boyish chest. His long hair is

swept back. His face is carefully made-up in the tasteful way teen magazines instruct their readers. The result is not the Janus-like head of a drag queen with the male features protruding through the obvious artifice of cosmetics, but something far more disturbing—a very womanly if somewhat stressed man. The companion photograph shows him in a leather jacket, a dark shirt, his hair in a pompadour that descends down his forehead, and a cigarette dangling from his lips. But the effect is not a mock-biker. The hair is not greased; the face far from menacing. Since both photographs are shot in soft focus, the nude seems silky; while the portrait in leather appears vulnerable and delicate. Mapplethorpe has thrown into question the naturalness of the androgyne and savageness of the biker by gaily inverting our expectations of inversion. In yet another photograph, a double portrait of Brian Ridley and Lyle Heeter (1979), Mapplethorpe captures an S-M couple. The older man stands in leather holding chains that are connected to a younger man who is seated, his hands and feet manacled, his neck collared and chained as well. But what keeps this portrait from becoming a Diane Arbus study in the pathological is the young man's face—it is as quiet, calm, and self-possessed as the boy's next door. His slightly rumpled hair gives him a boyishness that goes along with his tired eyes. These are not monsters born from the sleep of reason, but humans who do not fit the mold.

Mapplethorpe is most disturbing not because he sets up the simple-minded demonology that has proved so popular with heavy-metal bands—a self-conscious immorality—but because the glossy surface of his fashion photographs of the latest vinyl suits for masochists into water sports provides no easy resting place for his ironies. As Kiernan points out, the ideal camper possesses a "shameless love of all that is exaggerated" and an "amoral mode of laughter" (16).

Through the studied avoidance of the usual gargoyles, Mapplethorpe retains the carnivalesque atmosphere in *Certain People* that a less subtle and more conventional artist would reduce to the pathological. Gilbert and George, for example, turn their gallery of working-class boys into the predictable chorus of fallen angels which reflect heterosexual stereotypes of homosexuals. Mapplethorpe approaches each subject as a separate aesthetic and erotic object, freed from all but formalistic concerns. The only category that embraces these subtly unclassifiable portraits is the aesthetic. As Sontag noted in her preface to the collection, Mapplethorpe is not looking for the decisive moment. His photographs do not claim to be revelatory. He is not in a predatory relation to his subject. He is not voyeuristic. He is not trying to catch anyone off-guard. The rules of the game of photography, as Mapplethorpe plays it, are that the subject must cooperate—must be lit. Mapplethorpe wants to photograph everything, that is, everything that can be made to pose.

All of Mapplethorpe's people are poseurs: gothic and classic alike.

Mapplethorpe is heir to a long line of gay photography that has played with the aesthetic tensions between the classic and gothic. At the turn of the century Frederick Rolfe, better known as Baron Corvo, Fred Holland Day, Wilhelm von Pluschow, John Gambril Nicholson, Vincenzo Galdi, and perhaps most famous, Wilhelm von Gloeden recorded beautiful young men in the nude or nearly so. Often they posed the models in classical positions, as a young Bacchus, or as Pan playing on his pipe, or else in the presence of classical statuary. The result never quite managed, however, to achieve the right Hellenic sweetness and light—and even they seemed to feel some humor in the situation. Roland Barthes, writing about von Gloeden, has accurately put his finger on the camp effect of these fin de siècle photographs:

> The Baron's photographs are of a *ruthless* kind. And the sublime legend enters in collision (one has to use this word to understand our astonishment and perhaps our great joy) with the realism of the photography; for what is a photograph thus conceived non[e] other than an image where *all is seen;* a collection of details without hierarchy, without 'order' (the great classic principle). These little greek gods (already contradicted by their darkness) have dirty peasants' hands, badly cured fingernails, worn out and dirty feet; their foreskins are swollen and well in evidence, no longer stylized, that is, pointed and smaller; they are uncircumcised, this is all one sees. (21)

Barthes concludes that these photographs—indeed the very medium von Gloeden used—was a "carnaval [sic] of contradictions" (21). In these portraits we see at once why photography, rather than painting or drawing, has been the best medium for the erotics of camp, for by pitting classic and grotesque versions of the body together and rendering them both as mere poses it was able to create a "carnàval of contradictions" beyond even Bakhtin's inverted hierarchy. This tradition of mixing classical and grotesque images continued unbroken through the works of Cocteau, George Platt-Lynes, and Cecil Beaton, so that

when Mapplethorpe shot his now famous portraits of black men in severely classical poses, he alluded to what was already an on-going
"carnaval of contradictions." Thus, as we adjust our eyes to the dark
1981 picture of Ajitto in fetal position, we come to note below the X
formed by his arms and legs the enormous silhouette of his genitals. In
the double portrait of Ken Moody and Robert Sherman (1984), the
faces have become so severely and chastely sculptural, shorn of any
hair at all, that he has blended grotesque and classical images of the
body into an entirely camp category of the mannequin. This confusion
is heightened by Mapplethorpe's practice of photographing actual
classical sculpture as though it were human. Perhaps the epitome of
Mapplethorpe's playful confusion between Gothic and classic, human
and sculpture, natural and artificial is in his "Man in Polyester Suit"
(1980) in which the enormous black penis hanging out of the pants
seems constructed from the same materials as the suit which failed to
contain it. Although the human, real, and natural has erupted from
the synthetic, man-made, and unnatural, those categories seem inverted or meaningless. In such pictures Mapplethorpe has replaced the
diadic structure of the carnivalesque with the triadic oscillations of
camp.

Some may object that much of what I have identified as camp is not
funny, and camp, they would argue, is essentially silly. But the humor
of camp, while it may be full-throated, can also leave a lump. As Andrew Holleran says of Charles Ludlam's Theatre of the Ridiculous
performances, "He played both tragedy and Farce and refused to tell
us which was which. He died onstage of tuberculosis, or heartache,
and left us not knowing whether to laugh or to cry, suspended somewhere (with parted lips) between the two; so when he raised his gloved
hand to his lips, as Camille, and coughed those three coughs—just
three—the audience both howled and stopped laughing altogether"
(*Zero*, 97). Richard Howard describes the impulse behind Mapplethorpe's witty flower pictures—which identify the buds not with
female genitalia as is usually the case, but with the phallus—as part of
"Mapplethorpe's task . . . to restore the gravity which has leaked out
of what is unspeakable" ("Mapplethorpe," 155). The word "restore"
implies that the "unspeakable" has been trivialized. Camp, then, is not
trivial, but a reaction to trivialization. Its sacred parodies are a
strategy to reinvoke a divinity that has fled; it seeks entrance to the
Dionysian mysteries through its bawdy revelries.

Camp finds itself today at a crisis. Many of the social conditions for which camp was an adequate, even successful, response no longer obtain, at last with the same urgency. Most gay people no longer feel the terrible need to hide homosexual communication for fear of blackmail or criminal prosecution. Indeed, gay men now prefer to assert their political strength by making themselves visible. Again, camp's appearance of powerlessness, which gay men and women affected to make themselves less threatening to the heterosexual majority and avoid retaliation, is a strategy that the AIDS crisis and organizations such as ACT UP have found to be counterproductive.

But the crisis in camp goes further than the change in political climate. Andrew Ross's "Uses of Camp" presents a rather critical view of the style. For Ross, camp is co-opted by bourgeois values insofar as it has tried to appeal to the broad spectrum of the American public or to the lower classes. It pays tribute, he claims, "to the official national ideology of liberal pluralism" in its very attempt to short circuit established categories (6). I think Ross underestimates the provocative nature of such camp works as John Waters's *Pink Flamingos,* in which the transvestite Divine eats a dog turd to prove once and for all that she *is* the filthiest woman in the world. Ross also points out that camp's commitment to the marginal dooms it forever to a certain elitism and insignificance, its very process of challenging the categories of bourgeois seriousness already foreshadowing its failure to dislodge those categories. Ross's argument against camp duplicates the argument raised against the carnivalesque: Can such "licenced release"—as Stallybrass and White call it—really alter the dominant culture, or does it merely serve as a safety valve that, in fact, helps the dominant culture continue? Can there ever be an opposition to the codes of the dominant culture that is not committed to its own marginality? The only answer is that cultural codes do alter, and it is impossible to say whether they have changed only through their own internal evolution or through a dialectical operation that involves opposing values. What is clear is that an elite, however marginal, is not insignificant and that camp has had its rippling effect throughout the culture.

Ross does not, it seems to me, appreciate fully that a style can be destabilizing without being overtly oppositional. Gay people have recognized that they can achieve their rights not by becoming the majority, but by finessing the entire issue of power. Or to put it another way, were gay culture to develop a discourse of power in parity to the dominant society's discourse, it would only end up reproducing the machismo which has oppressed it. The aggressive passivity of camp has been among its most potent tools in giving gay people a voice that we ourselves could hear and then use to speak to others.

At a recent Gay Pride Day celebration in Baltimore, a drag queen in an elaborate lamé gown pried himself into a dunking booth to raise money for a special AIDS ward at Johns Hopkins Hospital. Having straightened his tiara on top of his puffed-up tresses, he barked at the gathering crowd, "Which of you brutes is going to make my mascara run?" It was a scene that typified not only the aggressive passivity of camp, but quite literally the carnivalesque world Bakhtin so much admired. It broke down the categories of brutality and cultivation and mocked the very notions of opposition it so gaily employed. It testified to the fact that camp is far from dead and celebrated the life of a community beset by the morbid.

In many ways, it strikes me that camp is the voice of survival and continuity in a community that needs to be reminded that it possesses both. It has come to serve those purposes before AIDS, and it will probably do so again. Camp appears in the most unlikely places. Allen Ginsberg is not a poet usually associated with camp, yet *Howl* is a supremely campy poem, and as time has gone on, Ginsberg has recited it with greater and greater emphasis on its comically carnivalesque tone. And in Ginsberg's "A Supermarket in California," a poem wistful and joyous, comic and sad by turns, the powers of camp to bind wounds and unsettle expectation, to destabilize even as it seems most accommodating are clearly in evidence:

> I saw you, Walt Whitman, childless, lonely old grubber,
> poking among the meats in the refrigerator and eyeing the
> grocery boys.
> I heard you asking questions of each: Who killed the
> pork chops? What price bananas? Are you my Angel?
> I wandered in and out of the brilliant stacks of cans
> following you, and followed in my imagination by the store
> detective.
> We strode down the open corridors together in our
> solitary fancy tasting artichokes, possessing every frozen
> delicacy, and never passing the cashier.

(136)

D. A. Miller might find in the reference to the store detective a clear sign of the importation of normative justice into gay society. The detective reminds us of the codes this poem so gaily transgresses, for

Ginsberg and Whitman float through the store without passing the cashier. Camp does not do away with the dominant society, but rather finds a way to live within it. It also knows that its salvation is not found in that dominant society. Camp may ask the grocery boy "Are you my Angel?" but the question is all but rhetorical. He is not. And though Ginsberg shares the supermarket—symbol of petit bourgeois society—with "whole families shopping at night! Aisles full of husbands! Wives in the avocados, babies in the tomatoes!" his words are saved for Whitman and García Lorca "down by the watermelons."

7

Larry Kramer and the Rhetoric of AIDS

JUST as "the love that dare not speak its name" became the love that won't stop talking about itself, so, too, the disease that no one wished to discuss has become the subject on everybody's lips. The bibliography on AIDS grows geometrically, and now even the most devoted student could not possibly keep up with all that is written. Virtually every discipline claims an area of the subject to bring the elusive figure of AIDS into manageable and recognizable shape, creating what Paula A. Treichler has called "an epidemic of signification" (42). Physicians, biologists, psychiatrists, public health officials, ethicists, sociologists, economists, marketing analysts, political scientists, anthropologists, theologians, and artists of all kinds have sought to leave their stamp on the topic. To the silence that was death now comes the babel which is itself a plague.

I embark on this effort, then, with a good deal of trepidation, and I want first to address the compulsion to add to the growing discourse on AIDS. ACT UP, the political action group devoted to AIDS issues, has appropriately adopted the Beckett-like slogan "Silence = Death," suggesting that what is said is far less important than the fact of speaking. We may judge its wisdom by the CEO of the Kellogg company, Bill LaMothe, who has been attacked at stockholders' meetings by gay activists (including a seventy-year-old descendant of the company's founder) alleging that the ads for *Nut & Honey Crunch* are homophobic. LaMothe admitted, "When the noise level reaches a certain point, then perhaps that's a noise level we have to address" (Wockner, 4). LaMothe judges gay criticism not on its merits, but on its loudness; content is subordinate to volume; he hears either noise or silence.

But the benefit of speaking about AIDS may more properly obtain to the speaker than the listener. For the mourner, words both release and relieve grief. For those who feel the moral obligation to do something, writing may fulfill such an obligation. I know from my own experience that there is an irrational feeling that by speaking about AIDS, one wards off the disease. Much of the vehemence of AIDS rhetoric may be attributable to the belief in language's magical prophylactic powers.

Not everyone, of course, thinks that the ceaseless discussion about AIDS is helpful or desirable. Susan Sontag, for example, longs for a day when AIDS will become as "ordinary" as leprosy has become in our own time, a subject rarely discussed and free of stigma (*AIDS,* 93). "But the metaphors cannot be distanced just by abstaining from them," she acknowledges. "They have to be exposed, criticized, belabored, used up" (*AIDS,* 94). For Sontag, the road to silence is paved with exhaustive analysis. Lee Edelman worries that since gay writers will always find their discourse "subject to appropriation by the contradictory logic of homophobic ideology" and since "there is no available discourse on AIDS that is not itself diseased" (315–16), it may be best to follow Freud's advice to H.D. on how to respond to the Nazi threat and remain quiet. Most writers, however, have come to believe that the urgency of the epidemic requires neither the austere objectivity of Sontag, nor "the verbal terrorism" Frances Fitzgerald lamented in her study of the Castro (109), but a pragmatic language that motivates people to helpful action.

No one is more responsible for the rhetoric of AIDS than Larry Kramer, whose pronouncements, ultimatums, vilifications, lampoons, and dramatizations seemed ubiquitous in the early years of the epidemic. He has secured himself a place in the history of AIDS as a writer: as founder of the Gay Men's Health Crisis (GMHC), the largest private service organization dedicated to helping people with AIDS; and of the community protest group AIDS Coalition to Unleash Power (ACT UP). Kramer is a controversial figure more for his delivery than for the content of his statements. Are his methods successful? It is conceivable that without his confrontational tactics, AIDS services and research might have developed more quickly; more probable, however, is the idea that his methods hurried things along. And in *The Normal Heart,* Kramer not only addressed social responses to AIDS before audiences that usually ignore such issues, but created one of the more powerful artifacts of its period.

In a symposium on the role of theater in AIDS Kramer gave a speech, collected with his other political pronouncements in *Reports from the Holocaust,* in which he said: "I don't consider myself an artist. I consider myself a very opinionated man who uses words as fighting tools" (145). He described himself to that gathering as "a message queen" (146). I wish to discuss his writings in that light: not as art, but as action. Did he make something happen, or were his tools unfit for the job? Is he the queen of the message queens, or their ugly stepmother?

To answer such questions we must look at his entire career as an AIDS activist, a career that has passed through three or four stages. Initially he focused the gay community's attention on AIDS and raised money for research and services for the ill. His early broadsides also attacked what became a long list of "enemies," including Mayor Koch, the *New York Times,* the Center for Disease Control (CDC), and the National Institutes of Health (NIH). "I was out to attack every perceived enemy in sight," he admits (*Reports,* 32). After his break with the GMHC, Kramer entered the second stage of his activist career, in which the GMHC, along with the Mayor and the *Times* became his principal targets. In the third stage, Kramer directed his attacks primarily on Washington and the Federal bureaucracy, especially NIH, its program director Dr. Anthony Fauci—whom he named "Public Enemy Number One" (*Reports,* 188)—and the Federal Drug Administration's (FDA) Dr. Frank Young. Finally, *Reports from the Holocaust* ends with a recent essay, less strident in tone than any of the earlier writings, which sets down the logic behind Kramer's political positions. However, with the possible exception of this final essay, Kramer's writing has changed little and displays a striking uniformity of style; for example, his attacks in the late eighties on Fauci, Reagan, and Koch as "megalomaniacs playing God," recapitulate a theme first announced in his 1969 screenplay for *Women in Love.*

Before examining in detail the patterns of Kramer's polemics, in fairness I should note that his consistency of manner is typical of the rhetoric surrounding AIDS, which has struck most analysts as a predictable rehashing of very traditional tropes. "It is almost impossible to watch the AIDS epidemic," Allan M. Brandt comments, "without a sense of *déjà vu*" (152), and Sander L. Gilman has also found that the representation of AIDS "clearly repeats the history of the iconography of syphilis" (107). The depiction of AIDS "reminds" Charles A. Rosenberg "of the way in which society has always framed illness" (51). Martha Gever bemoans that the public is "reassured" by "the containment of knowledge . . . within familiar structures" and does not seek more appropriate ways of understanding AIDS (110). Virtually all the writers on AIDS are prisoners of long-ingrained ways of looking at disease, and Kramer's writing is at once symptomatic of that cultural problem and heroic in the ways it struggles to free itself from such tropes.

Kramer responded to the first announcements of AIDS with an alacrity which can only be partially explained by his friendship with some of the first identified cases. The first official notice of the disease appeared on 5 June 1981 in the CDC's *Morbidity and Mortality Weekly Report* (30:21, 250–52). On 3 July, the same day that *MMWR* reported cases of both Kaposi's sarcoma and *Pneumocystis* pneumonia in New York and California, the *New York Times* reported "Rare Cancer Seen in 41 Homosexuals." Kramer weighed in with his first article in the *Native* in the 24 August–6 September issue. Thus three months after the first obscure report in a journal read by a handful of specialists, Kramer was already making "A Personal Appeal" to the gay men of New York City, warning them that "the many things we've done over the past years may be all that it takes for a cancer to grow from a tiny something-or-other that got in there who knows when from doing who knows what" (*Reports,* 8). Kramer could address AIDS with such speed and force because the disease served as an objective correlative for many of the ideas and attitudes he already had; AIDS was the triggering agent for a set of preexisting responses.

Kramer's "Personal Appeal" drew swift and powerful responses from gay readers. In a letter to the *Native,* Bob Chesley was the first to argue that Kramer's response to the crisis was of a piece with his earlier criticisms of the gay community: "The concealed meaning in Kramer's emotionalism is the triumph of guilt: that gay men *deserve* to die from promiscuity. . . . Read anything by Kramer closely, I think you'll find that the subtext is always: the wages of gay sin are death" (quoted in *Reports,* 16). Chesley's attack stung Kramer, who at some pains countered it in a subsequent *Native* article. But the hyperbole of Chesley's charges of "gay homophobia and anti-eroticism" contains more truth than Kramer admits, even as it fails to grasp the correctness of much of Kramer's analysis and the urgency of AIDS.

Andrew Holleran, in his introduction to *The Normal Heart,* also finds the roots of Kramer's response to AIDS in his 1978 novel *Faggots* (27). *Faggots,* a would-be Waughian satire of the New York homosexual life, is a phantasmagoria of rape, incest, drug addiction, coprophilia, pedophilia, and torture, and I have difficulty imagining how Kramer expected readers to find the mordant comedy he intended for the novel. Like Thackery's *Vanity Fair, Faggots* has no hero; its protagonist, Fred Lemish, Kramer's alter ego, is a successful screenwriter trying to find love with Dinky Adams, a handsome, charmingly manipulative, and utterly self-destructive nonentity. We follow Fred and Dinky and dozens of drugged and barely differentiated characters on a four-day odyssey that takes us through bus station tea rooms, gala openings of discotheques, S-M sex clubs, steam baths, Manhattan luxury apartments, and finally to the opening of the Fire Island season, which an aged Jewish businessman mistakes for a concentration camp because so many men are dressed in leather with Nazi insignias (287). Though participating in the orgy of sex, drugs, and violence, Lemish keeps himself aloof from its more sordid aspects. In the end, Fred, who suffers from constipation and believes that "one of these days we must stop shitting on one another," defecates as an act of defiance, disdain, and fertility in a garden Dinky designed (301).

Chesley's contention that Kramer believes promiscuous gays are responsible for their own deaths is best supported by a relatively tame episode in which Dinky tries to convince Fred of friendship's superiority to love. Dinky argues that the scarcity of happy couples "should tell you something." Fred replies:

> Yeah . . . It tells me no relationship in the world could survive the shit we lay on it. It tells me we're not looking at the reason why we're doing the things we're doing. It tells me we've got a lot of work to do. A lot of looking to do. It tells me that, if those happy couples are there, they better come out of the woodwork fast and show themselves pronto so we can have a few examples for unbelieving heathens like you that it's possible. Before you fuck yourself to death. (265)

Though Kramer strenuously denies it, such a passage does come perilously close to saying "the wages of gay sin are death." Kramer's one alternative to "fuck[ing] yourself to death" is a marriage-like relationship between men, suggesting that gay survival relies on approximating heterosexual behavior. Kramer blames the victims of lovelessness for their own predicament, and their deaths on a life of mindless, unrestrained sexuality. In *The Normal Heart,* Ben, the heterosexual brother of Ned Weeks, says "You guys [homosexuals] don't understand why there are rules and regulations, guidelines, responsibilities," and Ned lamely agrees (68). For Kramer, gay sexual behavior is "the equivalent of eating junk food" (*Normal Heart,* 79), irresponsible because it disobeys the rules, regulations, and guidelines that govern heterosexual relations. He fears, as I will discuss later, its very uncontrollability.

If Kramer's insistence that gay men temporarily forgo all sexual activity could be justified in the early stages of the health crisis as a reasonable response to a disease whose cause and mode of transmission were unknown, his continued sexual abstinence cannot be so easily explained and suggests rather strongly that beneath his earlier position lay a latent antipathy toward sex. He admits at the end of *Reports from the Holocaust:* "It is very difficult for me to make love, even 'safely,' when the very act is now so inextricably bound up with death. . . . I mean the very act itself—of kissing, of gently masturbating each other, of sweating bodies lying side by side. All the educational material in the world proclaiming that 'safe sex' is possible does not reduce the fear that some slipup might occur" (227). His neurotic fears of contagion, exacerbated by his refusal to be tested for HIV antibodies, further support the contention that Kramer used AIDS to mask his sexual discomfort. Yet, attacking Kramer for internalizing homophobia and antieroticism is an empty charge since we have all internalized the values of a society that considers sexuality sinful and homosexuality as worse. Just as no American is free of racism, so, too, no one is free of internalized homophobia. Where Kramer may be faulted is that by denying such latent tendencies, he can neither root them out nor make allowances for their persistence in his thinking, and so he allows his homophobic feelings to color not only his attitudes, but the very style of his polemic.

Kramer believes that the criticism leveled against *Faggots,* as well as the rest of his writing on AIDS, is an angry response to the truth he dared to report: the lovelessness that lay behind homosexual licence. "I have touched some essential painful truth that some do not want to look at," he writes (*Reports,* 20). Yet the anger Kramer arouses cannot be so easily explained away. Much of it came from sensitive and discerning writers. For example, George Whitmore—who died of AIDS and wrote one of the best and most moving accounts of the epidemic, *Someone Was There*—urged his readers to boycott *Faggots*. Moreover, 1978, the year *Faggots* was published, also saw the appearance of Edmund White's *Nocturnes for the King of Naples* and Andrew Holleran's *Dancer from the Dance,* works sharing the same decadent New York scene and critical attitude, but arousing little hostility. What separates White and Holleran from Kramer and what freed them from an angry backlash is that they possess a lyric sympathy for their wayward characters, while Kramer, at best, musters an angry identification. Unlike Evelyn Waugh, Kramer's artistic model, Kramer never gained the requisite satirical distance or clinical detachment. His personal involvement interferes with both his sympathy and objectivity. Where White and Holleran are sweetly elegiac, Kramer is bitterly censorious.

Kramer's habit of responding to political events as personal affronts, of transforming impersonal bureaucracies into individual bogeymen, of subsuming all conflicts into a version of the Freudian family romance is the source of both the power of his political polemics and of the problems with them. His broadsides derive much of their creepy insistence from their intimacy. So often does Kramer remind readers that the GMHC was born in his living room that we begin to sense that he felt betrayed when it left his apartment. In *The Normal Heart* and *Reports from the Holocaust,* Kramer weaves in his conflicts with his brother as if the AIDS epidemic were an episode in a continuing family squabble. Indeed, both of these books end, not with Kramer addressing the gay community, but with him embracing his brother and sister-in-law. Kramer's tendency to place the gay community within the bosom of the heterosexual family is, I think, the reason his work speaks so powerfully and uneasily to gay readers, for it suggests a vision of reconciliation both keenly desired and frustratingly delayed. As Seymour Kleinberg has noted: "Society has not acted as the surrogate family in which we all develop our loyalties and moral sense. In fact, too often it acts just like the families of gay men: filled with contempt and indifference" (59).

The voices of the family float up through the various articles, speeches, and essays contained in *Reports from the Holocaust.* I can detect at least three major strains: the grating soprano of the enraged child, the wounded contralto of the guilt-inducing mother, and the rasping bass of the humiliating father. Because I hear these voices coming not only from Kramer's page, but also from my own head,

I respond to them with an unusual intensity. Kramer's ability to address the subconscious of gay readers accounts, I think, in large measure for his nagging power and the anger he arouses.

The enraged child is perhaps the most obvious and embarrassing of his voices. A self-conscious profanity peppers his articles as though Kramer were a teenager trying to shock his respectable parents. He calls Dr. Anthony Fauci, for example, a "FUCKING SON OF A BITCH OF A DUMB IDIOT" (*Reports,* 194); Gary Bauer and Doctors Bowen, Windom, and Harmison, "four monsters" (*Reports,* 168); and Mayor Koch in *The Normal Heart,* "that cocksucker . . . he's a heartless, selfish son of a bitch" (90). "If I use gross language," he dares us, "go ahead, be offended" (*Reports,* 171). Later he admits: "Yes, I am screaming like a hysteric. I know that. I look and sound like an asshole. . . . I am going to go out screaming so fucking rudely that you will hear this course, crude voice of mine in your nightmares. You are going to die and you are going to die very, very, soon unless you get up off of your fucking tushies and fight back" (*Reports,* 172–73). The childishness of this rage can be measured by Kramer's use of "tushies," a word that deflates by its baby-talk connotations the fierceness of the jeremiad. Like an infant throwing a tantrum, Kramer screams, "I hate you. I hate you. I wish you were dead."

If Kramer often sounds like a child, he even more often strikes the note of a stereotypical Jewish mother complaining: "How could you do this to me after all I've done for you?" During his running feud with the GMHC, he sent an open letter to its then director Tim Sweeney:

> I love GMHC as much as, if not more than, most. After all, it was founded in my living room, I gave it its name (for better or worse), I arranged for my brother's law firm to be its legal counsel pro bono, which they [sic] still are, and I gave it two years of my life, full time. I am very proud that the organization is there partly because of me, and I am conscious of the many fine deeds it has accomplished over the years. If I have pain and anger and frustration as well, it is very much like that of a parent toward a wayward and unfocused child who is not growing up the way I want it to. (*Reports,* 119)

In another open letter, this time to Richard Dunne, the Executive Director of GMHC, he writes as though the organization's existence was a personal labor: "I am ashamed of the whole lot of you. I did not spend two years of my life fighting for your birth to see you turn into a bunch of cowards" (*Reports,* 110). The basic strategy of Kramer's

Jewish mother voice is to spread guilt as generally and liberally as he can, especially in reference to his own suffering. "I don't know how much longer I have to live," he writes pathetically, "and I would like to devote what time I have left to trying to contribute something more personally meaningful to this strange, perplexing world" (*Reports,* 146). Usually, however, the tone is less lachrymose, as when he tells the readers of the *Native:* "I am angry and frustrated almost beyond the bound my skin and bones and body and brain can encompass. My sleep is tormented by nightmares and visions of lost friends . . . I know that unless I fight with every ounce of my energy I will hate myself. I hope, I pray, I implore you to feel the same" (*Reports,* 49).

Even when Kramer accuses his "enemies" of heinous crimes, he makes them personal affronts: "Until the day I die, I will never forgive [the *Times*] and this mayor [Ed Koch] for treating this epidemic, which is killing so many of my friends, in such an irresponsible fashion" (*Reports,* 70). Kramer's personalization of guilt is a useful tactic for keeping the attack from becoming vague, abstract, and distant. Yet it is a dangerous rhetorical ploy since so many gay men, subjected to it since birth, resist being made to feel guilty.

The effectiveness of Kramer's guilt-tripping is offset by his compulsion to humiliate his gay readers with familiar fag-baiting terms. He often sounds like a football coach rousing the team by insulting its manhood, or a father striking out at his effeminate son. In *Reports from the Holocaust* he asks the GMHC, "Why are you such sissies!" (106) and compares it to "a sissy run[ning] away from a fight" (110). In *The Normal Heart,* Ned Weeks yells at one character: "Bruce, for a Green Beret, you're an awful sissy!" (91). He tells Richard Dunne to "weed out the wimps on your Board of Directors and among your staff. Replace them with fighters" (*Reports,* 113). He attacks them for being "cowards" and for growing "weak" (*Reports,* 109, 112). What makes Kramer's recourse to this homophobic language particularly odd is his clear understanding of its insidiousness. In his concluding essay in *Reports from the Holocaust,* he writes: "The concept of 'man-liness' is the stereotypical straight expectation for all males; somehow, all gay men are therefore 'sissies.' (How gay men hate this word!)" (236). Yet Kramer cannot resist using such stereotypes and regretfully acknowledges: "I still am unable to resolve this fundamental problem —how to inspire you without punishing you" (186).

This need to provoke gay men as sissies comes from a very deep source: his "awe of power, of those who have it," and his anger over his perceived powerlessness (*Reports,* 135). "I have learned, during these past seven years, to hate. I hate everyone who is higher in the pecking order and in being so placed, like some incontinent pigeon, shits all over all of those below" (*Reports,* 180). These twin obsessions generate some of the most bizarre episodes of Kramer's involvement as an AIDS activist.

The one I find the most disturbing is his break with GMHC, a break that not only occasions much of his journalism, but also forms a large part of *The Normal Heart.* According to Kramer, he was maneuvered into resigning from the board when he was excluded from a meeting with Mayor Koch because of his abrasive and confrontational manner. After he quit, he tried several times to rejoin, but was repeatedly rebuffed. In frustration, Kramer wrote a series of open letters in which he argues that GMHC had forsaken its original path and succumbed, in Kramer's suggestive phrase, to "the 'fuck the founding father' syndrome" by committing itself to patient services instead of political action (*Reports,* 138–39). In his open letter to Richard Dunne, he wrote: "I think it must come as a big surprise to you and your Board of Directors that Gay Men's Health Crisis was not founded to help those who are ill. It was founded to protect the living, to help the living go on living, to help those who are still healthy to stay healthy, to help gay men stay alive" (*Reports,* 103). He goes on in the same letter:

> GMHC has also placed itself in thrall to forces other than its Board. Somewhere along the line, the organization was completely taken over by Professional Custodians—social workers, psychologists, psychiatrists, therapists, teachers—all of whom have vested interests in the Sick, in the Dying, in establishing and perpetuating the Funeral. You help people to the grave, to face death. GMHC was founded for life. (*Reports,* 112)

Kramer distorts here the history of GMHC, which by his own account began in reaction to Dr. Friedman-Kein's request for someone "to organize a solicitation of funds [for] several patients who had no medical insurance, and . . . his own research" (*Reports,* 12), and thus, as a form of patient services. Even more disturbing, however, is his rejection of the sick and dying, his the-dead-should-bury-the-dead attitude. For a man who insists that gays "take responsibilities for our own lives," he has a strangely cavalier attitude to those with AIDS (*Reports,* 128). Kramer is not really as cold-hearted as he makes himself appear—he meticulously records the names of his dead friends on index cards—yet he seems compelled to deny his concern by striking a tough guy attitude.

Part of the explanation for Kramer's attitude toward people with AIDS is what Judith Wilson Ross has called "the Death Metaphor," that to be diagnosed with AIDS is to be dead already. According to Ross, we come to think of AIDS as death because it alleviates the pain of watching others die, and because "it better fits the drama that we have constructed about the coming of and the meaning of AIDS" (40). But Kramer's attitude also derives from his notions of masculinity: care of the sick is "women's work," a sign of weakness. In *The Normal Heart,* the GMHC's devotion to patient services is developed in a scene between Ned and Dr. Emma Brookner. Ned recounts his frustration in getting the board to take political action in sexist terms: "I thought I was starting with a bunch of Ralph Naders and Green Berets, and . . . they turn into a bunch of nurses' aides." Emma replies: "You've got to warn the living, protect the healthy, help them keep on living. I'll take care of the dying" (79). Kramer, the adaptor of D. H. Lawrence, follows Lawrence's archetypal scheme: women are the devotees of thanatos, men the celebrators of life.

Yet Kramer's attitude toward AIDS patients, I think, turns on still another part of the stereotypical code of masculinity, and the clue is found in his rejection of the "Professional Custodians." One key lesson AIDS mental health programs try to teach persons with AIDS is accepting the inevitable loss of control that comes with being ill, especially as the disease progresses (Acevedo, 100). George Whitmore has caught the fear and anger of men who, in their thirties and forties and used to managing not only their own but corporate responsibilities, find themselves unable to work, walk, or simply get out of bed: "I very much like being in control," admitted one media executive, "the control was taken away" (26).

"AIDS is about shit and blood," Whitmore tells us (24), and one of the most potent symbols of the loss of control that AIDS patients face is incontinence. The loss of bowel control is the obligatory scene in the AIDS literary drama—a horrifying moment, humiliating to the patient, if not to the caregiver. Barbara Peabody, the mother of an AIDS patient, writes that the major conversation of her support group for caregivers was about diarrhea: "how to pretend it doesn't bother us" (94). Whitmore writes about a nurse opening the door to her favorite patient's room to find it "full of shit and blood. Shit and huge clots of blood covered the floor. It covered the bed. . . . [the patient's] body was twisted across the bed. Shit and blood were still pouring out of him. His feet were slipping and sliding in it" (153). Kramer's obsession with bodily elimination appears even before the advent of AIDS. *Faggots* opens with Fred Lemish—who suffers from both constipation and a shy bladder—being peed on, and it ends with him defecating. In *The Normal Heart,* one of the most moving passages is a speech in which Bruce speaks of his lover, Albert:

> His mother wanted him back in Phoenix before he died, this was last week when it was obvious, so I get permission from Emma and bundle him all up and take him to the plane in an ambulance. . . . Then, after we take off, Albert loses his mind, not recognizing me, not knowing where he is or that he's going home, and then, right there, on the plane, he becomes . . . incontinent. He starts doing it in his pants, and all over the seat; shit, piss, everything. I pulled down my suitcase and yanked out whatever clothes were in there and I start mopping him up as best I can . . . and I sit there holding his hand, saying, "Albert, please, no more, hold it in, man, I beg you, just for us, for Bruce and Albert." (105–6)

Caring for the sick and dying means confronting in the most graphic ways the loss of control and with it the loss of masculinity (Schofferman, 56). Kramer, who is in "awe of power" and wishes GMHC to be a "powerful" organization, fears that its attention to patient services will make it and him weak. In doing so, he appears to suffer from a reaction fairly common in those who work with the terminally ill, what William Horstman and Leon McKusic have identified as "Helper Helplessness Syndrome" (63).

It would be mistaken, however, to see Kramer as lacking in compassion even if he does turn his back on the sick and dying while urging them to "rage, rage against the dying of the light." Were he truly so heartless, Kramer would be more of a monster than he accuses Mayor Koch or Anthony Fauci of being. Rather Kramer flirts with losing control even as he argues for the need for discipline and power; he is drawn to the dying even as he speaks of devoting himself to the living. What makes a Kramer performance fascinating to watch is the drama of his attempts to yoke contradictory forces, and the extremities to which he is driven in this mad attempt.

Kramer's rhetoric is filled with binary oppositions: masculine / feminine, living / dead, gay / straight, love / sex, relationships / promiscuity, friends / enemies. In this respect, his language differs little from the general rhetoric of AIDS (Treichler, 63–64). But whereas most writing on AIDS tries to maintain these oppositions, Kramer constantly conflates them. For example, many commentators have drawn attention to the very arbitrary distinction between "general population" and "risk groups" (Grover, 22; Ross, "Ethics," 45; Treichler, 66). As evidence developed of heterosexual transmission between intravenous drug users and their sexual partners, the "risk groups" were expanded to protect the concept of "general population." With the World Health Organization estimating current AIDS cases at 450,000 and projecting five million cases by the year 2000 (*New York Times,* 19 May 1989, D16), it is hard to maintain such distinctions. Kramer distinguishes between the "living" and the "dying," but his refusal to be tested for HIV infection is based not so much on his fears that the test would exclude him from the "living," but on his desire to keep open the prospect that he is one of the dead. His famous dictum that *"Each and every minute of my life, I must act as if I already have AIDS and am fighting for my life"* conflates the categories even as it insists upon them (*Reports,* 91).

Kramer's favorite form of address—the open letter—is also contradictory, repeatedly exposing that most private of written expressions to the scrutiny of the world. The open letter throws into question what is usually the simplest issue of letter writing—who is its reader. The persons explicitly addressed in his open letters are not especially his readers. Written to his "enemies" to tell them how evil they are, the letters never give up trying to convert them into allies. Perversely, the one open letter sent to a supposed friend, Max Frankel—who had replaced the reviled Abe Rosenthal as editor-in-chief of the *New York Times* and who had extended an olive branch to Kramer—summarily rakes Frankel over the coals. It is as though Kramer, having worked so hard to establish polarities, is not content until those polarities are made to collapse, and once collapsed, is more energetic than ever in reestablishing them.

Kramer's difficulties with conventional categories is nowhere more apparent than in his attitude toward gay marriage and family. Kramer wants the state to allow gay marriages, and he concludes *The Normal Heart* with the symbolic marriage of Ned Weeks to Felix as though the ceremony were necessary to legitimize the relationship (122). He contends that because gays cannot marry, they "were forced into AIDS" (*Reports,* 180). Kramer argues: "Had we [gays] possessed these rights you denied us, had we been allowed to live respectably in a community of equals, there would never have been an AIDS [*sic*]. Had we been allowed to marry, we would not have felt the obligation to be promiscuous" (*Reports,* 178–79). For Kramer, gays achieve "respectability" by imitating the disreputable heterosexuals who deny gays their rights. Kramer also struggles with the illusion that somehow marriage will protect people from AIDS: "I used to encourage friends," he writes, "to settle down into relationships. . . . While filling my index cards [of those who had died of AIDS], it upset me to note several couples I'd encouraged who had perhaps then infected each other" (*Reports,* 221). Kramer never quite sees that promiscuity may result as much from searching for a pseudo-spouse as from avoiding the commitment of a relationship, and he only belatedly realizes that the worst enemies of the homosexual are those, like Adolf Eichmann, who act to protect the family:

> The Family. The family. How these words are repeated and repeated in America—from campaign rhetoric to television commercials. This is a country that prides itself on proclaiming family values, as if there were no others, as if the family was homespun and united and loving, as if it is necessary to produce a child—like a product—to justify or countenance a sexual act. . . . Well, I am a member of a family, too. Or I once thought so. . . . How convenient for them all to have disposed of us so expeditiously, just when we need them most. But the ranks are closed, something is happening to gay men, and we are suddenly no longer affiliated with *the* family. Where do they think we came from? The cabbage patch? (*Reports,* 271)

Kramer both desires to be incorporated into the family and recognizes that the "values" that make the family desirable are hollow. As Simon Watney has pointed out, the state has used the family as an excuse for remaining silent about AIDS and for further stigmatizing homosexuals (82). Reading Kramer, I have the sense that he uses "family" metaphorically to describe an idea of a community which retains its original idealism, purged of hypocrisy, but such a formulation would mean abandoning the oppositional rhetoric that informs not only his writing on AIDS, but also traditional political polemic.

Kramer's concern with the family, which predates the AIDS epidemic, has taken on new urgency since the health crisis, for AIDS has forced gay men to reconsider their relationship with their families and with the nonhomosexual community. As Frances Fitzgerald points out, gay men in the 1970s were evolving in the larger urban centers a separatist lifestyle, living and working in gay ghettos, patronizing exclusively gay stores, restaurants, lawyers, and stockbrokers, attending gay concerts, sporting events, and churches (116). AIDS broke the spell of gay self-sufficiency. Suddenly, gay men needed government services and family support. However, their experience of independence led gay men to demand help as fully enfranchised citizens and fully accepted sons. Such changes have, in turn, altered gay political thinking and rhetoric.

Yet what sort of rhetoric might replace traditional oppositional language? If the sharp division between "them" and "us" is no longer useful or accurate, but the conflation of opposites into a unified society is also far from being achieved, then it becomes virtually impossible to speak, especially in Kramer's habitually passionate way. If his pronouncements of 1987 appear, even to Kramer, to be among his angriest and most hyperbolic, it may be the result of his increasing frustration in his failure to find language that is urgent without being oppositional. If he seems shriller in his call for force, going so far as to praise Zionist terriorist organizations (*Reports,* 191), it may be because gay power has become more diffuse as the epidemic has proceeded. In this respect the problems in Kramer's writings become symptomatic of the difficulties of the gay movement, which has witnessed simultaneously both its greatest successes in legitimizing itself before the American public, and its greatest failures in protecting its own population.

Seymour Kleinberg, one of the most cogent and sensitive commentators on homosexuality, has addressed these gay social and rhetorical problems.

> Not only must gay men refrain from what alone gave them a powerful enough identity to make a mark on the consciousness of society, a behavior that replaced society's contempt with the much more respectable fear and anger, but they must cease to think of themselves as unloved children. And they must do both before they have evidence that society accepts them or that their behavior has meaning for each other more nurturing than it has been (59)

In short, Kleinberg suggests that the gay movement needs a visionary polemic which will speak of the desired changes in social structure as though they have already occurred. Gay men must act and speak as though society is a family that loves them even as they recognize this attitude to be wishful thinking. The very tortuousness of Kleinberg's prose with its elegant, if confusing ellipses, suggests the difficulty of such a rhetorical and psychological stance.

How does one integrate the social role of gay people into a culture which has not yet accepted them? In her study of the gay movement in the Castro district of San Francisco, Frances Fitzgerald notes the changes in the way various gay groups communicate among themselves and to the heterosexual population. Gone is the "verbal terrorism" that marked the debate on whether to close gay bath houses. Replacing it has been a rational discussion of issues "without discovering 'enemies' and building up factions." One leader whom she interviewed went as far as stating "that gay politics as such [is] dead" (113).

Kramer, however, believes that gay political action is just beginning, and he hints that a possible model for the relationship between hetero- and homosexuals may be found in the relationship between gentiles and Jews. The analogy between Jews and homosexuals is long-standing. Proust develops it at great length at the beginning of *Cities of the Plain* (25). Even so sophisticated a theorist as Eve Kosofsky Sedgwick finds the analogy useful to explore ("Epistemology," 45–59). As the title of his collection states, Kramer compares the AIDS epidemic and the Holocaust. Borrowing from Hannah Arendt's analysis of the Holocaust, Kramer argues that gay people can avoid genocide only by demanding their political rights. By capitulating to hostile authority because they trusted its essential benevolence, Jews sealed their downfall; and by believing in the responsiveness of the federal government, gays allowed AIDS services and research to be ignored, underfunded, and subjected to unconscionable delays. "Every pariah," Kramer quotes Arendt as saying, "who refused to be a rebel was partly responsible for his position" (*Reports,* 254). Kramer wants not separatism, however, but for heterosexuals to accommodate and accept homosexuals. Just as Jews have preserved their ethnic, cultural, and spiritual difference, even as they have found a place within the American polity, so will homosexuals preserve their cultural and social identity; and just as Jews have had to remain vigilant against anti-Semitism, so, too, must gay people keep a sharp eye out for homophobia. As one gay activist has argued, according to Fitzgerald, "the solution [for the gay community is] to build philanthropies on the model of Jewish organizations" (113).

A nonseparatist political action is already emerging. Its most astounding success has been the NAMES Project, an ongoing activity

about which Kramer, as well as other radical gay theorists, have remained remarkably silent. The NAMES Project has encouraged individuals and groups in the creation of fabric pieces as memorials for
those who have died of AIDS, and it assembles and exhibits these
pieces as The Quilt, an enormous patchwork of grief and hope. Begun
by Cleve Jones, who, according to Randy Shilts, enjoys a "legendary
reputation as a media-savvy street activist" (600) and who once served
as a chief aide to California Assembly Speaker Leo McCarthy, The
Quilt, despite its grassroots reputation and folksy appearance, serves
as a highly sophisticated piece of political symbolism, engineered by
someone who knows the hard realities of both media exposure and
backroom politics (Ruskin, 9). Its first appearance on the Washington
Mall in October 1987 created a picture that was captured by all of the
networks and front pages of the major newspapers. Unlike other mon-
uments, The Quilt is no fixed pile of marble, but something more
human, vast, and flexible. Quilting, so long a symbol of the American
home, has also had political significance. As Elaine Hedges has noted:
"Through their quilts women became, in fact, not only witnesses to
but active agents in important historical changes" (11). The magnitude of The Quilt, while acknowledging a debt to women and to feminist struggles, provides it with a particularly masculine dimension. At
once extremely personal and utterly public, The Quilt integrates personal grief and public outrage, the fear of the closeted and the aggression of the activist, the solidarity of gay friends and the sympathy of
straight family, individual continuity and communal loss. Unlike so
many public protests, The Quilt is quiet, and those who come to witness it are hushed by its magnitude, its seemingly unlimited detail, and
its inescapable unity of effect. Stretched out between the rows of
autumnal trees, The Quilt turned Washington into both a bed and a
grave. Beyond the lines of people weeping or with heads bowed, the
Capitol rose small and grand, solid and toy-like, distant and inescap-
ably connected. The NAMES Project has struck a new chord in the
American psyche: a way to incorporate gay people into the fabric of
society while recognizing—even commemorating—their contributions
and sufferings. It forms the type of statement gay writers are only
beginning to stitch together with words.

8

Cannibals and Queers: Man-Eating

WHILE a student in middle school, the highly autobiographical
narrator of Yukio Mishima's *Confessions of a Mask* develops
anemia brought on, he and his doctor believe, by "self-pollution." Although he enjoins himself to practice "earnestness" to be rid of this
habit (100), the narrator instead accelerates his bouts of masturbation
by engaging in more and more rococo sadistic sexual fantasies based
on icons of St. Sebastian and episodes from *Quo Vadis* (91–92).
Without having read Sade, he invents a "murder theater," in which "a
Grecian soldier, many white slaves of Arabia, princes of savage tribes,
hotel elevator-boys, waiters, young toughs, army officers, circus
roustabouts" are systematically executed in a manner that would provide "a spectacle of outpouring blood" and an opportunity to "kiss the
lips of those who had fallen" as they spasmodically writhed on the
ground (92–93).

These daydreams culminate in a vision the narrator is pleased to
imagine as "probably one of the basest of which man is capable,"
namely, eating another human being, specifically, a fellow student
who was "a skilled swimmer, with a notably good physique" (94). In
the fantasy, the narrator hosts a dinner party whose guests grow
restive during the meal's long delay. To placate them, the narrator
goes to speak to the surly chef at the very moment that a second cook
leads his classmate into the kitchen. While the narrator diverts the stu-

dent, the cook places the swimmer in a stranglehold and then lashes the unconscious boy to "a large foreign-style platter" drilled on each side with five holes through which the bindings are laced. The cooks carry the student into the dining room where the narrator proceeds to carve him up. "Where shall I begin?" he asks his guests, and when he receives no reply, he "thrust[s] the fork upright into the heart. A fountain of blood [strikes him] full in the face," but he continues slicing the body "gently, thinly at first . . ." (94–97).

This passage is striking not for its horrific vision of cannibalism, which is in fact deferred by Mishima's ellipses, but for its prissy decorum, of which the ellipses are such a telling example. I find Mishima's calculated attempts to shock less disturbing than he intends, for if all self-conscious Satanism is a bit silly—evil in the twentieth century is almost by definition banal—Mishima's variety is particularly susceptible to bathos since it relies so heavily on literary and artistic allusions which steer it toward parody. The teenage daydreamer locates his fantasies in a theatrical space inspired by *Quo Vadis,* St. Sebastian, and the medical textbooks consulted by his doctor. The adult narrator adds Sade and Wilde as additional inspirations. As he later admits, his entire knowledge of sexuality is based on "the many novels I had read, a sex encyclopedia for home use, the pornography that passed from hand to hand, and an abundance of naive dirty jokes" (108).

We should not, however, ascribe this episode to Mishima's quirky sensibility. Mishima's case is far from unique. Melville, Charles Warren Stoddard, Tennessee Williams, Gide, Michel Tournier, Pasolini, all have written about cannibals or cannibalism, and the tradition continues in such writers as Daniel Curzon and Tobias Schneebaum.

Here I wish to explore how the association of cannibalism and homosexuality has developed, and what uses gay writers have made of it in their representation of themselves. In so doing I am continuing to examine the ways in which gay rhetoric, even while emerging out of the dominant culture's language, develops, at least partially, a way to express gay men's views of themselves. I have shown that gay rhetoric is compromised by its origins in the dominant culture's language and always feels the pull of the dominant even as it tries to spin away from it. The trope of gay cannibalism never extricates itself from the homophobic sentiments that gave it birth. Even in the case of *Suddenly Last Summer* when it is converted into camp, the voice which ought most effectively to distance it from the dominant culture, the trope never pulls entirely free. If I emphasize here as elsewhere, the extent to which gay writers have defused and transformed the homophobic origins of their language, it is because I find even partial success more interesting and worthy of note than the inevitable partial failures of these strategies.

That being said, I do not want to suggest that homosexuality and cannibalism are phenomena that are linked in actuality. Cannibals are not any more likely to be homosexual than heterosexual, and gay people are not inclined to eat their lovers any more than straight people are (though, of course, cases of both homo- and heterosexual cannibalism arise both in life and in art). In fact, Eli Sagan has argued on psychoanalytic grounds that cannibalism is an attempt by a male "who carries with him an ideal of masculine, independent behavior . . . to prove his masculinity and his independence of feminine support" (92), and consequently this behavior is *less* likely to occur in homosexuals who are less dependent on such heterosexual models. Like Peggy Reeves Sanday, I regard cannibalism as a "tangible symbol that is part of a system of symbols and ritual acts that predicate consciousness," and by studying cannibalism's entanglements with homosexuality, I want to see how such a symbolic complex can "reproduce consciousness in the ritual domination and control of the social order" (26). In short, I want to see how tropes of cannibalism and homosexuality intertwine and what such braiding has come to mean.

To be sure, cannibalism is not confined to gay literature. Native American captivity narratives contain many stories of heterosexual rape and cannibalism. Dickens was fascinated by cannibalism and appeared in Wilkie Collins's *The Frozen Deep,* a play about the unsuccessful Franklin expedition which sought to find a northwest passage through the Arctic and ended, it was rumored, by Franklin consuming his men in a vain effort to achieve his goal. Twain wrote "Cannibalism in the Cars," a potboiler about a train trapped in the Rockies during a blizzard. There is *Robinson Crusoe* and quite recently the controversial film *The Cook, The Thief, His Wife and Her Lover,* which ends with a scene of cannibalistic revenge. These heterosexual narratives concern people who either revert to cannibalism to survive or who are unwilling captives of cannibals or are forced to perform cannibalistic acts as punishment. Women are rarely eaters or the eaten in either homo- or heterosexual cannibal narratives; in fact, cannibalism is not so much the eating of humans (anthropophagus) as it is the eating of males. Unlike straight cannibal narratives, gay narratives usually have their protagonists seek out cannibals as in Melville's *Typee* and in Stoddard's tales of the Pacific, or their protagonists seduce the cannibal as in Williams's "Desire and the Black Masseur" or are even seduced by them as in Schneebaum's *Where the Spirits Dwell.*

The correlation of homosexuality and cannibalism is quite old. Among the earliest works to associate them—at least within the Christian tradition—is *The Panarion of Epiphanius of Salamis.* Epiphanius, an early anti-Gnostic church father, accuses the Gnostics or Borborites of both homosexuality and cannibalism (as well the violation of many other taboos). According to Epiphanius, the Borborites worship a prophet Barkabbas whose name is a multilingual pun on fornication and murder. These Gnostics "foul their assembly . . . with dirt from promiscuous fornication; and they eat and handle both human flesh and uncleanness" (84). The central act of the Borborites is a feast in which "the woman and man receive the male emission on their own hands," and standing with "their eyes raised heavenward," offer their semen to God and eat it (86). The Borborites practice all nonprocreative sexual acts. Occasionally, however, a women does get pregnant, and then according to Epiphanius, "they extract the fetus . . . cut it up. . . . And they mix honey, pepper, and certain other perfumes and spices . . . and each eats a piece of the child with his fingers," declaring the meal "the perfect Passover" (86–87). Thomas Aquinas also links sodomy and cannibalism in his *Summa Theologica* during his discussion of intemperance. Intemperance can be divided into two groups: (1) the excessive use of objects whose moderate use is good, or in St. Thomas's words "those human passions which to a certain extent are in conformity with human nature;" and (2) the use of those objects which under no condition are good or "exceed the mode of human nature." In the second group, St. Thomas believes, are such sins as "eating human flesh, or . . . committing the unnatural vice" (q. 142, art. 4, ad. 3). In short, sodomy and cannibalism are acts which "exceed the mode of human nature" by taking inappropriate objects, a categorical mistake.

The very word "cannibal" is of Renaissance fashioning and directly linked with sodomy. "Cannibal" is a corruption of "Carib," and the early chroniclers of Amerindians such as Cieza de León and Oviedo reported the wide practice of both man-eating and sodomy (Pagden, 176). As Anthony Pagden explains, the Amerindian tendency toward both cannibalism and sodomy were used by the Spanish—even the most enlightened of its jurists, such as José de Acosta—for justifying the enslavement or servitude of Amerindian tribes, since for Acosta these sins were destructive of the family upon which all culture is based (178).

Homosexual writers did not choose to represent themselves as cannibals or the lovers of cannibals; they inherited the representation from Christian and pagan tradition, reenforced by ethnographers. The conflation of homosexuality and cannibalism continues into modern times. For example, in *De la justice* (1860), Proudhon worries about whether sodomy will lead to cannibalism (Greenberg, 353; Aron and Kempf, 85), and in 1914, Paul Claudel insists to André Gide that "if one person claims to justify sodomy, another will justify onanism, vampirism, rape of children, anthropophagy" (Russell, 205). Yet despite the unsavoriness of the association, gay writers have explored it with a penetration, intensity, and frequency which is itself notable. Like so many elements of gay self-representation, it has been forced from without but reshaped from within. One of the ironies of this association is that for the gay writer, cannibalism is more acceptable than homosexuality. Mishima's *Confessions of a Mask* is an excellent case in point: his narrator finds it more flattering to his ego to imagine himself as a cannibal than as a queer; he can more easily and pleasurably dream about eating the breasts of his fellow students than fondling them. Within the patriarchy, violence between men is more acceptable than affection between them. Gay writers who represent themselves within the discourse of cannibalism rarely escape those patriarchal values, even as they try to find within the cannibals' society a value system other than the Western patriarchy they wish to reject.

Perhaps no one has so valiantly tried to escape the dubious values of American society and been more aware of their inescapability than Herman Melville, who at the very outset of his literary career jumped (almost literally) into cannibal society in *Typee*. The title was derived from the tribe with whom Melville lived, a tribe that "enjoy[ed] a prodigious notoriety all over the islands" as the "most inveterate gormandizers of human flesh." The tribe's name—according to Melville—is the Marquesan word for "lover of human flesh" (60–61). It turns out, in fact, that Melville invented the derivation, but that indicates how much he wished the book to be read as an extended meditation on man as eater and eaten.

Typee begins with Tom or, as he's called by the natives, Tommo (Melville's fictional alter-ego) on board ship in a state of near starvation. The crew has exhausted all the fresh provisions and for weeks is

reduced to eating only salt-horse and sea-biscuit (35). The ship is literally consuming itself—its inside scraped off for kindling or "gnawed
off" by the captain's pig, who has long since been consumed (36). The
hunger has led to a sort of castration, for "the gay and dapper young
cock" has become the sole inmate of the chicken coop, his "companions literally snatched from him one by one," and the crew awaits the
captain's orders for "the decapitation of this luckless Pedro." The
hardship of shipboard starvation makes Tom yearn for land, even the
Marquesas where the "Naked houris" sway before "'horrible idols'
that guard *heathen rites and human sacrifices*" (37, Melville's italics).

Throughout the opening chapters of *Typee,* people have a strange
way of turning into food, and food into people. The leg Tom hurt in
his escape from the *Dolly* becomes by the time he reaches the Typee an
"unfortunate limb . . . left much in the same condition as a rump-steak
after undergoing the castigating process which precedes cooking"
(127). The "small, broken, flinty bits of biscuit" he gathers before his
desertion are called "'midshipmen's nuts,'" an obscene pun on their
testicles (75). Toby, his companion, is said to be "ripe for the enterprise" (71), and the food and tobacco Toby had hoped to preserve
from the tropical storm becomes an ugly mass that appears to be a
cross between a turd and a fetus. From "beneath his garments, he produced a small handful of something so soft, pulpy and discoloured,
that for a few moments he was as much puzzled as myself to tell by
what possible instrumentality such a villainous compound had become engendered in his bosom" (82). Melville's intended comic treatment of male pregnancy—indeed, what "instrumentality" could have
engendered such an abortion!—takes on a ghoulish quality as Tom
and Toby proceed to divide these "midshipman's nuts" and eat them.
No wonder the Typee imagine that Tom and Toby are "a couple of
white cannibals who were about to make a meal of them" (113).

Robert K. Martin suggests that Tom and Toby are "almost attracted
by" the terror of cannibalism (*Hero,* 27). I would go further; they are
obsessed by eating and being eaten long before they reach land. In
fact, like all obsessions theirs disguises a repressed desire, and the intensity of the desire may be measured by the intensity of the need to
deny it. By fleeing the Typee, Tom escapes his homoerotic attraction
to a people who "in beauty of form . . . surpassed anything [he] had
ever seen" (193).

Tom's fears of being eaten are clearly irrational. They are based on
rumor, and the only physical evidence of cannibalism he witnesses ap-

pears during the Feast of the Calabashes when he sees three smoked human heads, one of which he is certain "was that of a white man" (309). He insists on this identification even though the heads are highly decorated, mummified, and "quickly removed from [his] sight" (309). The evidence is extremely shaky. Tommo is so overwrought with anxiety that the sight may well be a product of his fevered imagination. Nor does the existence of heads prove cannibalism. They may well be ancestral heads preserved for ritual purposes. In Tom's calmer moments, he recognizes that at worse only the chiefs and priests would eat their victims and then only "to gratify the passion of revenge upon their enemies," a minor defect in his opinion when compared with the decapitation, auto-da-fé, disembowelment, and pillaging "which only a few years since was practiced in enlightened England" (180).

In the course of the novel, Tom develops relationships with three male islanders, and by examining these relationships, we can discover not only a pattern to Tom's—and by extension Melville's—homosexual desires, but also the connection between homosexual desire and cannibalistic fears.

Tom's closest sexual relationship is with Kory-Kory, whom he first describes as "a hideous object to look upon" because of the tattoos that cover all of Kory-Kory's body (130). Yet, as Tommo comes to know Kory-Kory, he can look beneath the tattooed surface—which covers the skin of all the Typee males—to discover a young man some twenty-five years of age, "about six feet in height, robust and well made," who in addition is "the most devoted and best natured" person in the world (130). But to appreciate their relationship, one must understand Typee marriage customs. According to Melville, the Typee engage in a form of polyandry:

> The girls are first wooed and won, at a very tender age, by some stripling in the household in which they reside. This, however, is a mere frolic of the affections, and no formal engagement is contracted. By the time this first love has a little subsided, a second suitor presents himself, of graver years, and carries both boy and girl away to his own habitation. This disinterested and generous-hearted fellow now weds the young couple, marrying damsel and lover at the same time—and all three thenceforth live together as harmoniously as so many turtles. . . . No man has more than one wife, and no wife of mature age has less than two husbands,— sometimes she has three, but such instances are not frequent. (261)

Melville emphasizes that a wife has two husbands, but from his description it would appear to be more accurate to say that older men have both a wife and a male consort. So, at least, it seems when Tom describes Mehevi's household which contains "the damsel Moonoony" and "a young fellow of fifteen, who . . . was decidedly in her good graces." According to Tom, "I sometimes beheld him and the chief making love at the same time. Is it possible, thought I, that the valiant warrior can consent to give up a corner in the thing he loves?" (259) The language is unusually murky for *Typee*. Tom's somewhat surprised tone leaves open the question of what is the "thing" Mehevi loves. Moonoony or the young man? Nevertheless, the question shows Melville's adherence to the Western code of conjugal ownership, which assumes that the presence of another man in the marital bed constitutes a sharing of proprietary rights, not an enlargement of conjugal pleasures. Although Melville never explicitly states that Tom has a similar arrangement with Kory-Kory and the young girl Fayaway, he does refer to the three sleeping and living together in Marheyo's house. The homoerotic relationship is comically suggested by the fire-making scene in which Kory-Kory "drives [his] stick furiously along the smoking channel" with a "rapidity of movement," which produces "as he approaches the climax of his efforts, . . . pants and gasps of breath and his eyes almost start[ing] from their sockets with the violence of his exertions" (165).

Tom's strongest and most openly expressed erotic response is to Marnoo, who strictly speaking is not a Typee, but an outcast from another tribe who is permitted to wander freely across the island and even take up with white men. According to Tom, Marnoo's "unclad limbs were beautifully formed" and "might have entitled him to the distinction of standing for the statue of Polynesian Apollo" (193). Tom even jokes about his attractions to Marnoo. When Marnoo ignores Tom's offer for Marnoo to sit next to him, Tom is filled with jealousy: "Had the belle of the season, in the pride of her beauty and power, been cut . . . she could not have felt greater indignation than I did" (195).

But Tommo's relaxed attitude with both Kory-Kory and Marnoo does not extend to Mehevi. There is tension from their very first meeting when Mehevi's "severe expression" causes Tom to "quail." "Never before," Tom comments, "had I been subjected to so strange and steady a glance; it revealed nothing of the mind of the savage, but it appeared to be reading my own" (116). At their second meeting the following day, when Mehevi appears in all his ceremonial regalia, Tom fully experiences the twin emotions of sexual attraction and fear. Tom's lengthy description of Mehevi is rife with symbols of his sexual and political potency. Around Mehevi's neck hung "several enormous necklaces of boar tusks . . . disposed in such a manner as that the longest and largest were upon his capacious chest" and matched the "finely-shaped sperm whale teeth" whose cavities were "stuffed with freshly-plucked leaves," and his ankles and wrists were adorned with ringlets of "curling human hair" (124). In the end, Tommo decides that "the warrior, from the excellence of his physical proportions, might certainly have been regarded as one of Nature's noblemen" (125).

Why, we must ask ourselves, is Tommo's more explicitly sexual relationship with Kory-Kory free from the anxiety of cannibalism, while his implicit erotic interests in Mehevi—which are never clearly realized—are mixed with the ever-increasing fear of being eaten? What is different about his erotic relationship with Kory-Kory that makes it less phobic? And what about Mehevi makes him so frightening a person?

The answer is not Mehevi's greater physical and political force: though Mehevi is described as "the most influential of all the chiefs" (203), in point of fact, all the chiefs hold equal weight insofar as they hold any weight at all. As Tommo acknowledges: "the influence exerted over the people of the valley by their chiefs was mild in the extreme; and as to any general rule or standard of conduct by which the commonalty were governed in their intercourse with each other . . . I should be almost tempted to say, that none existed on the island" (271). In all of Tommo's time among the Typee he sees no "court of law or equity," trials, or punishments. Mehevi's authority is so light that Tommo remained for weeks "ignorant of his regal character" because of "the simplicity of the social institutions" (255). Tommo must admit that the equality of Typee life makes priests and chiefs "hard to be distinguished from the rest of their countrymen" (299). Thus, Tommo's obsessive fears of being eaten by Mehevi cannot be ascribed simply to Mehevi's superior status. Rather the very equality that Tommo elsewhere regards with such approval, seems to be the source of his discomfort.

Tommo's relationship with Kory-Kory is quite literally (but also symbolically) mediated by a woman. Because Fayaway is present, Tom does not feel anxious about his sexual relations with Kory-Kory.

When she is absent, Tommo consistently thrusts Kory-Kory in the feminine role and is unrelentingly condescending to him. To be sure, at the beginning of the relationship Tommo is a sort of helpless baby that must be cared for, but Kory-Kory performs the traditional feminine role of feeding and cleaning. From the outset, Kory-Kory is "my savage valet" (131). Similarly, Marnoo, with his "matchless symmetry of form," his "beardless cheeks," his face "of a feminine softness and . . . free from the least blemish of tattooing" is an androgynous figure, and his history of being snatched up by an English sea captain and carried off for three years in Sydney makes him sound more like a modern Ganymede than a "Polynesian Apollo" (193–99).

Tommo's relationship with Mehevi stands in sharp contrast to his friendships with Kory-Kory and Marnoo. Tommo neither regards him with the affectionate condescension with which he treats Kory-Kory, nor relegates him to a feminine position. Tommo at first regards Mehevi as a "confirmed bachelor," (often used as a code word for homosexual) and as "the president of a club of hearty fellows, who kept 'Bachelor's Hall' in fine style at the Ti," a sacred all-male preserve (258–59). Tommo corrects the impression when he witnesses Mehevi having sex with Moonoony and a "fellow of fifteen," but clearly Moonoony plays no mediating role between Mehevi and Tom, both of whom stand on the basis of equality. Tom's cannibalistic phobia is a screen for anxiety about the desire for egalitarian sexual relations with Mehevi. Despite Tommo's approval of sexual and political equality, the reality of it frightens him for it means the loss of his control and powers to distance and disengage himself emotionally. Indeed, as much as he desires such an equality, he is unable to imagine it, and therefore, converts it into a relationship in which—though inserted into another man's body—he is an entirely passive agent.

In his study of Indian captivity narratives, Richard Slotkin argues that the terror was a fear of "merging." "In cannibalism, the image of merging is heightened and intensified . . . beginning with the acquiring of special powers by consuming parts of the slain (hearts, hands), it culminates in the total absorption of the eater and the eaten in each other, a total sharing of identities" (125). Tommo feels a similar, but increased terror as he contemplates intimacy with Mehevi. He suffers not only from the fear of merging, but also from the fear of male passivity, since as Leo Bersani has forcefully argued, "To be penetrated is to abdicate power" (212). Cannibalism becomes for Tommo a marker for the anxiety he feels at equality with a homosexual partner, since such equality would mean becoming the occasional passive receptor of another man's desire.

In *Typee* Melville presents two sorts of homosexual relations: those egalitarian in nature, and those mediated by the feminine. The latter are free of anxiety because they reproduce the familiar privileged relations of male power. But the prospect of an egalitarian homosexual relationship fills Melville with terror—a terror he converts to the more understandable and acceptable fear of being eaten—for such equality represents for him a new, untried loss of power and privilege. The novel dramatizes his conflicts: his desire for an egalitarian relationship with other men and his fear of being destroyed in such relations; his desire for the social openness of the primitive and his horror that the primitive was merely a mask for a savagery even worse than in supposedly civilized society. As F. O. Matthiessen—who, as we have seen, searched for a relationship of equality—commented: "In *Typee* Melville's most serious scrutiny was given between civilized and savage life, to the frequently contaminating effects of the white man. . . . [Melville] could never be a savage; his background of Presbyterian orthodoxy, though in obeyance now, was soon to reassert itself in his meditations on innate depravity" (*Renaissance,* 375–76). Melville was never to trust that even among the Typee there could be sexual relations between men that were truly equal.

For the gay writer, the trope of homosexual cannibalism becomes a way to work through his desire for communion with other men and his anxiety about the equality such communion implies. For homosexuality, as I discussed when I looked at the structure of its discourse, is both distinguished by the equality of the men involved, and made anxious by the difference such equality imposes. The equality between gay men is a quality both hard won and disturbing. Cannibalism becomes a screen on which gay writers can project both desire and fear.

When Sigmund Freud takes up the interrelationship between cannibalism and homosexuality, he also locates the juncture in the desire for male equality, an equality always threatened by sexual and physical rivalry. Admittedly, Freud does not directly address this issue of homosexuality, cannibalism, and social equality. But Freud's conceptualization helps throw light on why cannibalism and homosexuality are so persistently linked and is itself a modification of the trope.

In *Totem and Taboo* Freud explains the transition from what he calls the "father horde" to the "brother clan" (188). Following Darwin, Freud posits that society was originally organized along the lines of many simian groups: a single male—the father—would control all the females and exclude his sons from access to his harem until the father grew so weak through sickness or age or one of the sons grew so strong that he could overcome and kill the father and establish himself as the sole authority. Thus one tyranny replaced another. This structure fosters a two-tiered structure of male sexuality. On the one hand, the father is heterosexual, limiting his homosexual conduct—if he has any at all—to those times when he wishes to show his dominance over other males. On the other hand, the sons are forced into institutionalized homosexual behavior if they permit themselves any sexual outlet. Freud speaks of the "homo-sexual feelings and activities which probably manifested themselves among [the sons] during their time of banishment" (186).

At first the sons probably squabbled among themselves, the stronger sexually dominating the weaker. But at some time, the sons developed a sense of solidarity and equality. Only by joining forces as equals can the brothers permanently overthrow the rule of the father. Freud writes:

> One day the expelled brothers joined forces, slew and ate the father, and thus put an end to the father horde. Together they dared and accomplished what would have remained impossible for them singly. Perhaps some advance in culture, like the use of a new weapon, had given them the feeling of superiority. Of course these cannibalistic savages ate their victim. This violent primal father had surely been the envied and feared model for each of the brothers. Now they accomplished their identification with him and each acquired a part of his strength. The totem feast, which is perhaps mankind's first celebration, would be the repetition and commemoration of this memorable, criminal act with which so many things began, social organization, moral restrictions and religion. (183)

But eating the father does not end Freud's scenario of how father horde turns into brother clan. As the sons traded their enforced homosexuality for access to the female harem, enormous tensions welled up among them.

> Though the brothers had joined forces in order to overcome the father, each was the other's rival among the women. Each one wanted to have them all to himself like the father, and in the fight of each against the other the new organization would have perished. . . . Thus there was nothing left for the brothers, if they wanted to live together, but to erect the incest prohibition . . . through which they all equally renounced the women whom they desired. (186)

The establishment of the brother clan is, for Freud, one of the central events of civilization. Not only does this "memorable, criminal act" establish the patriarchy through the incest taboo (the equivalent of exogamy since all the members of the brother clan are related), but it also establishes totemic laws controlling (though not eliminating) the symbolic cannibalization of the father through his animal substitute. Moreover, this scenario relates the origins of another taboo—the control (though not elimination) of sexual relations between men.

In one of those hauntingly pessimistic pronouncements which have been the source of untold speculation about his own personality, Freud declares in regard to the sons' revolt against the father, "Sexual need does not unite men; it separates them" (185). Competition over the harem would have led to countless internal battles. The only solution was to forbid access to any women in the clan—the establishment of the incest taboo.

But the renunciation of sexual relations would have had to extend not only to the women, but also to the men. The brother clan would have had to ban or strictly control homosexual activities for several reasons. As brothers, they would have been covered by any rule that banned sexual relations between members of the clan. Also those brothers who had been satisfied with homosexual relations would not have conspired in the murder of the father, and since the guilt of eating the father solidifies the clan around the totem, those who had murdered the father would resent the guiltless, accusing their more peaceful brothers of cowardice and uncooperativeness. Furthermore, continued sexual relations between some of the brothers would disturb the equality among them all. It would be feared that lovers were collaborating against the others (as Mehevi fears the erotic attraction of Tommo and Marnoo). Especially at the early stages of the brother clan, such real or imagined factionalism would threaten the harmony of the tribe. Finally, since the tyrannical father had forced his sons into homosexual activity by forbidding them access to his harem, the sons would tend to scorn such activities once they had liberated themselves from the father's rule. The sons would not entirely renounce homosexual relations—the very nature of the brother clan was, according to Freud, "based upon the homo-sexual feelings" that originally unified them—but once they had overthrown the father, such relations would be viewed as a remnant of their father's oppression and symbolize *not* the sons' equality, but their subservience. Thus while the homosocial component of the brothers' original fellowship was necessary for the success of the brother clan, actual homosexual activity had to be either limited to specific occasions, places, or classes of men or else banned completely. David F. Greenberg presents the process most succinctly as his anthropological principle: "If men are accustomed to compete with one another for status, and conceive of sex in terms of domination, then egalitarian relations must be asexual if they are to continue" (72).

Freud's scenario helps to explain why the taboo on homosexual relations is as varied as totemic taboos though not as harsh as the ones on incest. Homosexuality does not pose the political or psychological threat that incest poses to the brother clan. Its dangers may be handled in several ways whereas exogamy appears to be the only restraint on fraternal rivalry for control of the harem. After all, male homosexual activity itself does not cut down the ability of the clan to maintain its population (Greenberg, 10). More important, the exclusively homosexual man is not an economic threat to the heterosexual. Up to and throughout the eighteenth century, the childless man was at a relative economic disadvantage because he was without the free labor for farming, hunting, and protection that children provided. Indeed the economic disincentive of exclusive homosexuality may be one of the reasons it appears so rarely in preindustrial society. Only after industrialization do children become an economic burden because of their sustained economic dependence. Unsurprisingly systematic oppression of homosexuals began when men without children became an economic threat to those who had them.

Freud provides yet another way to view Tommo's anxiety about cannibalism. Freud's scenario of the defeat of the father horde may be broken down into three major phases: (1) the phase of brotherly homosexuality during banishment, (2) the murder and cannibalization of the father, and (3) the assertion of heterosexuality among the brothers and the imposition of the incest and totemic taboos. For Freud, cannibalism (at least of the father) is inconsistent with sexual relations between male equals. Indeed, it is the "memorable, criminal act" of eating the father which ushers in the period of general heterosexuality. As a member of the patriarchy, Tommo regards unmediated homosexual relations as a regression to a more primitive state. Equality between homosexual males seems to require moving through a cannibalistic phase—a rite of passage which the "poor European" rarely survives.

Speculation on the social organization of the primal horde is a notoriously inviting and slippery subject. With no way to prove or disprove any hypothesis, such speculation becomes an easy target for the projection of one's personal values. But that is also its chief attraction, and we have seen how attractive it was to such diverse thinkers as Bachofen, Morgan, Engels, and Carpenter. Much of the value of Freud's scenario lies not in whether it corresponds to the reality of those lost ages of prehistory—as such his theory would ever be subject to doubt—but in providing a window on how homosexuality and taboos against homosexuality fit into twentieth-century views of human history, in short, on how we make sense of and come to represent ourselves to ourselves. The narrative he tells satisfies us insofar as it embodies a useful way of conceptualizing and extending our already existing sense of society and sexuality, and as it provides lines for the further development of gay representation.

Tennessee Williams's "Suddenly Last Summer" brings together Freud and Melville in yet another work that explores homosexuality, cannibalism, and social equality. According to Williams, the play was produced immediately after he had undergone "a term of Freudian analysis" with Dr. Laurence Kubie (*Memoirs,* 175). He described his sessions as the "mistake of strict Freudian analysis," since as Williams wrote in his *Memoirs,* Kubie taught him "much about my true nature but . . . offered me no solution except . . . a thing that was quite untenable as a solution" (173). The equally ineffectual character, the psychiatrist Dr. Cukrowicz, may well be based on Dr. Kubie. Melville appears even more overtly in the text. Not only is Melville referred to by name, but his description of the Encantadas, the islands where Sebastian and Violet witness the attack of flesh-eating birds on the innocent sea turtles, is quoted at some length (116–18). In a play whose setting Williams describes as "surrealistic as the decor of a dramatic ballet" (113), these references locate the play's intellectual coordinates. In "Suddenly Last Summer," as in so many of his plays, Williams continues the critique of the "primitive" and the "civilized" which stands at the heart of Melville's early fiction and Freud's anthropological speculations. An angry and vengeful God—not unlike the father of Freud's primal horde or the Puritanical diety who figures in Melville's fiction—rules the universe of Violet and Sebastian Venable. And as both Freud and Melville do, Williams represents homosexuality as a respectful accommodation to the father and a rebellion against his tyrannical rule.

The Oedipal relationship between Sebastian and his mother is brushed in with extremely broad strokes. Sebastian completely replaces his father as the object of his mother's affections. She prefers to stay with her son even as she receives frantic telegrams of her husband's imminent death (120). Just as Sebastian cannibalizes his father's place, he also ingests his father's evils: Sebastian is a parody of the "ugly American," using wealth and power to satisfy his narcissistic needs and to maintain control over others.

Sebastian has inherited from his parents a belief in the social Darwinism underpinning free-market capitalism. As Catharine tells Dr. Cukrowicz, "We all use each other and that's what we think of as love, and not being able to use each other is what's—*hate*" (142, Williams's italics). Sebastian pretends to an entirely laissez-faire attitude toward life. According to Catharine he "thought nobody had any right to complain or interfere in any way whatsoever, and even though he knew that what was awful was awful, that what was wrong was wrong. . . . he thought it unfitting to ever take any action about anything whatsoever" (156). Yet, when the crowds become too threatening, he pays the restaurant staff to chase the hungry children away (157). The shift is fundamental, for "this was the first time that [he] had ever attempted to correct a human situation" (157).

In claiming control not only of his mother, but of Catharine, his father's niece, Sebastian establishes around himself something like the father horde's female harem and excites the jealousy of unattached males whom he can then manipulate sexually. The events of the summer sound remarkably like Freud's recreation of the sons' revolt against the father. Having grown old and weak—Sebastian is forty and developing heart problems—he can no longer exercise with impunity his power over the poor, who rise up and cannibalize him. Yet, vital differences exist between Freud's and Sebastian's scenario. Freud's primal father is heterosexual; he does not need his sons who are his enemies. Sebastian is homosexual and does not need his harem except as a means of trapping eligible young men, who are his object.

In these events, Sebastian's homosexuality plays a central, if ambiguous, role. Sebastian's purchase of sexual partners appears to be the ultimate expression of capitalism's decadence and corruption. But as such, it differs only in degree, not in kind, from heterosexuality—or at least the heterosexuality formed under capitalism. Sebastian's exploitation of the young men and children of Cabeza de Lobo is, in fact, achieved through his exploitation of Catharine and his mother as "procuresses" of males, and as such his actions are no worse than the rich young husband who seduces Catharine at Duelling Oaks and afterwards tells her "we'd better forget it . . . my wife's expecting a child" (144). Both hetero- and homosexual love are consuming passions on a par with the capitalist's passion to consume. The objectifying terms in which Sebastian regards his sexual male partners do not differ from the way heterosexual males often regard their female contacts:

> Cousin Sebastian said he was famished for blonds, he was fed-up with dark ones and was famished for blonds. All the travel brochures he picked up were advertisements of the blond northern countries. . . . Fed-up with dark ones, famished for light ones: That's how he talked about people, as if they were—items on a menu.—"That one's delicious-looking, that one is appetizing," or "that one is *not* appetizing"—I think because he was half starved from living on pills and salad. (130)

The cannibalism of his desires could as well be heterosexual as homosexual, for it is the color of hair and not the sex of people that distinguish them. Civilized men of capital—like the English of Swift's "A Modest Proposal"—cannibalize metaphorically the primitive in an unending need to maintain control over a world always on the brink of corruption.

If homosexuality is just one more of the perversions of civilizations, it is also the source of Sebastian's salvation. According to Catharine, he felt he had to make himself into a sacrifice to a terrible, cruel god (145), and his submission to the crowd, who has come to know him because of his sexual profligacy, carried out under the "great white bone of a giant beast that had caught on fire in the sky" seems as close to the beatific as is possible in Williams's cosmos (158). Moreover homosexual desire drives Sebastian across the social and class boundaries clearly marked in "Suddenly Last Summer" not just by Mrs. Venable's treatment of her in-laws or of her servant Foxhill, but by the literal wall that separates the "free" public from the private beaches in San Sebastian or by the wall at the restaurant that separates the feasting rich Americans from the starving masses (131). By seeking situations that at once dissolve and recognize class and racial boundaries, Sebastian reenacts Christ's love for the poor. Sebastian's final meal—his last supper, so to speak—is spent not in a posh restaurant, but in some cheap fish house, which though cheap is still too dear for the starving, penniless masses who live around it. Out on the street, Sebastian does not take Catharine's advice to go down to the harbor in imitation of the sea-turtles who find momentary safety from the flesh-eating birds (Catharine describes the children as "a flock of black plucked little birds") by entering the sea; rather, he goes up the mountain to the sounds of a brass band as though participating in some Latin Quarter funeral (158). When Catharine finally sees Sebastian after his attack he looks "like a big white-paper-wrapped bunch of red roses" (159). Though Sebastian resists his martyrdom and scorns the hungry, his homosexual desires draw him to the poor who transform him in ghastly communion: he has moved through hell to become the paradisal vision of the rose.

In Williams's other work that deals with cannibalism, the short story "Desire and the Black Masseur," homosexuality again leads the hero—if one may call either Sebastian or Anthony Burns a hero—to make his ultimate sacrifice for the injustices of the powerful, "civilized," Father. The sainted Anthony of the story burns with a desire that "swallowed him up," the desire for "atonement, the surrender of self to violent treatment by others with the idea of thereby clearing one's self of his guilt" (206). He falls in love with a black masseur who "was the natural instrument of" Anthony's atonement because by pounding his fist on Anthony's body, the giant black masseur was able to assuage his own abused pride (209). In the end the giant "devour[s] the body of Burns" and achieves momentary absolution (211). For Williams, the homosexual is sainted in two ways: first, like Christ he suffers the scorn of society for the sake of the love he bears for man, and second, because he pursues love not for what it might produce, but for itself alone.

In "Desire and the Black Masseur" cannibalism is both a cleansing act of reparations for the social injustices whites have perpetrated against blacks and an instrument of achieving egalitarian assimilation. Anthony's guilt is only partially guilt for his sexual attraction to men; more important is the original sin of all American white men—their traditional exploitation of blacks. Though Anthony Burns more explicitly gives himself up to martyrdom by loving and embracing his executioner, Sebastian pursues death and achieves through it the spiritual apotheosis for which he had been searching. Instead of acting like the father—selfishly hoarding the fruits of his productivity—the gay son sacrifices himself to his oppressed brothers, if not to achieve social and sexual equality, at least to pay reparations for the injustices of the father.

Like Melville, Williams believes that an egalitarian relation between so-called civilized men and their primitive brothers can be achieved only through an act of cannibalism in which the civilized will be consumed. Melville attempts to escape such relationships out of fear. Williams submits to them, and consequently finds himself speaking a truth that provided relief neither for himself, nor for those who came to hear him.

If Williams found the twin lines of homosexual egalitarianism and cannibal communion so hard to hold that he knotted them into short, lyric pieces of fiction and drama, Tobias Schneebaum has found them so difficult to put down that he has spun them across the three parts of his autobiographical trilogy, weaving them between the jungles of eastern Peru and the swampy villages of south-central New Guinea. Unlike Williams, Schneebaum not only survived among cannibals, but found in their presence a love and community, a sense of personal centeredness that he was unable to find in "civilized" society.

Like *Typee* and other gay works, Schneebaum's autobiographies fall between generic categories. *Keep the River to Your Right,* while it purports to be factual and anthropologically correct, is best read as a spiritual journey, and Schneebaum carefully orchestrates the work within the artifice of a journal letter to place it within its literary and religious context.

The books record Schneebaum's search for three conditions: (1) an individual whom he can love and who can love him in return as an equal, (2) a community that will accept him and his sexual orientation and with whom he can feel part, and (3) a spiritual state of integration with people and the world. Schneebaum recognizes he cannot find these three conditions in supposedly "civilized" culture. As a Jew, he will always feel on the margins of Christian society (especially since his notions of the Western tradition come from T. S. Eliot); as a homosexual he feels estranged from the orthodox Jewish community in which he has been raised; and as a twentieth-century New Yorker, he has lost contact with Whitmanian unity in the physical and spiritual universe. If "civilized" society does not hold promise of achieving these three conditions of life, perhaps "primitive" life will provide them.

Schneebaum approaches the "primitive" with very different expectations from either Melville or Williams. Melville and Williams have the "primitive" world forced upon them, while Schneebaum has gone out of his way to seek it out. "I came into a jungle," he explains, "to live a new incarnation" (181). Unlike Williams's Sebastian who is a kind of "ugly American," rich, powerful, Euro-centered, and self-centered, Schneebaum is already alienated or banished from the cultures that might have given him a sense of belonging. Unlike Tommo and Sebastian who fear the equality they desire, Schneebaum is hungry—and I use the metaphor advisedly—for inclusion into a society of equal males. He wants to be "a part of the family of Man" by becoming a part "of those men with whom I spent such days and nights of love" (181).

Consequently, cannibalism comes to have a different meaning for Schneebaum than for Williams or Melville. Like the earlier authors, Schneebaum views cannibalism as an erotic as well as a violent rite of passage by which he can take his place as an equal with other men. But as he comes to understand his own desires and those of the natives around him, cannibalism loses the retributive force it has for Williams and the fearful self-destructiveness it has for Melville. Indeed, for Schneebaum, cannibalism becomes an act or communion by which the gay man is fully constituted in his love for another. In *Keep the River,* Manolo, a lay missionary, tells Schneebaum: "I wanted you in possession, ownership. I wanted you to give yourself to me in a way, to such an extent, that I could even go so far as to eat you while you watched me do it" (151). At the end of *Where the Spirits Dwell,* Schneebaum imagines himself at Yaddo, the artists' retreat, having a cannibal feast with his Asmat lover Akatpitsjin eating Janet Frame, Georgina—"a painter of renown," and "the hand of Paul . . . a fine writer," in order to incorporate their powers into himself (202–3). Schneebaum focuses not on cannibalism's violence, but on its creative, self-constituting elements; it becomes for him a metaphor for adult nurturing.

Keep the River, the first and most famous of the volumes, takes place in 1955 in Peru, where Schneebaum studies on a Fulbright Fellowship. He later visits a remote mission on the eastern side of the Andes, then a village of the Akaramas, a cannibalistic tribe in the rain forests of the extreme western edge of the Amazon plain. *Where the Spirits Dwell,* the final volume of the trilogy, concerns his travels nearly twenty years later among the Asmat tribes in south-central New Guinea. The shift in locale corresponds to the shift in Schneebaum's conception of cannibalism from an act of destruction to an act of creation, from a form of retribution to a form of conciliation, from an actuality to a metaphor.

Schneebaum's shift is accelerated by his recognition that the Akaramas do not like to view people as individuals or individuals as valuable. Their indifference to individuality manifests itself subtly in at least three ways—their paternal behavior, their sexual expression, and their attitudes toward the dead and dying. In *Keep the River*, when Michii, one of Schneebaum's closest Akarama companions, fathers a child "he gave no sign of pride or pleasure" upon seeing it. "Though the mother and child were no more than ten feet away," Schneebaum comments with some distress, "he made no move to them" (86). That night, as Schneebaum lies in a sleeping pile with Michii and the other men of his compartment in the long house in which the entire village live, he comments on the lack of connection: "We live apart here, the men and the women. There are children and pregnancies. Yet in the middle of the night no one moves from his partition to seek out a partner. A partner is there next to you, arms and legs around you" (86). What Schneebaum had at first interpreted as the communal closeness of the long house, he now sees as being "apart" and indifferent. A man's erotic partner is not a particular person sought for intimacy, but the body in closest proximity, and not even the entire body is sought— a part will suffice. The metaphoric dismemberment of the passage prefigures the cannibal raid executed by his partition-mates, a raid that ends in a drunken orgy of eating their victims' remains and with Michii sodomizing his friend Darinimbiak, each growling with bestial delight. For a man who came to the jungle to find connectedness and wholeness, the Akaramas' indifference to individuality—even though it creates a certain equality—is disturbing, but for a man with Schneebaum's romantic needs, it constituted an insurmountable barrier.

Schneebaum becomes increasingly critical of Akaraman indifference during Darinimbiak's slow death from dysentery. Schneebaum, who had fallen in love with Darinimbiak, takes special care of his friend, but their other close companions act as though "he were not there among [them] or as if he had already gone to some forest" (129). Sadly and angrily, Schneebaum reports "Not Michii, or Baaldore or Ihuene or Reindude seemed to have him on their minds" (129). Nor is Schneebaum comforted with the chief's suggestion that Schneebaum overcome his grief by fathering a child, for the suggestion is premised on the beliefs not only that one life is as good as another, but also that all men are capable of having sex with women (172).

Unlike the Akaramas, the Asmats and the Asmat native, Akatpitsjin, with whom Schneebaum falls in love, have had contact with missionaries who have convinced most Asmat to stop intertribal wars, cannibalism, and wife-swapping. Luckily for Schneebaum, the missionaries have not put an end to the practice of *mbai*, or exchange friend. *Mbai* choose one another, usually in early childhood, and become life-long companions. They have sex with one another and exchange tribal responsibilities, food, work, and—in the past—wives. For Schneebaum, becoming a *mbai* subsumes the equality, communion, and belonging that he hoped to achieve in cannibalistic acts.

As presented by Schneebaum in *Where the Spirits Dwell, mbai* practices are a clear sublimation of cannibalistic desires. He describes a ritual called *mbi urum* that occurs when villages try to make peace with one another or as in Schneebaum's case, when a village wishes to make a stranger part of the community (189–90). The outsider is raised above the males of the village and then sucked all over as he is passed around. As Akatpitsjin explains, "When we suck on your chin and nose and penis and fingers, we take in some of your spirit with the waters of your body. This makes us strong and calms the spirits of the dead" (190). The Asmat perform a metaphoric cannibalization to forestall further violence.

This concern for the lives of individuals is reflected in their tenderness toward children. Akatpitsjin is an especially attentive father, who likes to feed both his male and female infant children (191). He is also the most considerate of lovers. Like a good *mbai,* he wishes to share his wife with his exchange friend. But when Akatpitsjin discovers that Schneebaum was "incapable of intercourse with *her,*" he exchanges places with Schneebaum and becomes Schneebaum's "proxy" (101). They enact not a mere substitution of one person for another as the Akarama chief had meant when he told Schneebaum to father a child, but an exchange that symbolically bridges and respects the differences between individuals.

Perhaps the central difference between the Asmat and the Akaramas is the Asmat notion of balance. During one of their nights together, Akatpitsjin declares, "I want balance." When Schneebaum indicates that he doesn't understand what Akatpitsjin means, Akatpitsjin "turned me around so that we reversed positions and he was on top. It was a startling moment, full of implications I could not then begin to think about" (192). Akatpitsjin insists that exchange friends exchange everything including their sexual roles. He forces Schneebaum—ever so gently—to give up the inserter role to become the receptor. It is Schneebaum's last lesson in egalitarian erotics.

Nearly twenty years after going into the Peruvian jungle, Schneebaum finds in his relationship with Akatpitsjin the values he was searching for.

It was [Akatpitsjin] who was the instigator, the one who moved me to new levels. It was he who induced me into adulthood, as if he were my mother's brother, my father. It was he who announced to one and all that I was his *mbai,* that I was related to him, as all others had such relations. It was he who provoked me into a new world by saying, "I must balance," and it was he who completed my initiation by taking me to his wife, even though I failed and he consummated the act in my place. (203)

He has a lover who returns his love, a community that accepts and values him despite his peculiarities, a feeling of unity with nature and a sense of belonging he had never felt before.

If the end of Schneebaum's search sounds triumphant—and Schneebaum certainly intends it to—let me voice my own reservations. His triumph of egalitarianism is achieved without any reference to women, who appear rarely and then as merely passive ciphers. In general the homosexual cannibalism trope is an all-male fantasy. Moreover, the trope appeals to gay writers who are still trying to free themselves from the stigmas of heterosexual discourse. Its major appeals are that the trope illustrates the "naturalness" of homosexuality by placing male-male love within the domain of the primitive, and the "masculinity" of the homosexual since cannibals escape the charge of effeminacy. Schneebaum's extreme anxiety about assuming the anal receptor role is of a piece with his refusal in *Keep the River* explicitly to acknowledge his homosexuality. Like Mishima, he finds it easier to be a cannibal than a queer.

The intersection of homosexuality and cannibalism began as a theme used to represent sodomy as horrible, "unnatural," and demonic. So terrible was the image it created that Melville comes to fear the very people he most desired. In Tennessee Williams it becomes part of the metaphorical cross homosexuals have to bear, and which by confronting—even to their own destruction—they achieve a grace which would otherwise be excluded from them. Finally, in Tobias Schneebaum's autobiographical trilogy, the trope of cannibalism is transformed into one of balanced exchange, a total mutuality that establishes rather than destroys the participants as individuals and extends rather than cuts off their human possibilities. Schneebaum has replaced the sword of retribution with the scales of justice and the blood of vengeance with the semen of affection. He has transformed the charge of sodomic cannibalism into the vision of gay communion.

The association of homosexuality and cannibalism provides us with a particularly good case of the gay transformation of heterosexual representation. Introduced by heterosexual theologians as a way to increase the horror of sodomy, the association was explored by successive generations of homosexual writers, who transformed it slowly, and with increasing skill, to reflect the ideals of homosexual love and affection. This process of transformation did not occur in isolation; it paralleled changes in Western views of both sexuality and the primitive. By interacting with these more general cultural changes, gay writers have transformed a representation that had been used to oppress them into one that in large measure is self-affirming. By such transformations, gay writers are proving to themselves and to the culture around them that they will no longer passively accept the dominant culture's representations, but actively develop their own.

9

The Agony of Gay Black Literature

ELDRIDGE Cleaver's attack on James Baldwin in *Soul on Ice* was, according to Baldwin's biographer W. J. Weatherby, extremely "important to Baldwin's development" and "helped to shape [Baldwin's] racial attitudes in middle age." It came "like a slap in the face bringing Baldwin to attention, making him reexamine his own situation" (334). At a distance of more than twenty years, Cleaver's "Notes on a Native Son" still seems a remarkable, forceful, but, in its way, perverse response to Baldwin, and one that functions to highlight the problem gay black authors face in writing gay black literature. Cleaver discredits Baldwin as a black writer, not because he ignores black issues, but because he is homosexual.

Cleaver begins respectfully enough. "After reading a couple of James Baldwin's books," he remembers like a latter-day Keats dipping into Chapman's Homer, "that continuous delight one feels upon discovering a fascinating, brilliant talent on the scene, a talent capable of penetrating so profoundly into one's own little world that one knows oneself to have been unalterably changed and liberated" (97). In a gesture of both humility and subservience, he imagines the pleasure of sitting "on a pillow beneath the womb of Baldwin's typewriter and catch[ing] each newborn page as it entered this world of ours" (97). But such obstetric fantasies do not last long, and the sex-change that this fantasy signals soon becomes "the racial death-wish" of "many

163

Negro homosexuals," who "unable to have a baby by a white man. . . . the little half-white offspring of their dreams . . . redouble their efforts and intake of the white man's sperm" (102). Cleaver's sympathy and appreciation is hampered and finally erased by Baldwin's "decisive quirk . . . which corresponds to his relationship to black people and to masculinity" (105); in short, Cleaver rejects Baldwin as homosexual, because as homosexual, Baldwin must be antiblack.

Although remarkably simple, Cleaver's sexual politics are central to his work. He argues that slavery has made the black man into "a black eunuch" who has "completely submitted to the white man" (107). Thus, all black people, both male and female, must help black men retrieve their masculinity. In "To All Black Women, From All Black Men," the concluding essay in *Soul on Ice,* Cleaver sees the black male crossing "the naked abyss of negated masculinity," afraid to look black women in the face because he might "find reflected there a merciless Indictment of my impotence and a compelling challenge to redeem my conquered manhood" (206). He, then, bids the Queen-Mother-Daughter of Africa, the Black Bride of His Passion: "Let me drink from the river of your love at its source, let the lines of force of your love seize my soul by its core and heal the wound of my Castration, let my convex exile end its haunted Odyssey in your concave essence which receives that it may give" (207).

In such a Freudian-charged atmosphere, it is no wonder that gay men threaten Cleaver. Uncertain of his own masculinity, he lashes out at what he fears he might himself be. Cleaver's paranoic anxieties are particularly excited by Baldwin's critique of racial anger, Cleaver's principal tool for rebuilding the edifice of black masculinity. When Baldwin comments that in Richard Wright's books "violence sits enthroned where sex should be" (108), Cleaver accuses Baldwin of engaging in a "despicable underground guerrilla war, waged on paper, against black masculinity" (109), and he defends Wright's characters on the grounds that though "shackled with a form of impotence, [they] were strongly heterosexual" (106).

Cleaver was not the only critic who had difficulty appreciating Baldwin's work because of his depiction of homosexuality. The white critic, Robert A. Bone also argued that Baldwin's homosexual viewpoint invalidated his art: "Few will concede a sense of reality, at least in the sexual realm, to one who regards heterosexual love as 'a kind of superior calisthenics.' To most, homosexuality will seem rather an evasion than an affirmation of human truth. Ostensibly the novel summons us to reality. Actually it substitutes for the illusions of white supremacy those of homosexual love" (283). I am uncertain what Bone really means in this crucial passage besides the fact that he thinks that writers who depict explicitly homosexual characters as good people are placing themselves beyond the pale of heterosexual sympathy, appreciation, and understanding. But I am not at all sure how such a depiction is "an evasion . . . of human truth." Does Bone mean homosexuals don't exist? Do not feel love? Are utterly deluded? Nor can I explain how "homosexual love" is a substitute for "white supremacy." But I don't want to leave the impression that Bone is the extremist and Cleaver the moderate. Toward the end of his essay, Cleaver pronounces: "Homosexuality is a sickness, just as are baby-rape or wanting to become the head of General Motors" (110). What is clear is that in the feverish atmosphere of the sixties, Baldwin's depiction of homosexuals disturbed both white and black readers and excited rather extreme examples of homophobia.

But in calling Baldwin's works homosexual, I am distorting them. Baldwin is careful to make all his characters bisexual: David and Giovanni; Rufus, Vivaldo, and Eric; Leo and Christopher; Crunch, Arthur, and Jimmy are never depicted as "faggots," by which Baldwin means exclusively and effeminately homosexual. Even in the case of *Just Above My Head,* in which Arthur Montana is never shown in any sexual relation with a woman, we are assured in the beginning that although "Arthur slept with a lot of people—mostly men," they were "not always" men, and although "he was a whole lot of things, he was nobody's faggot" (36–37). In fact, despite Bone's and Cleaver's assertions that Baldwin elevated homosexuality, gay black men such as Samuel Delany found his portraits far from affirming (Delany and Beam, "Possibilities," 196).

Even as late as 1984, Baldwin spoke of his discomfort with the term "gay." Asked if he felt "like a stranger in gay America," Baldwin answered: "Well, first of all I feel like a stranger in America from almost every conceivable angle except, oddly enough, as a black person. The word 'gay' has always rubbed me the wrong way. . . . I simply feel it's a world that has very little to do with me, with where I did my growing up. I was never at home in it" (Goldstein, 174). Moreover, he steers readers away from specifically gay interpretations of his work. He told Richard Goldstein, "*Giovanni* is not really about homosexuality. It's about what happens to you if you're afraid to love anybody. Which is much more interesting than the question of homosexuality"

(176). Though I understand and sympathize with Baldwin's desire to "universalize" the themes of his novels, I also feel that he is dulling their edge. For *Giovanni's Room* is not about just any obstacle to love, but quite specifically about internalized homophobia. To see it in any other way risks turning the novel into "a little morality play in modern dress, in which the characters tend to be allegorical," what Leslie Fiedler said of it in one of the novel's original reviews (147–48). Two of *Giovanni's Room*'s strengths are the realism and the historical precision of its sentiments and attitudes, for the novella makes sense only in a culture in which homosexual relations are relegated exclusively to the demimonde. As Claude Summers accurately states, "It reflects in its ambiguities the homophobic tenor of the Eisenhower years even as it challenges those assumptions" (174).

I cannot say to what extent Baldwin's resistance to calling himself gay or to reading his works within a gay context is an assertion of his personal beliefs or the result of homophobia in both the black and white communities. But after Cleaver's attack, Baldwin emphasized racial much more than sexual issues. To Goldstein, he stated, "The sexual question comes after the color question. It is simply one more aspect of the danger in which all black people live" (180). When sexual issues arise—as in the dialogue with Nikki Giovanni—Baldwin defends the male heterosexist position against Giovanni's black feminist criticism. Baldwin, however, admits that the homosexual theme in his writing threatened his career in ways the black theme did not. It lost him his first publisher, Alfred A. Knopf (Weatherby, 135), and by his own admission, "a certain audience . . . I wasn't supposed to alienate" (Goldstein, 177).

Baldwin does admit to a certain amount of fag baiting among blacks, but contends it is less than among whites. Asked if people ever called him "faggot" in Harlem, he answered: "Of course. But there's a difference in the way it's used. It's got less venom, at least in my experience. I don't know anyone who has ever denied his brother or his sister because they were gay. . . . a black person has got quite a lot to get through the day without getting entangled in all the American fantasies" (Goldstein, 179). Yet other accounts, even in his own fiction, suggest that gay black men are seriously oppressed by the black community. In an interview, Blackberri, a gay singer, remembers "the magic summer" of his teenage years in Baltimore when he fell in love with the boy "up the street." "We sat on the steps and talked all night long. He'd have his head in my lap, and we'd sit there until the sun came up." But when people saw them holding hands, "all hell broke loose. Lots of verbal attacks, people throwing rocks at us, being chased and stuff" (Branner, 172). The late Joseph Beam reflects in his essay "Brother to Brother" that the "fiery anger" that blazes as a result of racism "is stoked additionally with the fuels of contempt and despisal shown me by my community because I am gay. *I cannot go home as who I am*" (231, Beam's italics). So violent is the black reaction to homosexuality that even Cleaver deplores it as a scapegoating mechanism "not unrelated . . . to the ritualistic lynchings and castrations inflicted on Southern blacks by Southern whites" (106). Yet he admits that this "classic, if cruel . . . practice by Negro youths of going 'punk-hunting,' . . . seeking out homosexuals on the prowl, rolling them, beating them up" is not limited to the South but "a ubiquitous phenomenon in the black ghettos of America" (106).

Max C. Smith argues that homosexual African-Americans have developed two basic strategies to cope with homophobia in the black community: they become, in his words, either "Black gays" or "Gay Blacks" (226). "Gay Blacks are people who usually live outside the closet in predominantly white gay communities." Smith estimates they make up only 10 percent of all Black homosexuals. The vast majority are Black gays who, according to Smith, "are so strongly into our African-American identity that we would rather die than be honest enough with our homosexuality to deal with it openly" (227). Homosexual African-Americans, according to Smith, must choose between identifying themselves as gay or black; they cannot be both. As A. Billy S. Jones, whose own father was gay and advised his son "to be tough, to be discreet, to marry, and to have children" (144), laments: "The means by which we cope with our Blackness in mainstream America does not give us the means for coping with our gayness. Just because Black Americans have a history of being discriminated against, of being victims of institutionalized racism, does not automatically free us from other forms of prejudice nor give us an understanding of the oppressions and injustices waged against others—even other Black gays." In fact, Jones finds, "a strong sense of Black nationalism or separatism, which often does not embrace homosexuality, will give some of my children's peers enough reason to make their lives miserable" (150).

Throughout his career Baldwin insisted that homosexuality is a private matter and best kept away from public view. Although Baldwin took this position before Cleaver's attack, he held more tightly to it afterwards. Baldwin's analysis of sexuality stands in contrast to his analysis of race. Racial power relations, he argues, are not private matters, but are reflected in social institutions. One would think the same analysis would hold true for sexual power relations. Since for Baldwin "the sexual question and the racial question have always been entwined," it makes no sense to declare the former a private matter and the latter a public one (Goldstein, 178). Yet in 1954, he wrote that Gide's "homosexuality . . . was his own affair which he should have kept hidden from us" (*Ticket,* 102), and thirty years later he averred: "It seems to me simply a man is a man, a woman is a woman, and who [sic] they go to bed with is nobody's business but theirs. . . . that one's sexual preference is a private matter" (Goldstein, 183). In his last book, *The Evidence of Things Not Seen,* a jumbled account of the Atlanta child murder cases, he repeats speculation that Wayne Williams's motive for the murders—and Baldwin is uncertain of Williams's guilt —was to get back at his father, who frustrated over losing his job as a teacher, had "sodomized the son" (72). Nevertheless Baldwin castigates Williams's defense counsel for not finding a way to prevent "the question of homosexuality from being raised at all" since none of "the crimes for which Wayne Williams had been arrested . . . were classed as sexual crimes" (109). Yet even Baldwin admits that "a great deal" of the nonsexual classification of those crimes "depends on what one makes of the word, *sexual,*" since the bodies of the boys were found naked (75, Baldwin's italics). In short, Baldwin addresses the homosexual nature of the motive and the murders only briefly, and when he does, his contradictory stances show his discomfort.

Yet another measure of Baldwin's discomfort with the subject is that in all his voluminous nonfiction writing, only one short piece centers on homosexuality. This is his 1954 review of Gide's *Madeleine,* which while written at the same time as most of the articles published in *Notes of a Native Son,* was not reprinted until *Nobody Knows My Name.* Baldwin addresses sex between men almost exclusively in his novels, and in this one essay hardly articulates the belief that Cleaver accuses him of asserting, "that there is something intrinsically superior in homosexuality" (110).

To the contrary, in "The Male Prison" Baldwin writes: "The two things which contribute most heavily to my dislike of Gide were his Protestantism and his homosexuality," two of the attributes Baldwin held in common with him (*Ticket,* 101). What Baldwin found objectionable was not Protestantism and homosexuality considered separately, but the way they interacted in Gide's sensibility, since the battle between his sex and his religion limited Gide's capacity to be, "in the best sense of that kaleidoscopic word—a man" (103). In Baldwin's view, Gide's Protestantism forced him to separate erotic love, which in Gide's case was homosexual, from spiritual love, which for Gide took the form of a heterosexual love for Madeleine. Because Madeleine was his wife, Gide always felt guilty for failing to perform sexually while retaining her as a spiritual object. Yet because he preserved Madeleine as a spiritual ideal, Gide could minimize his homosexual guilt. As a result, Baldwin finds that Gide's "Heaven and Hell suffer from a certain lack of urgency" (104).

Baldwin's real objection is not that Protestantism and homosexuality are opposed, but that for Gide they so cunningly work together to exaggerate Protestantism's gynophobia and asceticism. Because Gide can so easily retain Madeleine as a nonsexual, spiritual object, he never has to perform the difficult task of loving someone both physically and spiritually. And yet, by making Madeleine his *wife* and thus retaining the possibility of heterosexuality—and here Baldwin exhibits his much-admired subtlety and complexity—Gide keeps open "a kind of door of hope, of possibility, the possibility of entering communion with another sex" (105). Baldwin praises Gide insofar as Gide entertains the possibility of heterosexuality and resists the Puritanism of his Protestantism, but he criticizes Gide for relenting too easily to the narcissism of homosexuality and the self-righteousness of Protestant self-sacrifice.

Baldwin ends his review with a paean to heterosexuality. Only heterosexuality can prevent Protestantism from falling into its latent homosexual asceticism, gnosticism, and narcissism. Only it can keep Protestantism from dividing the spiritual from the sexual: "When men can no longer love women," Baldwin writes, "they also cease to love or respect or trust each other, which makes their isolation complete. Nothing is more dangerous than this isolation, for men will commit any crime whatever rather than endure it" (105).

Although he does not mention bisexuality, one can see why it becomes so important to Baldwin: a homosexuality derived from a fear of the other sex, or a heterosexuality derived from a contempt of one's own are merely different forms of racism. Consequently, Baldwin sees Gide's prison as "not very different from the prison inhabited by, say, the heroes of Mickey Spillane" (105). Both the homosexual and the ultra-macho heterosexual are ruled by the need to control and contain their fears and contempt. Without such clear controls, when they find themselves "in a region where there is no definition of any kind, neither of color, nor of male and female," they feel as Vivaldo does in *Another Country,* "only the leap and the rending and the terror and the surrender" (255). Cleaver views Baldwin's critique of the reaction formation of machismo as an attack on black manhood and as an assertion of gay superiority. But the target of Baldwin's attack is the rigid exclusivity of either sexual orientation, which he maintains is an "artificial division" and "a Western sickness" that limits "the capacity for experience" (Goldstein, 182).

Baldwin's attitude toward Protestantism is extremely complicated, and as his article on Gide makes clear, it is inextricably tied to his attitudes toward sexuality. Insofar as Protestantism is Puritanical and polarizes concepts into a simple dualism—good from bad, spiritual from physical, heterosexual from homosexual, man from woman—it is destructive. But insofar as Protestantism breaks down these categorical barriers and teaches the need for love, understanding, and empathy, it is a source of enormous good. A world without religion disintegrates into the tyranny of narcissism, but a theocratic society soon becomes hypocritical, brutal, and self righteous.

The conflicts between religion and sexuality are central to Baldwin's early short story, "The Outing," included in *Going to Meet the Man.* "The Outing" tells of the Mount of Olives Pentecostal Assembly's boat trip to Bear Mountain one fourth of July. On board the little steamer, Father James gives a sermon whose effect is so intense that the congregation "might have mounted with wings like eagles far past the sordid persistence of the flesh, the depthless iniquity of the heart, the doom of hours and days and weeks; to be received by the Bridegroom where he waited on high in glory" (35). Baldwin's strategy in "The Outing" is to honor the high rhetoric and rich poetry of Pentecostal homiletics while exposing its hostility to the worldly and bodily. For Baldwin, the outing is a strangely ironic journey into the heart of darkness, since for the Assembly there is little difference between the Congo and the Hudson: "On the open deck sinners stood and watched, beyond them the fiery sun and the deep river, the black-brown-green, unchanging cliffs. The sun, which covered earth and water now, would one day refuse to shine, the river would cease its rushing and its numberless dead would rise; the cliffs would shiver, crack, fall and where they had been would then be nothing but the unleashed wrath of God" (36). For Father James, the Bridegroom's love is indistinguishable from His "unleashed wrath," and the beauty of the Hudson Valley is soon reduced to the wasteland of Armageddon.

Nowhere is the Pentecostal theology more destructive, in Baldwin's view, than in its attitude toward children. On the one hand, people are obliged to follow the divine injunction to be fruitful and multiply. Yet, on the other hand, siring children mires one further in "the sordid persistence of the flesh." Father James's love for his sons—particularly his eldest, Johnnie—is eaten away by the bitterness he feels in acknowledging that they represent his weakness before the "depthless iniquity of the heart." Baldwin's work from first to last is imbued with the deepest devotion to the family; no love can do more good than parental love, but parental hatred is the most destructive hatred of all. In his dialogue with Nikki Giovanni, Baldwin sees the biggest threat to blacks is that "in gaining the world," they may lose "the ability to love their own children" (25–26). In this regard, he has a place in a long line of gay writers whom I discuss in the closing chapter of this book, on family structure in recent gay novels. Baldwin's concern for the binding and healing love of parents (and conversely with the almost unclosable, festering wounds of parental hate) has its sources in his own life. He was the object of his father's violent paranoia, a paranoia whose magnitude required institutionalization. In "The Outing" as well as in another story in *Going to Meet the Man*, "The Rockpile," Baldwin exposes a father's hypocrisy in calling his brutal discipline of a son an act of love.

If the apocalyptic vision of Pentecostalism is inhospitable to nature and harmful to parental love, it is utterly destructive toward homosexual love, no matter how innocent or redemptive. "The Outing" narrates that crucial moment when the childlike love of one boy for another is transformed into the adult awareness of the sinfulness of same-sex affection. In transforming love into sin, the Puritanism of Pentecostalism warps the developing erotic and emotional life of the very children it claims to love and care for. Baldwin's resistance to the Puritanical pressures of Pentecostalism may be gauged by the names he gives the boys—Johnnie and David—names that resonate with biblical significance, alluding to both the beloved apostle and the king whose love for Jonathan "surpassed the love of women."

Baldwin, who was a preacher in his early teens, recalls the guilt and anguish that he felt about his developing homosexual feelings. "It hit me with great force while I was in the pulpit," Baldwin told Richard Goldstein. "I must have been fourteen. I was still a virgin. I had no idea what you were supposed to do about it. . . . Terrors of the flesh. After all, we're supposed to mortify the flesh, a doctrine which has led to untold horrors. This is a very biblical culture; people believe the wages of sin is death" (174–77). In "The Outing," the children must act "as though their youth, barely begun, were already put away." The elders find in the way the children moved, "no matter how careful their movements . . . a pagan lusting beneath the blood-washed robes." The adults "considering [the children] with a baleful kind of love, struggled to bring their souls to safety in order . . . to steal a march on the flesh, while the flesh still slept" (38). In *Just Above My Head* this twisted view of sexuality leads the father to commit incest with his preacher/daughter as a way of consummating a love that has no other outlet. "The Outing" ends with David embracing Johnnie, "but now where there had been peace there was only panic and where there had been safety, danger, like a flower, opened" (47). A religion that hates the flesh and abhors nature is exactly the sort of religion which will sow these particular *fleurs de mal,* and Baldwin abhors Father James as Blake abhorred the gray beadles for "binding with briars our joy and desire" and transforming the Garden of Love into a graveyard.

Many gay black writers have echoed Baldwin's difficulties with the black church. James S. Tinney, who ministers to the nation's first Pentecostal church for black gays, recalls how, in other Pentecostal churches he attended, "the 'holiness or hell' judgment was continually applied to homosexuals" (169). When Tinney informed his wife that he was gay, "she immediately called the pastor and his wife and other close confidants to pray for me. . . . Thus I was once a subject of an attempted exorcism. That in itself was extremely painful to my own sense of worth and well-being" (170). The hypocrisy of Pentecostals toward homosexuality pains Tinney still more. For while it is probably untrue that 70 percent of the Pentecostal congregation is gay—an estimate Tinney has heard—nevertheless, Tinney insists that "if our churches were to instantly get rid of the homosexuals in them, they would cease to remain 'Pentecostalist.' For the gospel choirs and musicians (the mainstay and pivot of our 'liturgy') would certainly disappear" (169). Tinney paints a portrait of an uneasy truce between the strictures of dogma and the demands of reality.

Despite the anti-sexual theme which characterizes much of Pentecostal preaching, a certain practical tolerance . . . exudes itself. The conscious

way in which the presence of homosexuality was recognized (whether approved or not) contributed to a feeling that it was really no worse than
women wearing open-toe shoes or saints missing a mid-week prayer
meeting. In such an atmosphere the mind easily reaches its own conclusions: either the church doesn't take seriously its own preachments or else
homosexuality is as culturally and temporally conditioned as the strictures against wearing red. (120)

But black Pentecostal churches are not alone in assuming this hypocritical attitude toward homosexuality. Leonard Patterson, who
served as an associate minister at the world-famed Ebenezer Baptist
Church in Atlanta, encountered the same experience. He was told, "in
effect, that as long as I played the political game and went with a person [unlike his white lover] who was more easily passed off as a
'cousin,' I would be able to go far in the ministry" (164). When Patterson refused to abandon his white lover, he was "attacked verbally
from the pulpit, forbidden to enter the study for prayer with the other
associate ministers, and had seed of animosity planted against [him] in
the minds of certain members" (165). The poisonous combination of
Protestantism and homosexuality seems not to be limited to Gide's
notebooks, but to extend to black churches as well.

I make this analysis fully aware of the danger Amitai Avi-Ram
warns white readers against falling into, namely, imposing the European Christian opposition of "soul and body or between the sacred
and sexual" on African-American religious beliefs, or conversely, of
"oversexualizing the Afro-American [concept of] 'soul'" in order to
distinguish it more easily from the dualisms of Euro-American theology (37). The very real problem that Avi-Ram locates is one I hope to
avoid. But it seems to me that Baldwin in "The Outing" and Tinney
and Patterson in their essays argue that black churches often themselves lose track of the continuum between body and soul when challenged by homosexuals who refuse to hide their homosexuality, and
that black preachers lapse into such dualism when faced with the
boundless gradations of sexual orientation. Black churches have trouble simultaneously honoring the continuum of sexual responses while
remaining true to the African-American religious beliefs that posit a
continuum of body and soul. And the difficulty of maintaining this
continuum of theological and sexual categories is reflected in Eldridge
Cleaver's response to Baldwin. By calling on "Queen-Mother-Daughter of Africa, Sister of My Soul, Black Bride of My Passion, My Eter-

nal Love" to heal his sexual and spiritual wounds, he exemplifies in secular terms the continuity between body and soul that is the hallmark of African-American theology, yet in his response to Baldwin he lapses into a strict dualism of sexual identity.

The reason these questions about dualisms versus continuums and European Christianity versus African-American theology play themselves out so directly in Pentecostalism is because, according to Tinney, "Historians of religion are pretty well agreed that there are more surviving Africanisms (the drums, the dance, the state of possession, the emphasis on spirits, the ecstatic speech known as tongues, the healing magic, the use of inanimate objects which are blessed and transmit blessing) in Pentecostalism than in any other religion in the diaspora." Thus Pentecostalism is a way not merely of being united with God, but of finding "continuity with the Africanity in my heritage" (169). Indeed as Tinney explains in another essay, "Why a Black Gay Church," one of the more difficult problems faced is how African a black Christian church can be before it descends into paganism (81).

Yet if one's "Africanity" and Christianity may not entirely blend, for Tinney, homosexuality and Africanity are continuous. Max C. Smith insists against the weight of black popular belief that "within some Black African societies homosexuality isn't legally and culturally condemned. The American Blacks' bias against gays is due to our forced socialization into Dixie Christian culture during slavery" (227). Thus gay black Christians wish to bring together their sexuality and their African heritage, and see the Puritanical nature of black Baptist and Pentecostal churches as falsely driving a wedge between black gays and their African heritage.

Eldridge Cleaver keeps his attack on Baldwin from becoming merely a homophobic exercise by situating Baldwin's homosexuality in relation to Africa. Cleaver argues that homosexuality blocks Baldwin's—and by extension, all black homosexuals'—identification with his African origins. The way this argument emerges in Cleaver typifies the breathtaking paradoxes of his thought. According to Cleaver, Norman Mailer is a better example of black manhood than James Baldwin: while Mailer, "the white boy, with knowledge of white Negroes [was] traveling toward a confrontation with the black, with Africa," Baldwin, "the black boy, with a white mind, was on his way to Europe" (105). The gay black men, like their counterpart in the black bourgeoisie—and Cleaver sees the two as identical—have "completely rejected their African heritage, consider the loss irrevocable, and refuse to look again in that direction" (103). For Cleaver the "only way out" of Baldwin's supposed problem of racial and sexual self-hatred, "is psychologically to embrace Africa, the land of his fathers, which [Baldwin] utterly refuses to do" (109). Thus Cleaver locates Baldwin's alleged homosexually warped vision of black culture not in *Giovanni's Room,* which he never mentions, nor in *Another Country,* but in Baldwin's essay "Princes and Powers," an account of the 1956 Conference of Black Writers and Artists, an essay in which sexuality never appears, but in which, according to Cleaver, Baldwin shows "revulsion . . . [for] Negritude and the African Personality" (99). Cleaver's equation of black homosexuality and anti-African sentiments may seem at first odd and strained, but it derives from a long and fascinating line and is perhaps Cleaver's most subtle and telling move in this strangely truculent essay.

This is not the place, nor am I the person, to argue whether homosexuality or other forms of sexual relations exist between men in sub-Sahara Africa. The issue is not, by any means, a literary or academic one. This very question has stymied AIDS researchers exploring routes of HIV transmission in Africa. Nevertheless, Gill Shepherd, an anthropologist, has extensively studied male and female homosexuality among the Swahili Muslims of Mambasa, a group of mixed-blood Arab-Africans, and reports that "Lesbians and homosexuals are open about their behavior" and that there are "well-established rules for fitting them into everyday life" (241). She also reports that "The Swahili for a male homosexual is *shoga,* a word also used between women to mean 'friend'" (250). I mention this because the street sense in the black community is that homosexuality is a habit picked up from whites, a remnant of slavery. Thus we have that voluble factotum of the rap music world, Professor Griff, lecturing the press:

> You have to understand something. In knowing and understanding Black history, African history, there's not a word in any African language which describes homosexual. You [journalists] would like to make them part of the Black community, but that's something brand-new to Black people. If you want to take me up on that, then you find me, in the original languages of Africa, a word for homosexual, lesbian or prostitute. There are no such words. They didn't exist. (quoted in *Outweek,* no. 54, 11 July 1990, p. 62.)

My point is not that Griff is a reliable expert, but rather that he speaks with such authority because, addressing blacks beyond the press, he states what is their received notion.

Even sophisticated black academics have difficulty maintaining the slippery hold on African mythology and anthropology when it comes to sexuality. The formidable Henry Louis Gates, Jr., for example, interrupts his discussion of Esu, the Yoruba god of interpretation, to state: "Despite the fact that I have referred to him in the masculine, Esu is also genderless, or of dual gender. . . . Each time I have used the masculine pronoun . . . I could have just as properly used the feminine" (29). Then Gates lapses back into the masculinist and heterosexist language he has used up to this point. Somehow the polymorphous perversity of Esu is lost in translation, and the continuum of African thought reduced to the binarism of Western ideology. Even for the best-intentioned black scholars, sexuality in Africa remains problematic.

The problem of the gay black's relationship to Africa begins in the work of Alain Locke—the Howard University professor, Rhodes Scholar, and Harvard Ph.D.—who was intellectually and sexually involved with various members of the Harlem Renaissance. His seemingly successful campaign to seduce the wary Hughes makes for interesting reading in Rampersad's biography of the poet (66–93). Locke is frequently, and in many ways correctly, viewed as one of the more forceful and articulate intellectuals to argue the need for African-Americans to study their origins in Africa, and "the most direct catalyst" of the Harlem Renaissance, which gave voice to the Negritude movement (Cureau, 77). Nevertheless, as James A. Barnes has pointed out, "Locke was often as ambiguous and enigmatic in his terms of definition as was the theme he was endeavoring to define" (104). Locke's interest in Africa and the ambiguity and enigmatic quality of his language about Africa are at least partly motivated by a desire to create a cultural context for black homosexuality, a subject that at the time could only be dealt with indirectly.

Locke's strategy is no different really from the strategy of upper-class gay Englishmen at the turn of the century, for whom, as David Halperin argues, "the Greeks provided an ideological weapon against the condemnatory reflexes of . . . Christian conscience, offering [them] in its place, 'a new guide for life'" (1). Group after group, as we have seen, tries to find cultural permission for homosexual behavior through recourse to some earlier—usually more primitive—state before Christian morality. Melville and Stoddard's journey toward the Polynesian derives from this impulse, as do many of Cavafy's lyrics and Lowes Dickinson's work on the Greek way of life. Similarly gay black men sought the same legitimization of desire in an African past and a cultural matrix. And like the "self-censorship" which, according to Halperin, "Lowes Dickinson evidently exercised" (2), Alain Locke found it advisable to couch his sexual politics in ambiguous and enigmatic terms.

The key to Locke's rhetoric may be found in the letters he wrote to Hughes in his campaign of seduction, a correspondence of which Rampersad gives a lively account. Early on, Locke tells Hughes of his identification with Germany, since "Germans had a gift for friendship, 'which cult I confess is my only religion and has been ever since my early infatuation with Greek ideals of life.' 'You see,' he went on, 'I was caught up early in the coils of classicism'" (68). In later letters, the two discovered they were "pagan to the core" (68). Rampersad believes this coding was so obvious that even the youthful Hughes was only "pretending not to understand" (68), coyly refusing to get the hint. In fact the polarities that Locke sets up between ancient and contemporary, classic and modern, Greek and American, pagan and Christian were the standard codes of the Uranian writers and such fellow-travellers as A. E. Housman, Countee Cullen's ideal.

Those enigmatic and ambiguous terms in Locke's criticism merely turn Greece into Africa. "What the Negro artist of to-day has most to gain from the arts of the forefathers," Locke wrote in "The Legacy of the Ancestral Arts," "is perhaps not cultural inspiration or technical innovation, but the lesson of a classical background, the lesson of discipline, of style, of technical control pushed to the limits of technical mastery" (256). The essay concludes with this peroration:

> If African art is capable of producing the ferment in modern art that it has, surely this is not too much to expect of its influence upon the culturally awakened Negro artist of the present generation. So that if even the present vogue of African art should pass, and the bronzes of Benin and the fine sculptures of Gabon and Baoule, and the superb designs of the Bushongo should again become mere items of exotic curiosity, for the Negro artist they ought still to have the import and influence of classics in whatever art expression is consciously and representatively racial. (267)

What makes African art classical is that it embodies "rigid, controlled, disciplined, abstract, heavily conventionalized" elements similar to the classical Greek plastic expression and its moral tone—"disciplined, sophisticated, laconic and fatalistic" (254)—bares a striking resemblance to the Hellenic temperament. Indeed, Locke makes quite explicit a comparison between Greek classicism and African classicism, a comparison that asserts that at the present, the African variety may be more useful:

> This artistic discovery of African art [by European modernists] came at a time when there was a marked decadence and sterility in certain forms of European plastic art expressions, due to generations of the inbreeding of style and idiom. Out of the exhaustion of imitating Greek classicism and the desperate exploitation in graphic art of all the technical possibilities of color . . . form and decorative design became emphasized. . . . And suddenly with this new problem and interest, African representations of form . . . appeared cunningly sophisticated and masterful. (258–59)

We should not ignore Locke's inbreeding metaphor because it provides a vital insight into his larger cultural politics. For Locke, African classicism enters as a *deus ex machina* to solve the incestuous problems of Greek classicism and European aesthetic inbreeding, and places the African-American at an advantage over the European in the coming years. To be sure, the black has suffered from the importation of European values (and Nordic blood), and the art of the blacks in America is a pale imitation of European artistic expression. However, that infusion of European influence has kept the African-American artist from suffering the degenerative inbreeding that has affected his European colleagues, and now black American artists stand to benefit, as no European could, from the rediscovery of their classical African roots.

One benefit, according to Locke, is that black Americans are better situated to throw off the shackles of Western oppression and participate in the austere, disciplined, and highly sophisticated paganism of African classicism. In "The Negro Spirituals," Locke writes:

> The universality of the Spirituals looms more and more as they stand the test of time. They have outlived the particular generation and the peculiar conditions which produced them; they have survived in turn the contempt of the slave owners, the conventionalization of formal religion, the repression of Puritanism, the corruption of sentimental balladry, and the neglect and disdain of second-generation respectability. They have escaped the lapsing conditions and the fragile vehicle of folk art, and come firmly into the context of formal music. Only classics survive such things. (199)

Locke's elegant periods emphasize both the process of the spirituals' transmission and their transformation into classics. The pagan source of the spiritual, its origin in African life, has survived "the conventionalization of formal religion" as well as "the repression of Puritanism." The Protestant message of black spirituals, like the Catholic interpolations in *Beowulf,* are merely recent excrescences on the classically stylized surfaces of the pagan originals, crude fig leaves across the heroic torso. Indeed, Locke divides the spiritual into four groups—ritualistic prayer songs, evangelical "shouts," folk ballads, and work songs—only to deny these divisions into secular and religious. "It is not a question of religious content or allusion,—for the great majority of the Negro songs have this—but a more delicate question of caliber or feeling and type of folk use" (205). In merging secular and spiritual concerns together, these classic works of art elude the conventions of Puritanism and formal European religions while suggesting a deeper and more flexible religiosity.

Yet Locke avoids the next logical rhetorical step: to see this classical African heritage as immediately connected to the American black. Some aspects of the African heritage have survived, according to Locke, like the rhythms of the spirituals, or their frighteningly rapid shifts of emotion. But Locke begins his "Legacy of the Ancestral Arts" by insisting that the thread connecting American blacks to Africa is virtually severed:

> Music and poetry, and to a certain extent the dance, have been predominant arts of the American Negro. This is an emphasis quite different from that of the African cultures, where the plastic and craft arts predominate. . . . Except then in his remarkable carry-over of the rhythmic gift, there is little evidence of any direct connection of the American Negro with his ancestral arts. . . . The characteristic African art expressions are rigid, controlled, disciplined, abstract, heavily conventionalized; those of the Aframerican,—free-exuberant, emotional, sentimental and human. Only by the misrepresentation of the African spirit, can one claim any emotional kinship between them. . . . The emotional temper of the American Negro is exactly opposite. What we have thought primitive in the American Negro—his naivete, his sentimentalism, his exuberance and his improvising spontaneity are then neither characteristically African nor to be explained as an ancestral heritage. They are the result of his peculiar experience in America and the emotional upheaval of its trials and ordeals. (243–45)

I have quoted Locke at some length because he echoes the position of many gay white intellectuals at the turn of the century and anticipates the problematic cultural issues Baldwin faced forty years later. Like

Symonds and Dickinson, Locke feels he lives in a sentimental, Puritanical, undisciplined society that needs both the chastening and the broadening of a classicism, which in turn would give room and support to homosexual feelings. But like Baldwin, Locke finds himself both attracted to and distanced from the African. While the African contains a grandeur missing in American black culture, it lacks the definitive agony that the "peculiar experience in America" forces on blacks. Baldwin, in particular, also doubts whether contemporary Africa really is less homophobic, more accepting than African-American society.

Homosexual desire, black Protestantism, and African classicism played themselves out in particularly stark and subtle ways in Countee Cullen, friend of both Langston Hughes and Alain Locke and boyhood teacher of Jimmy Baldwin. Cullen's poem "Heritage" introduces Locke's essay on "The Legacy of the Ancestral Arts" in the anthology *The New Negro* and forms—since Locke was the editor of the anthology—a gloss on Locke's position.

The poem begins with the school essay question: "What is Africa to me," but soon eroticizes the question: is it "Strong bronze men and regal black / Women from whose loins I sprang / When the birds of Eden sang?" (240). Within the first sentence, Cullen brings together images of Africa, homoeroticism, and allusion to the Judeo-Christian concept of the Fall. In the second stanza Cullen gestures to push Africa back into the geography books, but it cannot be so easily repressed. Like the snake, it naturally strips before him, and the opening question "what is Africa?" becomes by the end of the second stanza the more suggestive—and forbidden—question: "What's your nakedness to me?" (250).

Cullen links Africa and erotic fantasies by one of the oldest conventions of lyric poetry—the sleepless night:

> So I lie, who always hear
> Though I cram against my ear
> Both my thumbs, and keep them there,
> Great drums beating through the air.
> ·
> So I lie, and find no peace
> Night or day, no slight release
> From the unremittent beat
> Made by cruel padded feet,
> Walking through my body's street.

Up and down they go, and back
Treading out a jungle track.
So I lie, who never quite
Safely sleep from rain at night
While its primal measures drip
Through my body, crying, "Strip!
Doff this new exuberance,
Come and dance the Lover's Dance."

(251–52)

These neatly turned tetrameter lines echo with more than the jungle drums. One can hear some of Prufrock and perhaps a bit of "Sunday Morning" in the celebratory dance, but most of all Cullen has "caught the tread of dancing feet," that Oscar Wilde hears in "The Harlot's House." The pent-up sexual energy is not just the call of Africa, nor is its luridness justified by a heterosexual object. The homosexual implications freight the next short stanza that returns "Heritage" to its Christian mooring:

My conversion came high-priced.
I belong to Jesus Christ,
Preacher of humility:
Heathen gods are naught to me—
Quaint, outlandish heathen gods
Black men fashion out of rods,
Clay and brittle bits of stone,
In a likeness like their own.

(252)

Clearly heathen gods, far from being naught to Cullen, are very precious, especially if they look like the "strong bronze men" who haunt his imagination. The price for Christ is renouncing those rods fashioned by the men into gods, these phallic deities, and Cullen seems highly reluctant to pay it. The poem ends with the prayer, "Lord, forgive me if my need / Sometimes shapes a human creed" (253). Christianity of the Puritanical sort practiced by black churches does not allow Cullen the human need for humans. Its strict separation of spirit and matter does not satisfy Cullen's more pagan (and homosexual) requirements. Africa becomes both the despised Sodom and the long-sought Eden of the homoerotic against which Cullen stuffs his ears and for which his heart sings. In such ways Africa is far more problematical for the gay than for the heterosexual black American writer.

If Cullen and Locke feel themselves cut off as Christians and Americans from an ancestral identification with Africa, Langston Hughes feels alienated by race. Hughes's autobiography, *The Big Sea,* begins with his journey to Africa when as a young man he hired on as a seaman aboard the SS *Malone.* During the crossing, Hughes waits "anxiously to see Africa. . . . My Africa! Motherland of the Negro peoples!" (10). Putting in at Dakar, Hughes is disturbed that Africa looks nothing as he expected, a discomfort which is partly sexual, since "at first you couldn't tell if the Mohammedans were men or women" (11). But as the ship sails southward, he comes to recognize "The great Africa of my dreams." Yet now his pain is greater, for as Hughes writes, "there was one thing that hurt me a lot when I talked with the people. The Africans looked at me and would not believe I was a Negro" (11). Hughes's identification with an African ancestry is blocked not by his desire, but by Africans themselves who recognize in Hughes the admixture of many racial features—English, Jewish, and Cherokee. For Hughes, the American black can no longer claim an African motherland.

Although genes more than sex block Hughes's identification with an African heritage, Rampersad makes clear that the trip was a source of sexual anxiety for Hughes. During this trip Hughes first had sex with another man, "a swift exchange initiated by an aggressive crewman," according to Rampersad, who adds in case there was doubt, "with Hughes as the 'male' partner" (77). Later, according to Rampersad "to Langston's great disgust, one of the firemen openly brought young black boys to the ship and sodomized them for a shilling or so. Hughes longed for the ship to leave" (80). Hughes was not disgusted by the prostitution—accounts of which he gives quite casually, even mentioning his own occasional visits—but apparently by the openness of the sodomy. Or was it the low wages? What is clear is that Hughes found Africa off-putting, and that sex had some role in his alienation.

I hardly need mention that both these homosexual incidents are dropped from Hughes's account of the voyage in *The Big Sea.* Indeed, homosexuality, or rather transvestism, appears explicitly only once in *The Big Sea,* in a chapter ironically titled "Spectacles in Color." Hughes describes attending the annual Hamilton Club Lodge Ball, a drag affair in which "prizes are given to the most gorgeously gowned of the whites and Negroes." As if to distance himself, Hughes writes, "the pathetic touch about the show is given by the presence there of many former 'queens' of the ball, prize winners of years gone by, for this dance has been going on a long time, and it is very famous among the male masqueraders of the eastern seaboard" (273). This chapter is one of the clearest examples of Hughes's technique of indirectly and silently commenting on a subject by placing accounts in juxtaposition. In *The Big Sea,* the Hamilton Club Lodge Ball segues into Countee Cullen's lavish wedding to Yolande Du Bois, W. E. B. Du Bois's only child, as if the "male masqueraders" from one drag ball had merely waltzed over to another. Given the indirect way Hughes is forced to make his points about homosexuality, the sexual ambiguity of the Mohammedans begins to loom larger as a sign, as do other odd remarks. Hughes recalls docking at Horta where: "Some of the boys made straight for women, some for the wine shops. It depended on your temperament which you sought first. . . . I bought a big bottle of cognac" (8). What should we make of this sign of "temperament," or in this portrait of Ramon, Hughes's cabin mate: "he said he didn't care much for women. He preferred silk stockings" (7)? For a writer like Hughes who plays on an innocent ambiguity for his most sophisticated effects, Africa is a background at once too ambiguous and too clear for comfort.

When Cleaver attacked Baldwin, claiming his homosexuality was an obstacle to his identification with Africa, Cleaver's analysis hit rather strongly, not only at problems in Baldwin's own position, but at problems in other black writers and intellectuals who were gay or whose sexual orientation—like Hughes's—was ambiguous. Even after Cleaver's attack, at a time when Baldwin in his public statements attempted to side with the machismo of much black popular sentiment, Baldwin still was unable to see Africa in its own terms and without the aid of a specifically black American lens. His difficulties are quite evident in *Perspectives: Angles on African Art,* one of the last projects he worked on. Susan Vogel, a curator at the Center for African Art, selected a number of works, then asked ten individuals to choose the ones they liked best and write comments about their choices. The commentators, whom Vogel calls "cocurators," are an eclectic group, including David Rockefeller, William Rubin, Ekpo Eyo, and Romare Bearden. Baldwin's first choice is a wood statue from Madagascar in which a woman is kneeling on a man's lap, her head above his, her breast at hair level, so that the man must reach up to touch it. Baldwin identifies it as "a mother and child" although the man has an enormous erection that rests against the woman's hand which in turn rests beside her vagina. Baldwin's statement that the statue "speaks of a

kind of union which is unimaginable in the West" (117), though im-
plying a kind of intuitive sympathy, seems not only to beg the question
but to suggest his unwillingness to acknowledge what is before him.
When he turns to a Luba stool, he sees Samson, and illuminates the
work with references to Auden (118). In two women holding hands on
top of a Luba staff, Baldwin recognizes "the women who live in
Harlem" (119). A Djenne figural scene reminds Baldwin "of a song we
used to sing in church called Peace in the Valley" (122). In his final
selection, a Cameroon stool causes Baldwin to meditate that "the
Western idea of childhood, or children, is not at all the same idea of
childhood that produced me. . . . white people think that childhood is
a rehearsal for success. . . . But black people raise their children as a
rehearsal for danger" (127). Again Africa is seen as merely an extension of Harlem, though I doubt that even in Harlem "children" have
the thigh-long penis granted to one of the figures carved in the stool.
Despite Baldwin's repeated claims to have intuited the African spirit,
one is continually reminded by how obsessively he projects American
images—even negatively—onto African art, so that the footstool is
distinguished as "not like Mt. Rushmore" (127).

As I mentioned earlier, Cleaver locates Baldwin's deepest difficulties
with African identity in his essay "Princes and Powers," an essay
which does not deal with homosexuality explicitly. Yet I think Cleaver
recognizes the very subtle ways issues of gender get encoded, transformed, and deflected by black homosexual writers especially in the
repressive atmosphere of the mid-fifties. Cleaver's reading of "Princes
and Powers" as a homosexual text is his most daring insight into the
cultural politics of gender.

In a startling coincidence, Baldwin addresses the same issue of black
classicism that is so central to Locke, "classic here taken to mean," by
Baldwin, "an enduring revelation and statement of a specific, peculiar,
cultural sensibility" (*Ticket,* 50). Like Locke, Baldwin doubts that
African and black American art can meaningfully be connected. To
argue as Leopold Senghor does that Wright's *Black Boy* is "involved
with African tensions and symbols" is so to dilute the notion of a
classical heritage that it no longer contains any substance (50). Moreover as Baldwin points out, "In so handsomely presenting Wright with
his African heritage, Senghor rather seemed to be taking away his
identity" (51). A classicism so pervasive, so genetic, able to operate
even when all other cultural, social, and systemic reinforcement is
missing is nothing more than instinct, and one cannot claim that in-

stincts convey moral virtue. Like a posthypnotic suggestion, acts generated by an unconscious heritage cannot claim to be the work of the person who performed them. The writer merely becomes the instrument of a cultural force beyond his control; Baldwin rejects such a role for the artist and for the citizen. "A culture," he insists, is not "something given to a people, but, on the contrary and by definition, something that they make themselves" (52). Baldwin draws from the concept of individual volition two key beliefs: first, colonial attempts to Europeanize Africans cannot succeed unless Africans help make such a culture; and second, culture can never be something passively finished since it exists only as it is made. Baldwin takes Eliot one step further: the only tradition that counts is one of individual talent.

Baldwin rather self-consciously locates his cardinal virtues of individuality and volition within the Protestant ethic. His Gide essay indicates how problematic a move that is for him, and in "Princes and Powers" Baldwin is quite aware of the dangers since as he writes of the French, Christian apologetics have produced "a legal means of administering injustice" (*Ticket*, 56). Yet, whatever the sins of the European have been, "one of the results of 1455 [when the church had determined to rule all infidels] had, at length, been Calvin and Luther, who shook the authority of the Church in insisting on the authority of the individual consciousness" (58). In claiming the European culture was bad because it oppressed the individual wills of Africans, Africans were relying on the very cultural principle of moral persuasion they were rejecting. Christian culture, for Baldwin, provided the terms of its own critique and thus the means of its own correction, while relying on some intuited native African classicism that was transhistorical, transgeographic, even transracial created an authority with no internal mechanism for correction. Baldwin approvingly notes George Lamming when he quotes Djuna Barnes—and the sexual-political significance of the source should not be ignored: "Too great a sense of identity makes a man feel he can do no wrong. And too little does the same thing" (56). If Cleaver argued that Baldwin could not be an African because he was gay, Baldwin answers, at least in "Princes and Powers," that he can't be much of an African because he is too much of a Protestant.

Baldwin makes clear the tensions between the Protestant culture of American blacks and the pagan culture of Africans in yet another disagreement with Senghor. Though Baldwin was willing to concede that "The culture which had produced Senghor seemed, on the face of it, to have a greater coherence as regarded assumptions, traditions, customs, and beliefs than did the western culture," nevertheless "Senghor's culture . . . did not need the lonely activity of the singular intelligence on which the cultural life—the moral life—of the West depends" (*Ticket,* 48). Indeed, the coherence of African culture—and the authority of that coherence—produces, according to Baldwin, "necessarily, a much lower level of tolerance for the maverick, the dissenter, the man who steals the fire" (48). Baldwin sees only two alternatives: either a coherent culture of tribal conformity in which leaders control all values, or a more fragmentary culture of the West in which tolerance is required for the moral and creative acts of individuals. From a country where blacks are a minority and where the hierarchy oppresses homosexuals, Baldwin not surprisingly sides with the culture of tolerance for individual differences. As he did in the Gide essay, Baldwin finds in "Princes and Powers" that Protestantism is capable of producing—even if it has not always produced—not just the Puritanical seeds of sexual oppression, but the moral openness for tolerance to sexual minorities because of its self-correcting mechanisms. African culture, however, is potentially more homophobic, more racist, more intolerant than a Christian culture. Cleaver sees Baldwin's homosexuality at work in his advocacy of the liberal humanism of Protestantism, and by rejecting what he sees as a homosexual desire for "tolerance," Cleaver refuses to credit the other dimensions of Baldwin's position.

But it seems to me that, even within the context of "Princes and Powers," Baldwin is unwilling to settle for the either / or of Protestantism or Africa, homosexual tolerance or pan-African uniformity. "[Black Africans] were all now, whether they liked it or not," Baldwin insists, "related to Europe, stained by European visions and standards, and their relationship to themselves, and to each other, and to their past had changed" (*Ticket,* 54). Blacks—African or American— could not turn back the clock before the European invasion of their culture. In Aime Cesaire, Baldwin found a figure who seemed to bring together both the Protestant tolerance for difference and the African authority of origin. According to Baldwin, Cesaire "had penetrated into the heart of the great wilderness which was Europe and stolen the sacred fire. And this, which was the promise of their freedom, was also the assurance of his power" (54).

Baldwin posits in this passage the figure of a Black Prometheus, and the gay dimensions of such a figure should be obvious to us now, carrying with it both the Greek way of life and a tolerance for the oppressed (including, the sexually oppressed). It joins, as Locke did, both a Greek and African classicism—austere, disciplined, but open to difference and variety. It gives voice to the rebel, the maverick, the odd ball without placing the iconoclast outside of the culture it seeks to alter and whose errors it tries to correct. Baldwin, it is true, cannot sustain or even explore such a figure either in his essays or in his novels. The Black Prometheus—whose fires erotic and intellectual are never extinguished—is but the passing rhetorical gesture in an essay filled with rhetorical gestures. But it positions Baldwin within a line he nowhere acknowledges—a line of both gay *and* African-American writers—a line off of which Cleaver's essay seems to have driven him, a line that those after him have found difficult to trace and extend.

10

Alternative Service: Families in Recent American Gay Fiction

T OWARD the center of Andrew Holleran's novel *Nights in Aruba* the narrator and his friend Vittorio watch "a slender cocoa-colored youth in red polyester pants" give himself a bath from a water fountain in Union Square. "How beautiful he is," remarks Vittorio. "This is just what I live for. You see why I never want to go back to [my hometown]. You can have boys like that, or you can have the pleasures of family life. But you can't have both" (107). The narrator accepts this axiom of gay life and is agonized by it. "I was a man," he tells us, "whose past and present were divided by an abrupt schism" (107). Like Matthew Arnold, he finds himself "wandering between two worlds, one dead, the other powerless to be born."

What is most telling about this little incident—one of so many in both *Nights in Aruba* and Holleran's earlier novel *Dancer from the Dance*—is the extent to which it confirms the most antihomosexual prejudices, that gay society is irreconcilable to "family life," that those who choose boys have rejected not only the pleasures but the virtues of heterosexuality. "Homosexuality flies in the face of the one fact we know" writes no less an authority than Anita Bryant in her autobiography subtitled *The Survival of Our Nation's Families and the Threat of Militant Homosexuality*, "which is that male and female are

188

programmed to mate with the opposite sex. This is the story of two and half billion years of civilization, and any society that hopes to survive will have to recognize this" (115). She continues by quoting the psychiatrist Charles Socarides, who warns, "Homosexuality militates against the family, drives the sexes in opposite directions and neglects the child's growth and sexual identity" (115). The choice is dire. One can either select the boy in "red polyester pants" and with him chaos, anarchy, the end of civilization, or raise a family and preserve the universe from destruction. No wonder Holleran's characters are so uncertain, torn, plagued by guilt and doubt.

But though Andrew Holleran and Anita Bryant both agree that gay and family life are mutually exclusive, Holleran does not believe that one is the enemy of the other. Indeed, if anything his characters are sappily sentimental about the simple joys of familyhood. When his narrator-hero in *Nights in Aruba* goes out selling encyclopedias door-to-door, he is paralyzed by the beauty of the average American home:

> Sometimes I simply knocked on the door of a house to ask for a glass of water. I sat in the kitchen as the woman watched me drink, and the voices of children playing in the backyard, the flutter of a water sprinkler, mingled with the suburban silence. I liked clean kitchens, boxes of cake mix lined up on the Formica counter, paper cutouts taped to the refrigerator. Such a kitchen was as cool and clean as the kitchen of my dreams. But I saw no way to enter this domestic life. When I sat face to face with a husband and wife on the sofa, I felt a profound guilt stealing through me. How I could ask this pair of lovers to plunge themselves further into debt was beyond me. (94)

No heterosexual writer could produce so mournful a hymn to domestic bliss, for no heterosexual would feel so locked out of this particular conjugal paradise.

According to Jeffrey Weeks, antihomosexual sentiments derive from the desire to protect the family. "Increasingly over the past hundred years the reference point of anti-homosexual hostility has not been 'religion' or 'sin,' but 'family,' and in particular, the roles that men and women are expected to act out in the family" (5). The homosexual has been viewed, particularly by psychoanalysts, as an anomaly that is not so much a symptom as a cause of the family's breakdown.

Reviewing the psychological literature is both a frustrating and terrifying process, and with their accounts of treatments by castration, vasectomy, electroshock, insulin shock, lobotomy, and aversion therapy—to mention the least bizarre—the documents that Jonathan N. Katz and others have assembled read more like chapters in medieval history than in modern medicine. It is important to remember, however, that not only were these theories popular until quite recently and persist even today among some medical practitioners, but also that all gay writers have been brought up under their grim and horrifying shadow. The visit to the psychiatrist's office is one of the obligatory scenes of gay novels. As Edmund White puts in *A Boy's Own Story,* "My first sight of the analytic couch constituted the primal scene" (167).

One of the most important works was Irving Bieber's report, *Homosexuality: A Psychoanalytic Study,* issued in 1962 as an official publication of The Society of Medical Psychoanalysts. It codified the strong mother / weak father theory of homosexuality and asserted that "all parents of homosexuals apparently had severe emotional problems. *The H-son emerged as the interactional focal point upon whom the most profound parental psychopathology was concentrated*" (310, Bieber's italics). Homosexuality was the result of a pathology in parents and represented the failure of the traditional family structures. These "severe emotional problems" could according to Bieber and his associates, be passed on: homosexuality was a contagion spread from parents to their children.

Not surprisingly, Bieber's theories, while popular with straight readers, have had less effect on the gay audience. This lack of success is in contrast to that of other sexual theorists whose writing became the model for character analysis. As James Levin has pointed out in his exhaustive survey of American gay fiction, Karl Heinrich Ulrichs, the German amateur psychologist, not only affected other researchers including Kraft-Ebing and Magnus Hirschfeld, but such novels as Radclyffe Hall's *The Well of Loneliness,* Xavier Mayne's *Imre: A Memorandum,* and Blair Niles's *Strange Brothers* (20–21). Not that mothers disappear in gay fiction. To be sure they have a prominent place. But when one compares them to the mothers in such heterosexual novels as *Portnoy's Complaint, A Mother's Kisses,* or even Updike's *Of the Farm,* they hardly bear out the psychopathology Bieber and his associates claim they possess.

The only recent gay novel to follow the Bieberian scheme of weak father / strong mother is Andrew Holleran's *Nights in Aruba.* The narrator says he suffers from a "maternal obsession" (22) which leaves him unable to function on his own. He remembers proudly the intimacy he had with, and the power he had over, his mother as a child. He alone could persuade her to return to the house when she had had too much to drink. "It was understood," he informs us, "that I was my mother's and my sister my father's, and whenever someone had to go and get mother to bed, I was chosen . . . and [she] obeyed me without a word. I belonged to her, just as my sister belonged to my father" (50).

Nights in Aruba may be read as the narrator's struggle to free himself of the magnetic draw of his mother. Yet the mother does not wish to possess the force she exerts on her son. "You must remember you are a separate person," she advises, as he goes off to college (55). But her coaxing does no good, and by the end of the novel, he is as attached as ever. Hanging up from his annual Easter phone call to Mom, the narrator is still telling himself, "the life I must begin is my own—a separate person's" (240).

Yet the narrator's "maternal obsession" strikes me as being more an excuse than an honest analysis of his situation. It is easier for him to mouth Bieber's ready-made explanation than to develop one of his own. For he echoes in the phrase his mother's reasoning when she explains why her presumably gay brother has never married. "He loved my mother too much," is her thoughtful response, adding, "Your grandmother was very independent . . . but he was her favorite. He took care of her when she was sick and old. . . . After she died, we knew he would never marry" (17). It reads like a case study from one of Bieber's files at The Society of Medical Psychoanalysts.

All of Holleran's denizens of the gay underworld—who spend their nights at the baths, their summers on Fire Island, their evenings on the streets, and mornings at the toilets—are mama's boys in disguise, tied more tightly by apron strings than by leather and chains. It's unclear whether the service they give to their families, mixed as it is with equal doses of piety and humiliation, is no more than penance for the sin of being homosexual. For Holleran makes clear in *Nights in Aruba* what remains unspoken in his earlier novel, *Dancer from the Dance:* his characters suffer a deep Catholic guilt about their sexuality—a guilt which drives them into the worst sexual excesses and then delivers them into long periods of sexual renunciation. "I see so many boys your age," cautions Mr. Friel, possibly the most tortured of Holleran's Catholic homosexuals, "throwing away their youth in self-recrimination, unable to accept their sexual situation, shall we say. Stricken with self-loathing. Or lost like the little mermaid who fell in love with an inappropriate object. A human being!" (125). Friel, like Holleran, knows that in his own "guilt and self-loathing" he is only following a text someone else has written. He is unable to find another text or write a new one for himself. His book is bound—one is tempted to write "literally bound"—by the forces that have taught him "guilt and self-loathing," but though he is aware of his entrapment, he is unable to make the break, to forge a text of his own.

Holleran's characters absolutely separate the "pleasures of family life" from the pleasures of the homosexual world, not because they must be separate, but because of the fear of mutual contamination. Homosexuality is the characters' only expression of independence, and they fear that their parents might co-opt this arena of freedom. Yet they also fear that any involvement in the sexual demimonde might somehow dim the luminous and romantic wholesomeness of domesticity.

Holleran stands alone among contemporary gay writers in several respects. He is alone in his insistence that gay and straight worlds must and should remain separate. He is alone in throwing up his hands in desperation of ever bridging the gap between family life and gay life. He is alone in embracing the theory of the strong mother / weak father concept of homosexuality and the guilt that comes from enjoying forbidden pleasures. He is the novelist most dependent on hetero-sexist values and consequently one of the few gay novelists to have found recognition in the straight press.

Edmund White, of course, has received the most recognition and stands as the finest and best known of the middle generation of gay American novelists. (Of the older generation only William Burroughs, Gore Vidal, and James Purdy are better known.) White has received the praise of Vladimir Nabokov, Gore Vidal, and Susan Sontag, the approval of the *New York Times* and the *Washington Post*. White has not confined his energies to fiction. He is an indefatigable commentator on the gay world, having produced a fascinating travel book, *States Of Desire: Travels in Gay America,* hundreds of reviews and articles, and, with Charles Silverstein, the most famous manual of homosexual lovemaking, *The Joy of Gay Sex.*

Families loom as large in White's fiction as they do in Holleran's. But the families are different. It is the fathers who play the decisive role, and White's protagonists are as opposed to the Bieberian model as Holleran's characters are drawn from it. In *Nocturnes for the King of Naples* and *A Boy's Own Story,* White's gay narrators (both stories are told in the first person) are deeply attracted to their fathers. Nor is this the usual father-son affection. The narrators are erotically attracted. In fact, one protagonist finally lures his father to bed. The narrator of *A Boy's Own Story* sounds at one point like the woman in "Kubla Kahn" who is "wailing for her demon lover." "Once," the narrator recalls, "I'd wanted my father to love me and take me away. I had sat night after night outside his bedroom door in the dark, crazy with fantasies of seducing him, eloping with him, covering him with kisses as we shot through space against a night field flowered with stars" (27). Such a purple passion raises not the slightest blush on the narrator; to the contrary, he feels "sorry for a man who never wanted to go to bed with his father" (22).

Given the passionate intensity of this father-love, mothers count for little in White's fictional world. Mothers may hold sway over their children when no one else is there to turn to. "As long as I remained unpopular I belonged wholly to my mother," admits the narrator of *A Boy's Own Story,* but as soon as he acquires friends, he finds mothers "as uninteresting as the rich in novels of backstairs life; they were large naive personages who ask irrelevant questions" (127). Moreover, in the narrator's formative years his mother remained a distant, unreal figure. "As a little boy I'd scarcely known my mother; she'd seldom been home and I'd been left to my nurse" (71).

No, it is not mothers who dominate the novels of Edmund White; it is fathers, or rather one sort of father—a wealthy, slightly effeminate, sexually voracious, but essentially misanthropic WASP. In *Nocturnes* and in *A Boy's Own Story,* the fathers live in self-imposed exile, one in Europe, the other in an enormous mansion at the fringe of a city. Both fathers are loners, estranged from any close relationship but retaining retinues of servants, wives, and girlfriends to keep them amused during their sleepless nights.

The fathers in White's fiction are distinctly unlikable individuals, and their sons' continued wish to love them is perhaps the sons' most perverse desire especially since the boys are aware of how coldly manipulative their fathers are. The narrator of *A Boy's Own Story* is not merely a witness, but also an unknowing participant in one of his father's ruthless plans. One summer the father hires his son to run an addressograph in his office: the son is to help Alice, a woman whose "essential identity [was] her 'prettiness'" (37). Alice is soon fired after rejecting her boss's sexual advances, but not before the son has learned to run the office on his own. As the son ruefully observes, there was no interruption in the "endless mailings" (44). The Alice episode becomes paradigmatic of all the father's dealings with people, and a model which his son almost immediately emulates when he buys his first male hustler with his summer earnings. He has learned the lesson his father wanted him to learn—"the value of a dollar" (35).

Still, the sons in White's fiction eventually do achieve a measure of intimacy with their fathers, even if it takes an unexpected and unwelcome form. The narrator of *A Boy's Own Story* spends his nights with his father listening to Brahms. "I never showered with my dad," the narrator recalls. "I never saw him naked, not once, but we did immerse ourselves, side by side, in those passionate streams (of late Brahms) every night. As he worked at his desk and I sat on his couch, reading or daydreaming, we bathed in music" (22). Music brings father and son together and binds them in its warm embrace. Significantly, the son will betray his music teacher at the end of the novel, and the couch will reappear not only as the psychiatric couch on which the narrator will attempt another transference of affection, but the bed on which he finally makes love.

In *Nocturnes for the King of Naples,* father and son come together in a scene both lurid and pathetic, a mockery of love and paternity. The son is awakened by his father's attempts to enter the bed: having injected himself with an overdose of "tragic magic" (his name for heroin), the father is seeking comfort with his son:

> He slept with his huge bald head on my chest, and poked one fat finger into my mouth. Although I disliked the taste of his cold, salty finger, I submitted to it superstitiously, half-believing that my saliva was keeping him alive. At last he rolled away from me and began to breathe evenly. All along, I suppose, I had wanted this passionate, ridiculous pasha in my bed, had wanted him to hold me in his legendary arms. (114)

No scene in American fiction is quite like this one—a devastating parody of incestuous rape and paternal innocence, simultaneously chaste and pornographic. The father's fat finger stuck in his son's mouth is at once the child-man sucking his thumb and a substitute for fellatio in which the father's impotence is underscored by the salt taste of his sweat. Here is a scene in which saliva, semen, and blood all magically fuse into one life-giving fluid able—unlike the heroin, which the father has pumped into his own veins—to comfort, to satisfy, and to cleanse. Here is a scene that comes as close to child abuse as any in Bieber's gallery. Yet it is not a mother forcing enemas into her son, but a father, high on heroin, poking his sweaty finger into his son's mouth. This is not a mother binding her son closely in a humiliating violation, but a father giving his son a parody of nurturance.

For White's protagonists, the problem is not how to free themselves from domineering mothers but how to honor their fathers without becoming like their fathers. In both novels they fail. They have identified themselves too closely with their fathers, patterned their behavior too much on what their fathers have done. Contrary to Bieber's analysis, these boys have not "introjected" their mother's images—even though the narrator of *A Boy's Own Story* repeats his psychiatrist's theory apparently to win the doctor's favor; rather, they have suffered from an excess of father-worship.

One may pose the dilemma faced by the youthful protagonists in this way: How can I be a homosexual and be like my heterosexual father? And this question has its corollary: Can I love my father and still be a homosexual? The answer they give is a resounding NO! To be like father, these sons must deny the love they feel for the men in their lives. Systematically, they abandon or betray the various father-like figures who befriend them. Betrayal and rejection are the only ways these characters know how to "love men and not be a homosexual" (218).

One may argue just how marriage resolves the conflict between father and son. Whether marriage replaces the absent father, serves to return the son to his missing origins, or shows submission to the paternal law, marriage as an institution and ritual resolves and symbolizes the father / son relationship. But the self-identified gay man does not have marriage as a means of passage into manhood, and thus he exists in a limbo. As Holleran has Mr. Friel observe, "The unmarried have always occupied a place in human society similar to that of the undead" (142), and what Friel longs for is a stake through the heart which will end his existence as a vampire. Other gay writers have sought something less extreme than crucifixion, an alternative service by which the son may resolve his relationship to his father and restore the family to harmony.

In *Nocturnes for the King of Naples,* White attempts such an alternative symbolic pattern: the replacement of the biological heterosexual father with a surrogate homosexual father. The gay father almost literally rises out of the bed of the straight one, for the protagonist meets his surrogate dad on the very night his biological father, high on heroin, comes to the protagonist's bed. That shattering scene, in fact, ends on a blissful note. Disgusted and frightened by his biological father, the son escapes into the night, searches the empty streets of the city, has his shoes shined, and, in a gesture so unlikely it must be read symbolically, visits the botanical gardens where "under a banana tree . . . someone put a friendly arm around me. It was you at last" (115). Like Adam, the narrator awakes in the garden to the person of his dreams, his "perfect love." But, alas, the son has suffered such deep psychic damage that the lover is unable, despite his saintly efforts, to heal the young man's wounds. Ultimately, the gay son will revert to the model of his heterosexual father and abandon the persons who love him the best. The young man follows in his father's footsteps—a path of self-destruction.

One can only speculate why surrogate fathers have so little power in White's novels to reconcile the sons to homosexuality. But it is clear in the very structure of the work that the surrogate merely buffers the son temporarily from his father. The surrogate has not filled the place, re-placed the real father, but rather momentarily shields the son from his image. In *Nocturnes for the King of Naples,* the surrogate appears like some genie to wipe away the son's tears. The surrogate does not pro-vide the alternative service by which the young gay man may be recon-ciled to his father or integrated into the family.

If the conclusions of so many gay novels seem inadequate, the rea-son may be that gay writers have not yet created a myth which is not tragic, which does not follow the received heterosexual conception of gay man's fate. Without some integrating myths that will help bring together the sexual world and the familial world, the gay novel will be forever fractured, divided against itself, without a satisfactory resolution.

Frankly I know of no recent gay fiction that has solved the conflict between gay life and heterosexual forms, but Robert Ferro's *The Family of Max Desir* makes a bold attempt at forging what could be a truly gay novel, one which eschews the heterosexual mythic forms.

At first glance *The Family of Max Desir* is two different novels sandwiched between the same covers. One novel is a realistic account of an Italian-American family in northern New Jersey; the other re-cords the seemingly fantastic adventures of a man involved in voodoo. Max Desir is the youngest son of John and Marie Desir, a wealthy couple who reside in the sprawling suburbs of the East Coast, and the novel recounts how the family confronts Marie's death from brain cancer. Complicating this domestic tragedy is John Desir's inability to accept that Max is gay and has a lover of fifteen years named Nick Flynn. Tensions between Max and his father come to a head when John removes from a prominent place in the home an embroidered version of the Desir family tree on whose uppermost branches are paired the names of Max and Nick.

Interspersed through this realistic tale is a far more fantastic one. Max lives a charmed life full of wild and magical encounters. He meets Nick, for example, in a gothic Italian prison suggestively called La Stella Nera. They are rescued by the mysterious Lydia, "a sister of the President of Italy," a woman of enormous influence and few demands. In New York, Max gets involved with Clive, a black man devoted to the occult, who has turned his Harlem apartment into a small shrine dedicated to "Santa Barbara Africanna, the Black Madonna."

Yet on closer examination, the two strands are not so different. Primitive rites and mysterious coincidences occur in the domestic portions of the novel, and the gay narrative is replete with homey little details. Which is stranger: Max's visit to a Haitian medium who is possessed by the spirit of a small child named Gedde, or Marie's father's visit to the glass-lined crypt of his mother, a vacuum-sealed "grotesque waxen doll" whose "hair was dark and seemed firmly attached to the scalp" but whose lips were claimed by "the rictus of a kind of imminent scream" (28)? And which seems the more unlikely coincidence: that Nick is freed from jail by the sister of the Italian president or that Marie is nursed in her last illness by Madelaine, a protective angel, who under the name of Louella served the family twenty years prior to Marie's death when she was responsible for Max's sexual initiation? Clearly, the domestic scenes are as bizarre in their way as the gay scenes. Ferro has an uncanny way of making suburban Italian-American life seem strange and mysterious.

Throughout *The Family of Max Desir* and his last novel, *Second Son,* Ferro brings gay and family life together. Max does not try to keep his sexual identity a secret from his family as the characters in Holleran's novels do. He wants his family to accept him and Nick as a married couple. John Desir may, to satisfy his masculine ego, try to hide Max's sexual perference from friends, yet he never forgets his love for his son. "No matter what, you're my son," he assures Max (70). In time, John Desir grants his son and Nick a good measure of approval. "In the years Max and Nick had been lovers, John's attitude toward Nick has slowly evolved from coldly polite to cordial, and even to a level of respect—which seemed mutual—for each other's opposite" (94).

In contrast to the families in Holleran's novels or in Edmund White's, the Desirs want to integrate Max and Nick into the family. This may be an example of how the close-knit Italian family differs from the Anglo-Saxon family, or it may be an example of the more accepting nature of once lower-class families. Nevertheless, it is significant that Max maintains a fifteen-year-old relationship with Nick, while the nameless narrators in Holleran's and White's novels can sustain nothing. The Desir family supports the Max-Nick alliance in many ways. When John Desir is angriest at Max, Max's sister, Robin, gives the lovers a place to stay (81). Later, when Marie is ill, Max and Nick watch over the grandchildren so that Marie can rest. "Nick and Max were avuncular to a turn, parading their brood" (89). The conflict between Max and John Desir is not over acceptance, but concerns a complete, unconditional acceptance of homosexuality, which even Max comes to understand may be too much to ask of his father.

But *The Family of Max Desir* would be a far less interesting work were it merely the story of how Max wins his father's acceptance. *The Family of Max Desir* includes not merely his mother and father, brothers, sisters, nieces, nephews, and aunts, and Max's lovers—Nick, Clive, and Arthur. It also embraces a spiritual world of past ancestors never directly seen or known, ghosts and voices, Gedde who possesses the bodies of the Haitian fortune-tellers, and the "deux Femmes" who protect Max from danger. The gay family is not the biological family of the heterosexual novel. The gay family is made up of kindred spirits of the living and dead, real and imaginary.

Consequently, Robert Ferro does not end his novel with a touching vignette of the Desir family reunion, but with an episode from one of Max's stories, appropriately titled "The Tribe," a story we are to believe is suggested by historical fact. "The Tribe," addressed to Charles Darwin, is a fictional account of the first Caucasian to visit the Mato Grasso region of the Amazon, a man whom Darwin meets on his Beagle voyage. Max feels a remarkable affinity for this "blond man" who "walked through the Amazon in 1832, traveling from tribe to tribe as a sexual deity" (194).

In the story, the Amazonians mistake the blond man for a god, or more precisely "as one who had received the god and who might receive him again" (210). As a result, he is given food, shelter, gifts, and the sexual favors of a young boy. The man is not one god, but the vessel of all the gods. "Depending on the moon, I am the flood, the harvest, the hunter's god" (217). Nor does the incongruity of his humanity and divinity serve as an obstacle toward belief. If anything, it inflames devotion. "All that cannot be explained makes me holy— my arrival, my nature, my skin, my gold hair, my eyes, my placid acceptance of all attentions and offerings" (218).

Whether it is because the homosexual exists outside of the biological continuum, or for some other reason, Max feels himself to be the agent of a greater spiritual world, the vessel of the gods and the voices of destiny. In this regard Max (or more specifically Robert Ferro) stands in a long line of gay sibyls including Whitman, Hart Crane, and James Merrill. Even in the absence of the sibylline, gay authors identify to a degree not found in heterosexual fiction with an ancestral past, a primitive Dionysian force. Even Edmund White recognizes this otherworldly impulse. The narrator of *A Boy's Own Story* meets Fred, the owner of a bookstore, who disappears into the Mexican jungle never to reemerge. The narrator speculates:

> I've been told that in some Indian villages in Mexico homosexual men live in a separate compound where they take care of the tribe's children; is Fred still living as some ancient nanny respectably obscured by pure white veils of beard and hair, his glasses long since broken and abandoned, his constant murmur unheard below the swell of warm, naked toddlers who clamber over him as though he were nothing but a weathered garden god half-sunk into creepers and vines, his notebook of handwritten stories open to the elements to scatter its pages as the leaves of a calendar in old movies fly away to indicate the passage of years, even decades? (90–91)

White's vision of Fred is essentially the same as Ferro's vision of Max, the vision of the gay man who has not rejected his family, but has transcended it by giving himself to the entire community, to the whole tribe. He lives apart, but he shares the joys and sufferings of his people with whom he lives as a "weathered garden god," an incarnation of fertility. The fictions of the homosexual are "open to the elements," both reflecting the natural forces around the notebook and radiating its supernatural energy outward. It is the vision one finds in Whitman's barbaric yawp when he asserts himself as a kosmos and the vision of Merrill's *The Changing Light at Sandover,* which "must improve the line, in every sense of life." The direction of a great deal of gay fiction is toward the visionary, the ancestral, the communal. The gay protagonist moves toward an encounter with death, not as the person dying, but as the agent most knowledgeable in making the transition to death. Ferro's novel breaks new ground in the way it enacts this mythic movement. The novel begins typically enough with a character raised in a particular family in a particular social milieu, but ends with a different hero—a blond, blue-eyed westerner—serving as an idol for a "primitive" community, the vessel of their gods. This pattern appears to underlie the best works of the gay imagination. Works which fail to embrace this pattern have protagonists who are often self-destructive, self-hating, and emotionally paralyzed. The two novels that Ferro wrote after *The Family of Max Desir* and before his death from AIDS repeat to a large measure the mixture of visionary and realistic narrative, yet neither *The Blue Star* or *Second Son* pushes the formal and intellectual terrain beyond *The Family of Max Desir*.

Ferro, Holleran, and White were all friends, and with Christopher Cox, Michael Grumley, Felice Picano, and George Whitmore formed in the late 1970s and early 1980s a group called The Violet Quill. The group was united by friendship and a taste for sweet desserts, but also by the feeling that in the post-Stonewall decade a new gay literature had an opportunity to develop. Those of their works discussed at length here reflect a brief, if golden period between the onset of gay liberation and the AIDS epidemic, which has killed at this writing more than half of The Violet Quill. Yet their work strangely anticipates the epidemic that will so decimate their ranks. With their concern for building a gay community positioned within the heterosexual community to act as the bridge between the living and the dead, they put in place a mythic structure that would enable gay people to cope with AIDS. Such recent works as Michael Cunningham's *A Home at the End of the World* and David Feinberg's *Eighty-sixed* are more than indebted to the work of The Violet Quill; it is impossible to imagine their coming into being without them.

Among the finest works which embody this gay mythic structure is David Plante's trilogy, *The Francoeur Novels,* which tells the story of Daniel Francoeur, Plante's autobiographical hero, and his large and tragic French-American family. Daniel Francoeur, next to the youngest of seven sons, grows up—like his creator—to be a novelist living in London who returns periodically to Providence, Rhode Island, to visit his parents.

Until *The Catholic,* Plante's work was rarely classified as gay literature, although Plante in his book of nonfiction, *Difficult Women,* acknowledges his homosexuality. "Homosexuality" and "gay" are words
that never appear in the trilogy. Yet it is this very reticence that makes
The Francoeur Novels quintessentially gay. For gay statements—the
love that dares not speak its name—as we have seen repeatedly are
almost always unspoken subtext to be inferred from the literary context. As Max Desir, in Ferro's novel, is taught by his friend Arthur,
"One always has to read between the lines for the queer bits" (193).

In the Francoeur family the typical reticence toward homosexuality
is enhanced by the cultural habit of suppressing emotions. In his blue-
collar family, feelings are constantly denied until they burst out in terrible paroxysms of anger, guilt, and sadness. Even the smallest emotions are denied, as when Daniel returns home for a short visit: "My
mother, her head realized as if the tilt allowed more light into her eyes,
said, 'Why are you crying' 'I'm not,' I said. . . . My brother was behind
me with my suitcase, 'Where do you want this?' he asked. I was wiping
tears away with my knuckles, 'Put it here by the stove.' I said"
(408–9). Daniel cannot admit that he is brought to tears by the sight
of his mother, but attempts to hide his emotions in the banal details of
homecoming.

The most overtly gay character is Daniel's brother, Edmund, a tool-
and-die worker whose sexual predilection is apparently for youths. As
in so many families, Edmund's homosexuality is only tacitly recognized, sometimes with contempt but more often with indulgence. On
a visit home, Daniel asks Edmund if he still sees his teenage friend
Tommy Walters.

> No. You know, we used to do a lot together, Tommy and me, we'd go up
> to the shopping mall and play the pinball machines, have an ice-cream
> soda, and I'd buy him a model car, then we'd go to his house and watch
> television with his mother, or he'd come here and we'd watch television.
> But then when he became sixteen he bought a real car. Now he goes off
> on his own. I don't know where he goes. He was a good friend for a
> while, and I know that if I didn't use to have his company I would have
> gone crazy, with work and what I have to do for Mere and Pere that
> Albert doesn't do, but now he doesn't come around anymore. (431)

It sounds innocent enough until one remembers that Edmund is a man
in his forties, quite old enough to be Tommy's father, and that an

earlier friendship with a thirteen-year-old boy named Billy ended because Billy's parents forbade Edmund further contact with their son (485). The depth of Edmund's feelings can be gauged by Tommy's return when he hears that Francoeur Pere has died. "You see," Edmund explains, "he came back to his family. We're Tommy's family" (502). Before his father's funeral Edmund asks his brothers if Tommy can take a place with the grandsons in being a pallbearer, and the brothers acquiesce, "if it'd please you, Ed, . . . of course" (515). The unspeakable remains beneath the surface. Edmund's lover must find a place in this family's grief.

In the Francoeur family, the unmarried sons, who have no children of their own, are the ones who take care of the aging parents. Edmund lives with his mother and father; Albert, a retired military officer, stays not far away. In two parallel scenes Daniel cuts his father's nails (428) and bathes his mother. The veneration and care of parents is the role of the gay sons not only in *The Country*, the last of the Francoeur novels, but also in Ferro's *Family of Max Desir* and even in Holleran's *Nights in Aruba* in which Mr. Friel spends each Sunday with his parents preparing, in Tupperware containers, their dinners for the rest of the week. "One day," he tells the narrator, "I will find them not breathing. I will have to act. Go to the telephone, phone whom? The ambulance, the funeral home? I dread it more than my own death" (135–36). Since AIDS, this caregiving role has been extended to friends and lovers.

In his duty to his parents, the gay son expresses two of his mythic roles. He acts as agent for the family's ancestral past and as the one who oversees the transition of the living into the dead. It is no trivial matter for Max Desir that his father rejects his and Nick's place on the family tree, for it is their role to tend to its cultivation, not by continuing it, but by paying it homage. Similarly, it is the proper tale for the gay Francoeur sons to take care of their parents, since in doing so they obey "certain high principles . . . which exist above me and you and the whole country," principles which "make . . . another country" (482).

The entire action of *The Country* is Daniel Francoeur's attempt to gain access to these high principles, those tribal laws that can be met only in his father. Like Fred in *A Boy's Own Story* who goes to live as a "garden god" among the Mexican Indians, or like the blond-haired Englishman in *The Family of Max Desir* who lives among the Amazonian tribes, Daniel Francoeur tries to learn about his Indian past. He is one-quarter Indian, his grandmother having been "a full-blooded Blackfoot" (413). On one journey out to the country, Daniel gains a partial vision of his ancestral past.

> I stopped, turned, and saw, in the light, my father, standing alone. He was very straight. He was looking away from me. His lips were moving, I saw, standing in the woods behind him, his mother, large and dark, and deeper in, a larger, darker woman, and then another and another, each larger and darker, mothers and daughters, daughters and mothers, going back and back, to a great dark mother, to whom my father could pray in a language I did not know. (424)

The gay son does not view his father as the access to a patriarchy, but rather to a matriarchal line at once more potent and more mysterious. The vision is one Daniel can only see at the outset of the novel. He cannot participate in it because he does not know the language. Not until the last pages will Daniel gain a greater part of it, and again such access will be through the spirit of his father: "In the stillness of the woods there was the calm, clear space of a strange country, and though I could not see it, or hear it . . . I knew it was populated. . . . In almost dark, snow fell. The snow fell loosely; then, as I walked through the densest part of the woods, it revolved among the trees with a whish sound, and disappeared. I stood under a pine tree . . . I was with my father" (547). Unlike any of the other gay characters, Daniel is reconciled at last with his father—they have become two spirits inhabiting an ancestral wood. Though Daniel cannot at first "hear," at the end he does. The whish of snow, the breathing of the wind through trees or through the body, this is the Ur-sound, the common language which unites all children with their ancestors. Daniel comes to recognize through the death of his father how they are united: "My father was born as I was, among the ghosts of a small community of people of strange blood. They were people who saw that they were born in darkness and would die in darkness, and who accepted that. They spoke in their old French, in whispers, in the churchyard . . . in the snow, and with them, silent, were squaws with papooses on their backs" (522). The link of the gay son to his ancestral past transcends the Christianity which attempted to block the identification. The essential link that binds the gay writer with his past is pagan and forged out of the death with which homoeroticism is intrinsically bound.

This awful and terrifying vision that through orgasm—what the

Elizabethans called dying—one gains a vision of our ancestral past is central to Max Desir, who cannot reveal the vision to anyone.

> What Max couldn't say to Clive or Nick was that sometimes, on the point of coming, the floor opened and the image of his mother flew at him. Death, he thought. . . . The image did not linger. . . . When it happened again he stopped and looked. . . . She was dead. She was wearing a wig and a ruffled collar like Elizabeth I. The image seemed actual, like a theatrical production. Her eyes were closed. They remained closed. (178)

There is, however, a strong exception to this rule. In *Totempole,* Sanford Friedman's extraordinary novel, his protagonist, Stephen Wolfe, must break out of the totemic world of his ancestors and enter the rational world of science where sexual expression is freed from the irrational taboos of the tribe. The difference between Friedman and the others lies in the fact that Stephen Wolfe is not only gay, but Jewish. The Jewish writer, unlike his Gentile counterpart, is less able to entertain the romantic fiction of a tribal, pagan ancestry that antedates the Puritanical restrictions opposing him. Since Judaism has never lost its tribal structure or ethos, the Jewish writer is hard pressed to imagine a pre-Hebraic tribe which would accept such sexual variation. Friedman sees the tribe as being, if anything, more intolerant of homosexuality than modern man. In this regard Friedman is like Freud, who—as I indicated in the discussion of the intersection between cannibalism and homosexuality—fixes the origins of homophobia at the moment when tribal brotherhood overcomes parental tyranny. For Friedman, a return to the tribe is a return to irrational tabus, sexual restriction, and psychological repression. Yet, even *Totempole* senses that the homosexual must, to be free, find a place for himself in heterosexual society that strengthens the community's well-being. The Korean doctor, who extricates Stephen from the grasp of superstition, is dedicated to caring for his fellow Koreans. *Totempole* moves from the tribal to the communal, from senseless and exclusive hierarchy to rational and embracive egalitarianism.

We have observed repeatedly the tendency of gay writers to search in primitive cultures for role models. Writers such as John Addington Symonds, Havelock Ellis, and Edward Carpenter sought in the classical Greek a pattern for modern friendship. Alain Locke and Countee Cullen tried to find such models in classical Africa, and Francis Grierson explored the value of Native American culture. The anthropologist and philosopher Edward Westermarck noted in his influential study of the origins of ethics the high correlation between homosexuality and shamanism. In this, Westermarck followed the lead of traditional ethnographers and more contemporary anthropologists. As Gloria Flaherty has demonstrated, enlightened ethnography has always been fascinated by the correlation of shamanism and homosexuality, and though "deeply troubled" about the pederastic use of children, ethnographers "went on to make their reports and analyses according to the current state of scholarly methodology" (265). In short, according to Flaherty, ethnography has always been a rhetorical space in which homosexual practices were given more objective or at least less hysterical treatment than in other official discourses.

By the time Westermarck wrote, the subject had taken an even lyrical turn in such French writers as Elie Reclus, whose remarkably poetic work *Primitive Folk* formed a part of a series edited by Ellis. In the work, Reclus discussed the *choupans* who are Aleutian boys raised as girls because they have "a pretty face [and] a graceful demeanor": "The pretty youths . . . willingly dedicated themselves to the priesthood, and when their first youth is passed take orders . . . From time immemorial there has been a marked affinity between the minion and the servant of the altar, between prostitute and passacide" (68). Another initiation rite is even more explicit in its association of homosexuality, priestliness, and death. The young priest goes to an uninhabited island where a famous shaman's corpse lies hidden. The initiate then "sleeps the sleep of death, but only sleeps" (78). By beating on a magic drum, the *angakok* wakes the dead shaman: "At the noise the corpse starts, the feathers flutter, the mask shakes. The living salutes the dead by rubbing his nose against the nasal bone of the corpse. Then passes his hand across the stomach as much as to say, 'How delightful!'" (78–79). The *angakok* is not a typical tribal member. As a *choupan* he is raised as a girl and has sexual relations with the *angakok* who is his master. But neither man is an outcast. To the contrary, though "debarred from all official power, he is . . . consulted on every important occasion, and his advice is always followed" (80). He is, according to Reclus, "public counsellor, justice of the peace, universal authority, arbitrator in public and private affairs, artist of all kinds, poet, actor, buffoon" (81). With some irony, Reclus concludes his section on the *angakok* by noting: "The angakout themselves are always represented as being instruments of satan by the missionaries of the Greek, Lutheran and other churches" (81).

The most important proponent of the shamanistic role of the homosexual is Edward Carpenter who, throughout his career as poet, critic, and social theorist, wove anthropological fact into a myth of social transformation. In his remarkable study *Intermediate Types Among Primitive Folk,* Carpenter argues that the homosexual is the central figure in the transformation of society, responsible for leading the primal horde into the cooperative tribe. Carpenter argues that there are two species of homosexuals, or Uranians, as he prefers to call them. On the one hand are the supermasculine types who became the warrior clans of Dorian Greece and medieval Japan; on the other hand, are the feminized males who were inclined "to retire into the precincts of the Temples and the services (often sexual) of Religion—which, of course in primitive days, meant not only the religious like in our sense, but the dedication to such things as Magic, learning, poetry, music, prophecy" (12). Indeed, for Carpenter, gay men and women did not so much choose these roles as invent them because they were unable or unwilling to fit into the stereotypical, heterosexual models of warrior/hunter and domestic servant.

> When the man came along who did not want to fight—who perhaps was more inclined to run away—and who did not particularly care about hunting, he necessarily discovered some other interest and occupation—composing songs or observing the qualities of herbs or the processions of the stars. Similarly with the woman who did not care about housework and child-rearing. The non-warlike men and the non-domestic women, in short, sought new outlets for their energies. They sought different occupations from those quite ordinary men and women—as in fact they do to-day; and so they became the initiators of quite new outlets for their energies. (*Intermediate Types,* 58)

Despite the impression this passage gives of gay people as negations of the ordinary (nondomestic, nonwarlike), elsewhere Carpenter stresses that homosexuals differ from heterosexuals by being more intuitive and affectionate. "There is an organic connection between homosexual temperament and unusual psychic or divinatory powers," he insists in *Intermediate Types* (46), and in the concluding chapter to *The Intermediate Sex* entitled "The Place of the Uranian in Society," he argues: "Unwilling as the world at large is to credit what I am about to say, and great as are the current misunderstandings on the subject, I believe it is true that the Uranian men are superior to the normal men in this respect—in respect of their love-feeling—which is gentler, more sympathetic, more considerate, more a matter of the heart and less of mere physical satisfaction than that of ordinary men" (126). Clearly, the homosexual's greater psychic and affectional powers lead him or her to artistic and religious occupations. Gay people were not simply banned from traditional social functions; they evolved to create a more complex, varied, livelier, and more satisfying society. We have seen how F. O. Matthiessen has used the exceptional qualities of the Uranian to construct his notion of the writer.

Moreover, according to Carpenter, the homosexual is not finished with the job of transforming society. In the modern world, when the "religion of the body, and a belief in the essential sacredness of all its processes" has been lost, Carpenter calls upon the Uranian to show society how it may "adapt the free life to the open air and restore the healing and gracious sense of human community and solidarity" (*Intermediate Types,* 170). And when Love, instead of being "the binding and directing force of society" is only a "Cash-nexus," Carpenter argues that "the superior types of Uranians—prepared by society by long experience and devotion, as well as by much suffering" will play an "important part . . . in the transformation" of human relations (*Intermediate Sex,* 122–23). In short, because the homosexual has better psychic powers and more emotional sensitivity, he or she will not only awaken the religious sentiments of society, but also direct society from "property consideration" (126) to "more spontaneous and comparatively unrestricted associations" (127). Through sex, the nonreproductive sex of the homosexual, the homoerotic act moves retrograde —not to future generations, but back to former generations. The gay man or woman, unburdened of the forms of heterosexual love so easily degraded into property considerations, achieves a kind of communion with the dead and becomes the vehicle through which they speak and make themselves manifest.

The message that gay readers gain from their fiction is very different, then, from the message heterosexuals wish to communicate to the homosexual. Heterosexuals fear the homosexual as an enemy of the family who wishes to break the contact the young have with familial traditions. Heterosexuals view homosexuals as distant from their fathers, and obsessed with their mothers' "introjected" identity. According to heterosexuals, homosexuality exists outside of the social system since homosexuals do not produce families of their own.

Fiction is not merely reportage. No matter how realistic a work of fiction pretends to be, it is fundamentally linked to a myth and calls on its readers to emulate the protagonist's actions, to avoid his mistakes, or to accept his predestined fate. Gay fiction is no different.

Until recently, heterosexuals have produced the myths by which homosexuals lived. They have viewed the homosexual as an evil person or a helpless victim of fate. In either case, the gay protagonist will die or live life in isolation and unhappiness. In the straight myths, gays are so intimately attached to the images of their mothers that they have made themselves unfit for life within the family structure. Though this is paradoxical, its contradictions were accepted by gays (including gay authors). In Holleran's fiction, it necessitates that his characters keep their sexual life and their family life strictly separate. His characters obsessively fear that one life will contaminate the other. Clearly, gays who accept the straight myths of homosexual life will enact the self-destructive end such myths dictate. Their unhappiness is a self-fulfilling prophecy.

At the center of the straight myth, there is the belief that homage to the family can be shown only through duplication. The son must duplicate the act of father; he must create his own family on his father's model. In the heterosexual world, the failure to reproduce the family is an attack on the family. Homosexual sex is an act that goes to the etymological root of iconoclasm.

But, of course, there are more ways to show homage than through duplication. Though imitation may be the sincerest form of flattery, one does not need to flatter the household gods in order to respect them. What gay writers are attempting to do, it seems to me, is forge a mythos of their own which pays homage to the family without reproducing it.

The need for such a mythos is there. As Jacques Lacan and other psychologists have pointed out, our contemporary culture is weak in its symbolizations of death. It has forgotten how to make the transition from the living to the dead; thus it suspends the dying in a permanent coma in which they are neither buried nor paid respect. The liberating of the gay imagination will come when the homosexual sees that he plays a necessary role in the culture—that his relationship to the family and to his tribe is as the servant of the dead, the other, and as the person charged with the responsibility of transporting the living through the process of death. In recent gay fiction, the homosexual has become Charon, the ferryman, the sea captain. We may imagine him on liberty, his arms around his handsome sailors. In the new myth, Billy Budd need not be killed for his beauty; he will take his place in Captain Vere's bed where together they will set a steady course across the Lethe, the cabins booked by their mothers and fathers, brothers, sisters, uncles, and aunts.

A comic image? Yes, I suppose so. But the challenge of the gay writer will be to convert the heterosexual tragedy of gay life into a homosexual comedy. Indeed, the mythos of comedy is already better suited to the homosexual than tragedy since in comedy's mythos of eternal spring, transvestism, exile, and return have been firmly established. One need make room only for the unmasked lovers to be of the same sex, which was the case in Shakespeare's time when orgasm and death were more comfortably united. The comedic mythos will come, however, only when the homosexual accepts his homosexuality and recognizes it as an honor to his family. For the homosexual, as the final product of heterosexual duplication, is in effect its final achievement—the telos toward which process has been moving. As the blond Englishman recognizes at the conclusion of *The Family of Max Desir,* though he does not "understand all of what they think me to be, or wish me to do for them[,] I make every effort to bless them and to show them no fear. . . . All that cannot be explained makes me holy" (217–18).

BIBLIOGRAPHY

Abrams, Robert E. "*Typee* and *Omoo:* Herman Melville and the Ungraspable Phantom of Identity." *Arizona Quarterly* 31 (1975): 33–50.

Acevedo, John R. "Impact of Risk Reduction on Mental Health." In *What to Do about AIDS: Physicians and Mental Health Professionals Discuss the Issues,* edited by Leon McKusic, 95–102. Berkeley: Univ. of California Press, 1986.

Adorno, Theodor W. *Minima Moralia: Reflections from a Damaged Life.* London: Verso, 1974.

Adorno, Theodor W. "Subject and Object." In *The Essential Frankfurt Reader,* edited by Andrew Arato and Eike Gebhardt, 497–511. New York: Continuum, 1982.

Ahrens, W. *The Man-Eating Myth: Anthropology and Anthropophagy.* New York: Oxford Univ. Press, 1979.

Aquinas, St. Thomas. *The Summa Theologica,* translated by Fathers of the English Dominican Province. London: Burns Oates & Washbourne, 1896.

Arac, Jonathan. "F. O. Matthiessen: Authorizing an American Renaissance." In *The American Renaissance Reconsidered: Selected Papers of the English Institute, 1982–83,* edited by Walter Benn Michaels and Donald E. Pease, 90–112. Baltimore: Johns Hopkins Press, 1985.

Aron, Jean Paul, and Roger Kempf. *Le penis et la démoralisation de l'occident.* Paris: Grasset, 1978.

Ashbery, John. *April Galleons.* New York: Viking, 1987.

Ashbery, John. *The Double Dream of Spring.* New York: Ecco Press, 1976.

Ashbery, John. *Rivers and Mountains.* New York: Ecco Press, 1977.

Ashbery, John. "The Romance of Reality." *Art News* 15 (1966): 28–30, 56.

Ashbery, John. *Self-Portrait in a Convex Mirror.* New York: Viking, 1975.

Ashbery, John. *Some Trees.* New York: Corinth, 1970.

Ashbery, John. *A Wave.* New York: Viking, 1984.

Avi-Ram, Amitai. "The Unreadable Black Body: 'Conventional' Poetic Form in the Harlem Renaissance." *Genders* 7 (1990): 32–46.

Babuscio, Jack. "Camp and the Gay Sensibility." In *Gays and Film,* edited by Richard Dyer, 40–57. Rev. ed. New York: Zoetrope, 1984.

213

Bachofen, J. J. *Mother Right.* 1861.

Bakhtin, Mikhail. *Rabelais and His World.* Translated by Helene Iswolsky. Cambridge, Mass.: MIT Press, 1968.

Baldwin, James. *Another Country.* New York: Dell, 1962.

Baldwin, James. *The Evidence of Things Not Seen.* New York: Henry Holt, 1985.

Baldwin, James. *Giovanni's Room.* New York: Dell, 1956.

Baldwin, James. *Going to Meet the Man.* New York: Dell, 1965.

Baldwin, James. *Just Above My Head.* New York: Dell, 1979.

Baldwin, James. In *Perspectives: Angles on African Art,* 113–28. New York: The Center for African Art, and Abrams, 1987.

Baldwin, James. *The Price of the Ticket.* New York: St. Martin's, 1985.

Baldwin, James, and Nikki Giovanni. *A Dialogue.* Philadelphia: Lippincott, 1973.

Barnes, James B. "Alain Locke and the Sense of the African Legacy." In *Alain Locke: Reflections on a Modern Renaissance Man,* edited by Russell J. Linneman, 100–108. Baton Rouge: Louisiana State Univ. Press, 1982.

Barthes, Roland. *Wilhelm Von Gloeden.* Naples: Amelio Editore, 1978.

Bauerlein, Mark. "Whitman's Language of the Self." *American Imago* 44 (1987): 129–48.

Beam, Joseph. "Brother to Brother: Words from the Heart." In *In the Life: A Black Gay Anthology,* edited by Joseph Beam, 230–42. Boston: Alyson Publications, 1986.

Berger, Charles. "The Vision in the Form of a Task." In *Beyond Amazement: New Essays on John Ashbery,* edited by David Lehman, 163–208. Ithaca: Cornell Univ. Press, 1980.

Bersani, Leo. "Is the Rectum a Grave?" In *AIDS: Cultural Analysis/Cultural Activism,* edited by Douglas Crimp, 197–222. Cambridge, Mass.: MIT Press, 1988.

Bieber, Irving. *Homosexuality: A Psychological Study.* New York: Vintage, 1962.

Blau, Herbert. *The Eye of Prey: Subversions of the Post-Modern.* Bloomington: Indiana Univ. Press, 1987.

Bone, Robert A. "The Novels of James Baldwin." In *Images of the Negro in American Literature,* edited by Seymour L. Gross and John E. Hardy, 265–88. Chicago: Univ. of Chicago Press, 1966.

Boone, Joseph Allen. *Tradition Counter Tradition: Love and the Forms of Fiction.* Chicago: Univ. of Chicago Press, 1987.

Brandt, Allan M. "AIDS: From Social History to Social Polity." In *AIDS: The Burdens of History,* edited by Elizabeth Fee and Daniel M. Fox, 147–71. Berkeley: Univ. of California Press, 1988.

Brannan, Robert, ed. *Under the Management of Mr. Charles Dickens: His Production of "The Frozen Deep."* Ithaca: Cornell Univ. Press, 1966.

Branner, Bernard. "Blackberri: Singing for Our Lives." In *In the Life: A Black Gay Anthology,* edited by Joseph Beam, 170–84. Boston: Alyson Publications, 1986.

Bray, Alan. *Homosexuality in Renaissance England.* London: GMP, 1982.

Brodsky, Joseph. *Less Than One: Selected Essays.* New York, Farrar, 1977.

Bryant, Anita. *The Anita Bryant Story: The Survival of Our Nation's Families and the Threat of Militant Homosexuality.* Old Tappan, N.J.: Revell, 1977.

Cain, William E. *F. O. Matthiessen and the Politics of Criticism.* Madison: Univ. of Wisconsin Press, 1988.

Carpenter, Edward. *The Intermediate Sex: A Study in Some Transitional Types of Men and Women.* London: George Allen & Unwin, 1908.

Carpenter, Edward. *Intermediate Types Among Primitive Folk.* London: George Allen, 1914.

Carpenter, Edward. *Love's Coming of Age.* London: George Allen & Unwin, 1919.

Carpenter, Edward. *Selected Writings, Volume One: Sex.* London: GMP, 1984.

Castle, Terry. "The Culture of Travesty: Sexuality and Masquerade in Eighteenth Century England." In *Sexual Underworlds of the Enlightenment,* edited by G. S. Rousseau and Roy Porter, 156–80. Chapel Hill: Univ. of North Carolina Press, 1988.

Chester, Alfred. *The Exquisite Corpse.* New York: Carroll and Graf, 1986.

Chester, Alfred. *Head of a Sad Angel: Stories 1953–1966.* Edited by Edward Field. Santa Rosa, Calif.: Black Sparrow, 1990.

Chodorow, Nancy. *The Reproduction of Mothering: Psychoanalysis and the Sociology of Gender.* Berkeley: Univ. of California Press, 1976.

Cleaver, Eldridge. *Soul on Ice.* New York: McGraw-Hill, 1968.

Cohen, Ira. "Our Ancestor Alfred Chester." Appendix to *Head of a Sad Angel: Stories 1953–1966,* by Alfred Chester, Santa Rosa, Calif.: Black Sparrow Press, 1990.

Collecott, Diana. "What is Not Said: A Study in Textual Inversion," *Textual Practice* 4.2 (1990): 236–58.

Coote, Stephen, ed. *The Penguin Book of Homosexual Verse.* Harmondsworth: Penguin, 1983.

Craft, Christopher. "'Descend and Touch and Enter': Tennyson's Strange Manner of Address." *Genders* 1, no. 2 (1988): 83–101.

Cunningham, Michael. *A Home at the End of the World.* New York: Farrar Straus, 1990.

Cureau, Rebecca T. "Toward an Aesthetic of Black Folk Expression." In *Alain Locke: Reflections on a Modern Renaissance Man,* edited by Russell J. Linnemann, 77–90. Baton Rouge: Louisiana State Univ. Press, 1982.

Curzon, Daniel. *Curson in Love.* New York: Sea Horse Press, 1988.

Dank, Barry M. "Coming Out in the Gay World." In *Gay Men: The Sociology of Male Homosexuality,* edited by Martin P. Levine, 103–33. New York: Harper, 1979.

Delany, Samuel R., and Joseph Beam. "Samuel R. Delany: The Possibility of Possibilities." In *In the Life: A Black Gay Anthology,* edited by Joseph Beam, 185–208. Boston: Alyson Publications, 1986.

D'Emilio, John. *Sexual Politics, Sexual Communities: The Making of a Homosexual Minority in the United States 1940–1970.* Chicago: Univ. of Chicago Press, 1983.

Dickinson, Goldsworthy Lowes. *The Greek View of Life.* London: Methuen, 1909.

Dollimore, Jonathan. "The Dominant and the Deviant: A Violent Dialectic," *Critical Quarterly* 28, nos. 1–2 (1986): 179–92.

Dover, K. J. *Greek Homosexuality.* New York: Vintage, 1978.

Duncan, Robert. *Caesar's Gate: Poems 1949–50.* N.p.: Sand Dollar, 1972.

Duncan, Robert. "The Homosexual in Society." In *Young Robert Duncan: Portrait of the Poet as Homosexual in Society,* edited by Ekbert Fass, 319–22. Santa Barbara, Calif.: Black Sparrow, 1983.

Duncan, Robert. "Two Chapters from H. D." *Triquarterly* 12 (Spring 1968): 67–98.

Edel, Leon, ed. *Henry James Letters.* Vols. 3 and 4. Cambridge, Mass.: Harvard Univ. Press, 1984.

Edelman, Lee. "The Plague of Discourse: Politics, Literary Theory, and AIDS." *The South Atlantic Quarterly* 88, no. 1 (1989): 301–17.

Ellis, Havelock. *Studies in the Psychology of Sex, Vol. 1 (Sexual Inversion).* New York: Random House, 1936.

Ellmann, Richard. *Oscar Wilde.* New York: Knopf, 1988.

Engels, Frederick. *The Origin of the Family, Private Property, and the State.* New York: Pathfinder Press, 1972.

Epiphanius of Salamis. *The Panarion of Epiphanius of Salamis.* Edited by James M. Robinson and translated by Frank Williams. Nag Hammadi Studies, Vol. 35. Leiden: E. J. Brill, 1987.

Erikson, Erik. *Identity: Youth and Crisis.* New York: Norton, 1968.

Federman, Lillian. *Surpassing the Love of Men: Romantic Friendship and Love Between Women from the Renaissance to the Present.* New York: Morrow, 1981.

Feinberg, David B. *Eighty-Sixed.* New York: Viking, 1989.

Ferro, Robert. *The Blue Star.* New York: Dutton, 1985.

Ferro, Robert. *The Family of Max Desir.* New York: Dutton, 1983.

Ferro, Robert. *Second Son.* New York: Crown, 1988.

Fiedler, Leslie A. In *Critical Essays on James Baldwin,* edited by Fred L. Standley and Nancy V. Burt, 146–49. Boston: G. K. Hall, 1988.

Field, Edward. Personal interview, 7 June 1990.

Fitzgerald, Frances. "The Castro." In *Cities on the Hill,* 25–119. New York: Simon & Schuster, 1987.

Flaherty, Gloria. "Sex and Shamanism in the Eighteenth Century." In *Sexual Underworlds of the Enlightenment,* edited by G. S. Rousseau and Roy Porter, 261–80. Chapel Hill: Univ. of North Carolina Press, 1988.

Ford, Charles Henri, and Ira Cohen. Interview with Charles Henri Ford. In *Gay Sunshine Interviews,* Vol. 1, edited by Winston Leland, 35–66. San Francisco: Gay Sunshine Press, 1978

Foucault, Michel. *The History of Sexuality: Vol. 1: An Introduction.* New York: Vintage, 1980.

Freud, Sigmund. "Creative Writers and Day-dreaming." In *The Standard Edition of the Complete Psychological Works, Vol. 9,* edited by James Strachey, 143–53. London: Hogarth, 1959.

Freud, Sigmund. "From the History of an Infantile Neurosis." In *Collected Papers,* Vol. 3, 473–605. New York: Basic, 1959.

Freud, Sigmund. *Leonardo Da Vinci and a Memory of Childhood.* In *The Standard Edition of the Complete Psychological Works, Vol. 11,* edited by James Strachey, 59–137. London: Hogarth, 1957.

Freud, Sigmund. *Totem and Taboo: Resemblances Between the Psychic Lives of Savages and Neurotics.* Translated by A. A. Brill. New York: Vintage, 1946.

Fricke, Aaron. *Reflections of a Rock Lobster: A Story About Growing Up Gay.* Boston: Alyson Publications, 1981.

Friedman, Sanford. "An Interview with Richard Howard." *Shenandoah* 24 (1973): 5–31.

Friedman, Sanford. *Totempole.* San Francisco: North Point, 1984.

Fries, Kenny. *The Healing Notebooks.* Berkeley: Open Books, 1990.

Fuss, Diana. *Essentially Speaking: Feminism, Nature and Difference.* New York: Routledge, 1989.

Gates, Henry Louis, Jr. *The Signifying Monkey: A Theory of Afro-American Literary Criticism.* New York: Oxford Univ. Press, 1988.

Gever, Martha. "Pictures of Sickness: Stuart Marshall's *Bright Eyes.*" In *AIDS: Cultural Analysis/Cultural Activism,* edited by Douglas Crimp, 109–27. Cambridge, Mass.: MIT Press, 1988.

Gide, André. *If It Die.* Harmondsworth: Penguin, 1982.

Gide, André. *Travels in the Congo.* Harmondsworth: Penguin, 1986.

Gilman, Richard. *Decadence: The Strange Life of an Epithet.* New York: Farrar, Straus and Giroux, 1971.

Gilman, Sander L. "AIDS and Syphilis: The Iconography of Disease." In *AIDS: Cultural Analysis/Cultural Action,* edited by Douglas Crimp, 87-108. Cambridge, Mass.: MIT Press, 1988.

Ginsberg, Allen. *Collected Poems: 1947–1980.* New York: Harper & Row, 1984.

Gluck, Robert. *Jack the Modernist.* New York: Gay Presses of New York, 1985.

Goldstein, Richard. "'Go the Way Your Blood Beats': An Interview with James Baldwin." In *James Baldwin: The Legacy,* edited by Quincy Troupe, 173–85. New York: Simon & Schuster, 1989.

Greenberg, David F. *The Construction of Homosexuality.* Chicago: Univ. of Chicago Press, 1988.

Grierson, Francis. *The Celtic Temperament, and Other Essays.* Port Washington, N.Y.: Kennikat Press, 1970.

Grierson, Francis. *The Humor of the Underman, and Other Essays.* London: Stephen Swift, 1911.

Grierson, Francis. *Modern Mysticism and Other Essays.* Port Washington: Kennikat Press, 1970.

Grierson, Francis. *The Valley of Shadows.* 5th ed. Edited by Bernard de Voto, with an introduction by Theodore Spencer. Boston: Houghton Mifflin, 1948.

Grover, Jan Zita. "AIDS: Keywords." In *AIDS: Cultural Analysis/Cultural Activism,* edited by Douglas Crimp, 17–30. Cambridge, Mass.: MIT Press, 1988.

Gunn, Thom. *The Occasions of Poetry: Essays in Criticism and Autobiography.* Expanded ed. San Francisco: North Point, 1985.

Halperin, David M. *One Hundred Years of Homosexuality and Other Essays on Greek Love.* New York: Routledge, 1990.

Harry, Joseph, and William B. DeVall. *The Social Organization of Gay Males.* New York: Praeger, 1978.

Hartland, Claude. *The Story of a Life.* San Francisco: Grey Fox Press, 1985.

Hedges, Elaine. Untitled essay. In *Hearts and Hands: The Influence of Women And Quilts on American Society,* edited by Pat Ferrero, Elaine Hedges, and Julie Silver. San Francisco: Quilt Digest Press, 1987.

Herdt, Gilbert H. *Guardians of the Flute: Idioms of Masculinity.* New York: McGraw-Hill, 1981.

Hocquenghem, Guy. *Homosexual Desire.* Translated by Daniella Dangoor. London: Allison & Busby, 1978.

Holleran, Andrew. *Dancer from the Dance.* New York: Bantam, 1979.

Holleran, Andrew. *Ground Zero.* New York: New American Library, 1989.

Holleran, Andrew. "Introduction" to *The Normal Heart,* by Larry Kramer, 23–28. New York: New American Library, 1985.

Holleran, Andrew. *Nights in Aruba.* New York: Morrow, 1981.

Horstman, William, and Leon McKusic. "The Impact of AIDS on the Physician." In *What to Do about AIDS: Physicians and Mental Health Professionals Discuss the Issues,* edited by Leon McKusic, 63–74. Berkeley: Univ. of California Press, 1986.

Howard, Richard. *Fellow Feelings*. New York: Atheneum, 1974.

Howard, Richard. "The Mapplethorpe Effect." In *Robert Mapplethorpe,* by Richard Marshall, 152–59. New York: Whitney Museum, 1988.

Howard, Richard. "Preface: Considerations of a Transfuge." In *Homosexualities and French Literature,* edited by George Strombolian and Elaine Marks, 11–22. Ithaca: Cornell Univ. Press, 1979.

Howard, Richard. *Quantities*. Middletown, Conn.: Wesleyan Univ. Press, 1962.

Howard, Richard. "Translator's Note." In *Corydon,* by André Gide, vii–xvii. London: GMP, 1985.

Hughes, Langston. *The Big Sea: An Autobiography*. New York: Thunder's Mouth Press, 1986.

Hyde, H. Montgomery. *The Love that Dare Not Speak Its Name*. Boston: Little Brown, 1970.

Hyde, Louis, ed. *Rat and the Devil: Journal Letters of F. O. Matthiessen and Russell Cheney*. Reprint ed. Boston: Alyson Publications, 1988.

Isay, Richard. *Being Homosexual*. New York: Farrar Straus, 1990.

Jackson, Bruce. "Deviance as Success: The Double Inversion of Stigmatized Roles." In *The Reversable World: Symbolic Inversion in Art and Society,* edited by Barbara A. Babcock, 258–75. Ithaca: Cornell Univ. Press, 1978.

Jones, A. Billy S. "A Father's Need, A Parent's Desire." In *In the Life: A Gay Black Anthology,* edited by Joseph Beam, 143–51. Boston: Alyson Publications, 1986.

Katz, Jonathan N. *Gay American History: Lesbians and Gay Men in the U.S.A.* New York: Crowell, 1976.

Kiernan, Robert F. *Frivolity Unbounded: Six Masters of the Camp Novel*. New York: Continuum, 1990.

Kinsey, Alfred, et al. *Sexual Behavior and the Human Male*. Philadelphia: W. B. Saunders, 1948.

Kleinberg, Seymour. "Life after Death." In *AIDS: Ethics and Public Policy,* edited by Christine Pierce and Donald VanDeVeer, 56–60. Belmont, Calif.: Wadsworth, 1988.

Koestenbaum, Wayne. "Privileging the Anus: Anna O. and the Collaborative Origin of Psychoanalysis." *Genders* 1, no. 3 (1988): 57–81.

Kramer, Larry. *Faggots*. New York: Random House, 1978.

Kramer, Larry. *The Normal Heart*. New York: New American Library, 1985.

Kramer, Larry. *Reports from the Holocaust: The Making of an AIDS Activist*. New York: St. Martin's, 1989.

Kristeva, Julia. *Desire in Language: A Semiotic Approach to Literature and Art*. Edited by Leon S. Roudiez, and translated by Thomas Gora, Alice Jardine, and Leon S. Roudiez. New York: Columbia Univ. Press, 1980.

Lacan, Jacques. *Écrit: A Selection.* New York: Norton, 1977.

Levin, James. *The Gay Novel: The Male Homosexual Image in America.* New York: Irvington, 1983.

Locke, Alain, ed. "The Legacy of the Ancestral Arts." In *The New Negro: An Interpretation,* by Alain Locke, 243–67. New York: Albert and Charles Boni, 1925; reprint ed., New York: Arno, 1968.

Locke, Alain. "The Negro Spirituals." In *The New Negro: An Interpretation,* by Alain Locke, 199–213. New York: Albert and Charles Boni, 1925; reprint ed., New York: Arno, 1968.

Lowell, Robert. *Day by Day.* New York: Farrar, 1977.

Lynn, Kenneth S. "F. O. Matthiessen." In *Masters: Portraits of Great Teachers,* edited by Joseph Epstein, 103–18. New York: Basic, 1981.

McClatchy, J. D. *White Paper: On Contemporary American Poetry.* New York: Columbia Univ. Press, 1989.

McIntosh, Mary. "The Homosexual Role." *Social Problems* 16 (1968): 182–92.

Mapplethorpe, Robert. *Certain People: A Book of Portraits,* N.p.: Twelvetrees Press, 1985.

Marlow, James E. "English Cannibalism: Dickens after 1859." *SEL* 23, no. 4 (1983): 429–39.

Marlowe, Christopher. *Five Plays.* Edited by Havelock Ellis. New York: Hill and Wang, 1956.

Martin, Robert K. *Hero, Captain, and Stranger: Male Friendship, Social Critique and Literary Form in the Sea Novels of Herman Melville.* Chapel Hill: Univ. of North Carolina Press, 1986.

Martin, Robert K. *The Homosexual Tradition in American Poetry.* Austin: Univ. of Texas Press, 1979.

Marvell, Andrew. *The Poems & Letters of Andrew Marvell.* Edited by H. M. Margoliouth, 2 vols. 2d ed. Oxford: Clarendon, 1952.

Marx, Leo. "Double Consciousness: The Cultural Politics of F. O. Matthiessen." *Monthly Review* 34 (February 1983): 34–56.

Matthiessen, F. O. *American Renaissance: Art and Expression in the Age of Emerson and Whitman.* New York: Oxford Univ. Press, 1941.

Matthiessen, F. O. *Sarah Orne Jewett.* Gloucester, Mass.: Peter Smith, 1965.

Melville, Herman. *Typee: A Peep at Polynesian Life.* Ed. George Woodcock. Harmondsworth: Penguin, 1972.

Merrill, James. *The Changing Light at Sandover.* New York: Atheneum, 1982.

Miller, D. A. *The Novel and The Police.* Berkeley: Univ. of California Press, 1988.

Mishima, Yukio. *Confession of a Mask.* New York: New Directions, 1958.

Mitchell, Juliet. *Psychoanalysis and Feminism.* New York: Pantheon, 1974.

Moon, Michael. *Disseminating Whitman: Revision and Corporeality in Whitman's "Leaves of Grass."* Cambridge, Mass.: Harvard Univ. Press, 1991.

Moon, Michael. "'The Gentle Boy from the Dangerous Classes': Pederasty, Domesticity and Capitalism in Horatio Alger." *Representations* 19 (1987): 87–110.

Morgan, Lewis Henry. *Ancient Society.* 1884.

Newell, Gordon. *Ocean Liners of the Twentieth Century.* New York: Bonanza Books, 1963.

Newton, Esther. *Mother Camp: The Female Impersonator in America.* Chicago: Univ. of Chicago Press, 1979.

O'Hara, Frank. *The Selected Poems.* Edited by Donald Allen. New York: Knopf, 1974.

Packard, William, ed. *The Craft of Poetry: Interviews from the New York Quarterly.* Garden City: Doubleday, 1974.

Pagden, Anthony. *The Fall of Natural Man: The American Indian and the Origins of Comparative Ethnology.* Cambridge, England: Cambridge Univ. Press, 1982.

Patterson, Leonard. "At Ebenezer Baptist Church." In *Black Men/White Men: A Gay Anthology,* edited by Michael J. Smith, 163–66. San Francisco: Gay Sunshine Press, 1983.

Peabody, Barbara. *The Screaming Room.* San Diego: Oak Tree, 1986.

Plante, David. *The Catholic.* New York: Atheneum, 1986.

Plante, David. *The Francoeur Novels: The Family, The Woods, The Country.* New York: Dutton, 1983.

Pollak, Michael. "Male Homosexuality; or Happiness in the Ghetto." In *Western Sexuality: Practice and Precept in Past and Present Times,* edited by Phillippe Aries and Andre Bejin, 40–61. Oxford: Oxford Univ. Press, 1985.

Proust, Marcel. *Cities of the Plain.* Translated by C. K. Scott Moncrieff, 1927. New York: Vintage, 1970.

Radiguet, Raymond. *Count d'Orgel.* New York: Grove Press, 1969.

Rampersad, Arnold. *The Life of Langston Hughes: Vol. 1: 1902–1941, I, Too, Sing America.* New York: Oxford Univ. Press, 1986.

Reclus, Elie. *Primitive Folk: Studies in Comparative Ethnology.* 1891.

Rich, Adrienne. "Compulsory Heterosexuality and Lesbian Existence." In *Blood, Bread, and Poetry: Selected Prose, 1979–1985,* pp. 23–75. New York: Norton, 1986.

Rodgers, Bruce. *Gay Talk: A (Sometimes Outrageous) Dictionary of Gay Slang.* New York: Paragon, 1972.

Rosenberg, Charles A. "Disease and Social Order in America: Perceptions and Expectation." *The Milbank Quarterly* 64, suppl. 1 (1986): 34–55.

Rosenthal, M. L. *The New Poets.* New York: Oxford Univ. Press, 1967.

Ross, Andrew. "Uses of Camp," *The Yale Journal of Criticism* 2, no. 2 (1988): 1–24.

Ross, Judith Wilson. "Ethics and the Language of AIDS." In *AIDS: Ethics and Public Policy,* edited by Christine Pierce and Donald VanDeVeer, 39–48. Belmont, Calif.: Wadsworth, 1988.

Ruskin, Cindy. *The Quilt: Stories from the NAMES Project.* New York: Pocket Books, 1988.

Russell, John, ed. *The Correspondence Between Paul Claudel and André Gide 1899–1926.* Boston: Beacon Press, 1964.

Sagan, Eli. *Cannibalism: Human Aggression and Cultural Form.* New York: Harper & Row, 1974.

Sanday, Peggy Reeves. *Divine Hunger: Cannibalism as a Cultural System.* Cambridge, England: Cambridge Univ. Press, 1986.

Sarton, May. *Faithful Are the Wounds.* New York: Rinehart, 1955.

Schneebaum, Tobias. *Keep the River on Your Right.* New York: Grove Press, 1982.

Schneebaum, Tobias. *Where the Spirits Dwell: An Odyssey in the Jungles of New Guinea.* New York: Grove Press, 1988.

Schofferman, Jerome. "Medicine and the Psychology of Treating the Terminally Ill." In *What to Do about AIDS: Physicians and Mental Health Professionals Discuss the Issues,* edited by Leon McKusic, 51–60. Berkeley: Univ. of California Press, 1986.

Secret History of the London Clubs. Second Part. London, 1709.

Sedgwick, Eve Kosofsky. *Between Men: English Literature and Male Homosocial Desire.* New York: Columbia Univ. Press, 1985.

Sedgewick, Eve Kosofsky. "Epistemology of the Closet (I)." *Raritan* 8.2 (1988): 39–69.

Shilts, Randy. *And the Band Played On: Politics, People and the AIDS Epidemic.* New York: St. Martin's, 1987.

Shively, Charley, ed. *Calamus Lovers: Walt Whitman's Working Class Camerados.* San Francisco: Gay Sunshine Press, 1987.

Simonson, Harold P. *Francis Grierson.* New York: Twayne, 1966.

Sinfield, Alan. *Literature, Politics, and Culture in Postwar Britain.* Berkeley: Univ. of California Press, 1989.

Slotkin, Richard. *Regeneration through Violence.* Middletown, Conn.: Wesleyan Univ. Press, 1973.

Smith, Max C. "By the Year 2000." In *In the Life: A Black Gay Anthology,* edited by Joseph Beam, 224–29. Boston: Alyson Publications, 1986.

Sontag, Susan. *Against Interpretation and Other Essays.* New York: Farrar, Straus and Giroux, 1964.

Sontag, Susan. *AIDS and Its Metaphors.* New York: Farrar, Straus, 1989.

Sontag, Susan. "Certain Mapplethorpes." In *Certain People: A Book of Portraits,* by Robert Mapplethorpe, unpaginated. N.p.: Twelvetrees Press, 1985.

Stallybrass, Peter, and Allon White. *The Politics and Poetics of Transgression*. Ithaca: Cornell Univ. Press, 1986.

Stambolian, George, and Elaine Marks, eds. *Homosexualities and French Literature: Cultural Contexts/Critical Texts*. Ithaca: Cornell Univ. Press, 1979.

Stimpson, Catharine R. *Where the Meanings Are: Feminism and Cultural Spaces*. New York: Routledge, 1989.

Stoddard, Charles Warren. *Cruising the South Seas*. Edited by Winston Leyland. San Francisco: Gay Sunshine Press, 1987.

Summers, Claude. *Gay Fictions: Wilde to Stonewall: Studies in a Male Homosexual Literary Tradition*. New York: Continuum, 1990.

Summers, Claude, and Ted-Larry Pebworth. "'We Join the Fathers': Time and the Maturing of Richard Howard." *Contemporary Poetry: A Journal of Criticism* 3, no. 4 (1978): 13–35.

Sweezy, Paul M., and Leo Huberman, eds. *F. O. Matthiessen (1902–1950): A Collective Portrait*. New York: Henry Schuman, 1950.

Symonds, John Addington. *The Memoirs of John Addington Symonds*. Edited by Phyllis Grosskurth. New York: Random House, 1984.

Thurman, Wallace. *Infants of the Spring*. Lost American Fiction. Carbondale: Southern Illinois Univ. Press, 1979.

Tinney, James S. "Struggles of a Black Pentecostal." In *Black Men/White Men: A Gay Anthology,* edited by Michael J. Smith, 167–71. San Francisco: Gay Sunshine Press, 1983.

Tinney, James S. "Why a Black Gay Church." In *In the Life: A Black Gay Anthology,* edited by Joseph Beam, 70–86. Boston: Alyson Publications, 1986.

Treichler, Paula A. "AIDS, Homophobia and Biomedical Discourse: An Epidemic of Signification." In *AIDS: Cultural Analysis/Cultural Activism,* edited by Douglas Crimp, 31–70. Cambridge, Mass.: MIT Press, 1988.

Tuttleton, James W. "Politics and Art in the Criticism of F. O. Matthiessen." *The New Criterion* 7, no. 10 (June 1989): 4–13.

Van der Veen, Evert. "A Global View of the Gay and Lesbian Press." In *The Second ILGA Pink Book: A Global View of Lesbian and Gay Liberation,* edited by The Pink Book Team, 15–21. Utrecht: Interfacultaire Werkgroep Homostudies, 1988.

Watney, Simon. "The Spectacle of AIDS." In *AIDS: Cultural Analysis/Cultural Activism,* edited by Douglas Crimp, 71–86. Cambridge, Mass.: MIT Press, 1988.

Weatherby, W. J. *James Baldwin: Artist on Fire*. New York: Dell, 1989.

Weeks, Jeffrey. *Coming Out: Homosexual Politics in Britain, from the Nineteenth Century to the Present*. London: Quartet, 1983.

Weiermair, Peter. *The Hidden Image: Photographs of the Male Nude in the Nineteenth and Twentieth Centuries*. Cambridge, Mass.: MIT Press, 1988.

Westermarck, Edward. *The Origin and Development of Moral Ideas.* 2 vols. New York: Books for Libraries Press, 1971.

White, Edmund. *A Boy's Own Story.* New York: New American Library, 1983.

White, Edmund. *Nocturnes for the King of Naples.* Harmondsworth: Penguin, 1978.

White, George Abbott. "Ideology and Literature: *American Renaissance* and F. O. Matthiessen." In *Literature in Revolution,* edited by George Abbott White and Charles Newman, 430–500. New York: Holt, Rinehart and Winston, 1972.

Whitman, Walt. *Complete Poetry and Prose.* Edited by Justin Kaplan. New York: Library of America, 1982.

Whitman, Walt. "Democratic Vistas." In *Collected and Other Prose,* edited by Floyd Stovall. Vol 2. New York: New York Univ. Press, 1964.

Whitman, Walt. *Whitman's Manuscripts: Leaves of Grass (1869). A Parallel Text.* Edited by Fredson Bowers. Chicago: Univ. of Chicago Press, 1955.

Whitmore, George. *Someone Was There: Profiles in the AIDS Epidemic.* New York: New American Library, 1988.

Wilde, Oscar. *The Artist as Critic: The Critical Writings of Oscar Wilde.* Edited by Richard Ellmann. New York: Random House, 1968.

Wilde, Oscar. *De Profundis.* New York: Random House, 1954.

Wilde, Oscar. *The Importance of Being Ernest. Plays.* Harmondsworth: Penguin, 1971.

Wilde, Oscar. *The Picture of Dorian Gray.* New York: Modern Library, 1954.

Williams, Tennessee. *Baby Doll, Something Unspoken, Suddenly Last Summer.* Harmondsworth: Penguin, 1961.

Williams, Tennessee. "Desire and the Black Masseur." In *Collected Stories,* by Tennessee Williams, 205–12. New York: New Directions, 1985.

Williams, Tennessee. *Memoirs.* Garden City: Doubleday, 1975.

Williams, Walter L. *The Spirit and the Flesh: Sexual Diversity in American Indian Culture.* Boston: Beacon Press, 1986.

Wilson, Edmund. *Patriotic Gore: Studies in the Literature of the Civil War.* New York: Oxford Univ. Press, 1962.

Wittig, Monique. *The Lesbian Body.* Translated by David le Vay. New York: Avon, 1978.

Wockner, Rex. "Kellogg Shareholders Stunned by Gay Speech at Battle Creek Meeting," *The Baltimore Alternative,* 1 May 1989, p. 4.

Yingling, Thomas E. *Hart Crane and the Homosexual Text: New Thresholds, New Anatomies.* Chicago: Univ. of Chicago Press, 1990.

INDEX

225

THE WISCONSIN PROJECT ON AMERICAN WRITERS

A SERIES EDITED BY FRANK LENTRICCHIA

Gaiety Transfigured: Gay Self-Representation in American Literature
DAVID BERGMAN

American Puritanism and the Defense of Mourning: Religion, Grief, and Ethnology in Mary White Rowlandson's Captivity Narrative
MITCHELL ROBERT BREITWIESER

F. O. Matthiessen and the Politics of Criticism
WILLIAM E. CAIN

In Defense of Winters: The Poetry and Prose of Yvor Winters
TERRY COMITO

A Poetry of Presence: The Writing of William Carlos Williams
BERNARD DUFFEY

Selves at Risk: Patterns of Quest in Contemporary American Letters
IHAB HASSAN

Reading Faulkner
WESLEY MORRIS WITH BARBARA ALVERSON MORRIS

Repression and Recovery: Modern American Poetry and the Politics of Cultural Memory, 1910–1945
CARY NELSON

Lionel Trilling: The Work of Liberation
DANIEL T. O'HARA

Visionary Compacts: American Renaissance Writings in Cultural Context
DONALD E. PEASE

"A White Heron" and the Question of Minor Literature
LOUIS A. RENZA

The Theoretical Dimensions of Henry James
JOHN CARLOS ROWE